OUDTESTAMENTISCHE STUDIËN

DEEL XXV

# OUDTESTAMENTISCHE STUDIËN

NAMENS HET OUDTESTAMENTISCH WERKGEZELSCHAP

UITGEGEVEN DOOR

A.S. VAN DER WOUDE
GRONINGEN

DEEL XXV

# NEW AVENUES IN THE STUDY OF THE OLD TESTAMENT

*A Collection of Old Testament Studies*
*Published on the Occasion of the Fiftieth Anniversary*
*of the Oudtestamentisch Werkgezelschap*
*and the Retirement of Prof.Dr. M.J. Mulder*

EDITED BY

A.S. VAN DER WOUDE

E.J. BRILL
LEIDEN · NEW YORK · KØBENHAVN · KÖLN
1989

**Library of Congress Cataloging-in-Publication Data**

New avenues in the study of the Old Testament: a collection of Old Testament studies, published on the occasion of the fiftieth anniversary of the Oudtestamentisch Werkgezelschap and the retirement of prof. Dr. M. J. Mulder / edited by A. S. van der Woude.
p. cm.—(Oudtestamentische studiën, ISSN 0169-7226; d. 25)
ISBN 90-04-09125-4
1. Bible. O.T.—Criticism, interpretation, etc. 2. Mulder, M. J.
3. Oudtestamentisch Werkgezelschap in Nederland. I. Mulder, M. J.
BS1171.2.N48 1989
221.6—dc20 89-36225
CIP

**ISSN 0169-7226**
**ISBN 90 04 09125 4**



PRINTED IN THE NETHERLANDS BY E.J. BRILL

CONTENTS

# FÜNFZIG JAHRE OUDTESTAMENTISCH WERKGEZELSCHAP

Die Arbeitsgemeinschaft niederländischer und flämischer Alttestamentler und Orientalisten beging am 1. Juli 1989 ihr goldenes Jubiläum. Aus diesem Anlaß erscheint der vorliegende Band der *Oudtestamentische Studiën*. Es bereitet Genugtuung festzustellen, daß seit der Gründung der Gesellschaft durchschnittlich alle zwei Jahre ein neuer Band in der Reihe veröffentlicht werden konnte.

Die Verfasser der in *Oudtestamentische Studiën* erschienenen Aufsätze haben immer versucht, mit neuen Methoden und Ansichten in ihrem Wissenschaftsbereich Schritt zu halten. Auch der heutige Jubiläumsband dürfte zeigen, daß neue Wege nicht gescheut werden. Die jüngere Generation wendet ihre Aufmerksamkeit besonders strukturalistisch-synchronen bzw. synthetischen Annäherungsmethoden zu im Gegensatz zu älteren Generationen, deren Verfahren vorwiegend diachron-analytisch geprägt war.

Es ist nicht nötig, sich nochmals im einzelnen mit den Schicksalen der Gesellschaft in den ersten vierzig Jahren ihres Bestehens zu beschäftigen. DE BOER hat in Band XIV der *Oudtestamentische Studiën* über die ersten fünfundzwanzig Jahre berichtet und ich habe das für den Zeitraum bis 1980 in Band XXI fortgesetzt.

Auch jetzt soll zuallererst mit Wehmut und Dankbarkeit derer gedacht werden, die uns durch den Tod entrissen wurden: VRIEZEN (1981), RIDDERBOS (1981), BLOMMERDE (1982), NELIS (1982), JONGELING (1986), DAVID (1986), BRONGERS (1986), GISPEN (1986), BEEK (1987) und ALFRINK (1987). Insoweit ihre Gesundheit und ihr Aufgabenbereich es ihnen ermöglichten, haben sie sich voll eingesetzt für die Gesellschaft, die ihnen ans Herz gewachsen war. Was sie ihren Kollegen an Inspiration, Zuneigung, Ermutigung und Erkenntnissen gegeben haben, bleibt unvergeßlich.

Auch in den letzten zehn Jahren traten der Gesellschaft viele anerkannte und vielversprechende Alttestamentler bzw. Orientalisten bei: 1982 DIRKSEN, KOSTER, BEENTJES und OOST; 1983 HOLMAN und SMELIK; 1985 RENKEMA; 1986 VAN DER TOORN; 1987 VAN GROL, BECKING und VERVENNE; 1988 TALSTRA und ZUURMOND. Wegen ihrer Umsiedlung nach Heidelberg verließen Frau und Herr WEIPPERT den vertrauten Kreis.

Wie üblich wechselten auch im letzten Jahrzehnt alle drei Jahre das Präsidium und Sekretariat. Vorsitzender und Sekretär waren jeweils bis 1981 MULDER und BEUKEN, von 1981-1984 VAN LEEUWEN und TROMP, von 1984-1987 BREKELMANS und DEQUEKER und ab 1987 DEURLOO und SMELIK.

Die Gesellschaft hat sich dafür entschieden, ihren ursprünglichen Namen "Oudtestamentisch Werkgezelschap in Nederland" zu ändern, weil jener nicht länger der Tatsache gerecht wird, daß sie auch manche flämische Mitglieder zählt. Weil die niederländische Bezeichnung "Oudtestamentisch Werkgezelschap" genügend zum Ausdruck bringt, daß es sich um einen niederländischsprachigen Kreis von Fachkollegen handelt, wurde sie als künftiger Name gewählt.

Die Art und Weise, in der die Sitzungen der Gesellschaft stattfinden, hat sich im letzten Jahrzehnt nicht wesentlich geändert. Gelegentlicht unterbreitete Vorschläge, eine Anzahl von Tagen nacheinander zu konferieren, wurden mehrheitlich abgelehnt. Deswegen kamen die Mitglieder auch in den letzten Jahren dreimal pro Jahr zusammen, jeweils an einem Tag und in verschiedenen Universitätsstädten. Abgesehen von der Erledigung geschäftlicher Angelegenheiten blieb der Morgen dem "großen Vortrag" gewidmet, während der Mittag für kürzere Beiträge und Mitteilungen Gelegenheit bot.

Die engen Beziehungen, die seit 1970 mit der British Society for Old Testament Study bestehen, führten auch in vergangener Zeit alle drei Jahre zu einem Joint Meeting: 1982 in "Woudschoten" bei Zeist, 1985 im Fitzwilliam College in Cambridge und 1988 im "Doopsgezind Broederschapshuis" in Elspeet. Die an den zwei erstgenannten Tagungen gehaltenen Vorträge wurden in *Oudtestamentische Studiën* XXIII und XXIV veröffentlicht. Die Referate des Elspeeter Kongreßes sollen in Band XXVI erscheinen.

Mit Genugtuung kann unsere alttestamentliche Arbeitsgemeinschaft auf das hinter uns liegende halbe Jahrhundert zurückblicken. Die Inspiration und Ermutigung, die von den regelmäßigen Kontakten ausgehen, die freundschaftliche Atmosphäre, die die Sitzungen zu kennzeichnen pflegt, die engen Beziehungen mit unseren britischen Freunden und Kollegen und die günstige Aufnahme der Reihe *Oudtestamentische Studiën* stimmen uns dankbar. Trotz staatlicher Sparmaßnahmen an den Universitäten und drohender Verringerung von fakultärem Personal blickt die "Oudtestamentische Werkgezelschap" voller Zuversicht und Vertrauen in die Zukunft, weil sie davon überzeugt ist, daß sie auch künftighin einen Beitrag zur Erforschung unseres religiös-kulturellen Erbes und hoffentlich auch zur geistigen Orientierung von Generationen, die in einer pluriformen und säkularisierten Gesellschaft nach Sinngebung suchen, zu leisten vermag.

Der vorliegende Band enthält, abgesehen von Aufsätzen, die anläßlich des 50.jährigen Jubiläums verfaßt worden sind, in Übersetzung auch die Vorträge, die am 20. Januar 1989 bei Gelegenheit der Emeritierung von Professor MULDER von seinen Kollegen BEUKEN, DEURLOO, HOFTIJZER, DIRKSEN und VAN DER WOUDE gehalten wurden. In Anbetracht der Tatsache, daß Mulder sich in den letzten Jahren im besonderen der Erforschung der Bücher der Könige zugewendet hat, befassen sie sich ausnahmslos mit Themen, die diesen beiden Schriften entnommen worden sind.

Beim fünfzigjährigen Jubiläum unserer Arbeitsgemeinschaft ehren wir MULDER, dessen Abschiedsvorlesung sich auch in diesem Band findet, als einen der prominentesten Mitglieder, dessen durchgearbeitetes Oeuvre wegen seiner Verschiedenheit und seines Umfangs tiefste Bewunderung abnötigt. Es ist unser sehnlichster Wunsch, daß wir nach seiner Emeritierung noch lange die Früchte seiner reichen Erkenntnisse und langjährigen Erfahrung ernten dürfen.

A.S. VAN DER WOUDE

# NO WISE KING WITHOUT A WISE WOMAN (I KINGS III 16-28)*

BY

W.A.M. BEUKEN

*Nijmegen*

The scientific oeuvre of Martin MULDER extends from the Peshiṭta of Ezechiel to a commentary on the books of Kings, I and II, and from the history of the Canaanite religion to lexical contributions to *ThWAT*. A noteworthy gem among all of these remains his first inaugural address, titled "Het meisje van Sodom" ("The girl of Sodom", Free University, Amsterdam 1970). The title makes one suspect a piquant story, but it is exciting in another sense: MULDER succeeds in finding a virtuous woman even in Sodom, that pool of deprivation. When to my sincere happiness I received the invitation to read a paper on the occasion of MULDER's leave-taking which would in one way or another relate to his commentary on I Kings i-vii, I began searching spontaneously in the story of King Solomon and the two prostitutes (iii 16-28). What would MULDER, with his experience of women in a bad milieu, have to say about this story? I was not disappointed. MULDER offers a starting point by which the mother of the living child can be given a higher appraisal than is usual among exegetes. I would like to go into that further in the space afforded me here.

It is customary to interpret this story as if the narrator employs the trick used by Solomon to discern which of the women is the real mother of the living child, together with the subsequent judgement, as evidence that "the wisdom of God" was in him[1]. Martin MULDER questions this interpretation: "In this impasse the king lays down a sentence, decisive, but from our point of view rigorous. Actually this is not even a judgement but only a command that does not seem to have anything to do with the case, but which heightens the excitement in the story all the more: 'Bring me a sword'"[2]. MULDER is in good company when he doubts that the narrator wants to make us better appreciate

* Bible quotations basically according to RSV.

[1] C.F. KEIL, *Biblischer Commentar über die Bücher der Könige* (BCAT), Leipzig 1865, pp. 33 f.; A. SANDA, *Die Bücher der Könige* I (EHAT), Münster i.W. 1911, pp. 61ff.; M. NOTH, *Könige* I (BKAT IX/1), Neukirchen 1968, pp. 52ff.; H. BRONGERS, *I Koningen* (POT), Nijkerk 1967, pp. 56f.; E. WÜRTHWEIN, *Das Erste Buch der Könige. Kapitel 1-16* (ATD 11/1), Göttingen 1977, pp. 37f.; J. GRAY, *I and II Kings* (OTL), London 1970², p. 129; M. REHM, *Das erste Buch der Könige*, Würzburg 1979, p. 46.

[2] M. MULDER, *Koningen* I (COT), Kampen 1987, p. 136.

Solomon's trick. According to the Midrash Rabbah of Ecclesiastes (X, 16, §1) R. Judah remarked on behalf of R. Ilai the following in connection with this story: "If I had been there I would have wound a rope of wool around (Solomon's) neck, and when he said, '*Fetch me a sword*', had she (the child's mother) not been filled with compassion for the babe, he would already have been strangled"[3]. Next R. Judah applies to this judgement scene the verse concerned from Ecclesiastes: "Woe to you, O land, when your king is a child" (x 16). Finally he relates the following verse: "Happy are you, O land, when your king is the son of free men" (x 17) to the judicial verdict of Solomon: "Give the living child to the first woman, and by no means slay it" (I Kings iii 27). According to this midrash it was actually the Holy Spirit who cried out the motivation of the verdict: "She is its mother (of the living child)"[4].

In this article I would like to focus on some aspects of the story which qualify the explanation of Solomon's trick as a consequence of God's wisdom. Hopefully it will become obvious as a result that this story has more than one scope, that not everything turns around Solomon's exceptional ability "to render justice" (vs. 28). In this connection it should be noted that the story also functions as a counterpart of the story about David and Bathsheba (II Sam. xi), as FONTAINE has demonstrated in detail[5]. Without repeating the contents of this study here we can say that the latter story exposes the role of lady folly, while that about Solomon demonstrates the wisdom of YHWH at work.

## I. THE NARRATIVE PROGRESS OF THE STORY

When this story is often referred to as a pearl of ancient Eastern simplicity in the art of story-telling[6], it is partially the case because the number of words is limited and their placement and repetition are extremely effective. An example of this is formed by the sequence of verb forms at the beginning of the sentences in the narrative section (thus not in the direct address):

---

[3] *Midrash Rabbah VIII/2, Ecclesiastes*, transl. A. COHEN, Soncino Press 1983[3], pp. 277f.

[4] In Genesis R. (lxxxv 12) and Midrash Tehillim (lxxii 2), too, the last sentence is ascribed to the Holy Spirit, cf. *Midrash Rabbah II, Genesis II*, transl. H. FREEDMAN, Soncino Press 1983[3], p. 797, and *The Midrash on Psalms, I* (Yale Judaica Series XIII/1), ed. W.G. BRAUDE, New Haven 1959, p. 560.

[5] C. FONTAINE, "The Bearing of Wisdom on the Shape of II Sam. 11-12 and I Kings 3", *JSOT* 34 (1986), pp. 61-77.

[6] This characteristic of the story has most convincingly been described by B.O. LONG, *1 Kings with an Introduction to Historical Literature* (The Forms of the Old Testament Literature IX), Grand Rapids, Mich. 1984, pp. 67-70.

| | | | | |
|---|---|---|---|---|
| 16 | Then two harlots came to the king | *'āz* | *tābo'nâ* | A/B |
| | They stood before him | | *watta'^amodnâ* | B′ |
| 17 | The one woman said | | *watto'maer* | C |
| 22 | The other woman said | | *watto'maer* | C |
| | They spoke before the king | | *watt^edabbērnâ* | B′′ |
| 23 | The king said | | *wayyo'maer* | C′ |
| 24 | The king said | | *wayyo'maer* | C′ |
| | They brought in a sword | | *wayyābi'û* | A′/B′′′ |
| 25 | The king said | | *wayyo'maer* | C′ |
| 26 | The woman whose child was alive said | | *watto'maer* | C |
| | Truly, her heart yearned for her son | *kî* | *nikm^erû* | D |
| | She said | | *watto'maer* | C |
| 27 | The king answered and said | | *wayya'an . . .* | |
| | | | *wayyo'maer* | C′ |
| 28 | All Israel heard | | *wayyišm^e'û* | |
| | They stood in awe | | *wayyir^e'û* | |
| | Truly, they saw | *kî* | *rā'û* | D′ |

Sigla:
- A and A′ stand for the verb "to come/to bring" (*bw'* qal and hiph'il)
- B stands for verbs which in contrast to "to say" signify a part of the legal case: "to come", "to stand", "to speak", "to bring a sword"[7]
- C for the verb "to say" (*'mr*) as part of the legal procedure[8]: C with one of the women, C′ with the king as subject
- D for *kî* with the perfect form of verbs which are not a part of the legal case.

What does this pattern teach us? It shows regularity, but which meaning may we attach to it?

1. In the series of verbs which do not introduce direct address, the A-element (*bw'*) announces the entrance of the dramatis personae: the two women cause the impasse of the story (vs. 16a), the sword appears to resolve it, yet only intensifies it, since this alone does not bring about a real solution (vs. 24b). These two events at the same time form parts of the judicial procedure (B-elements), together with the others which mark the beginning and the con-

[7] Some scholars have noticed that I Kings iii 16-28 contains forensic terminology, but so far the phenomenon has not been investigated in a systematic way; cf. H.J. Boecker, *Redeformen des Rechtslebens im Alten Testament* (WMANT 14), Neukirchen 1964, pp. 73f., 85, 89, 96, 143, 150. The story has been described as a "concise record of a courtroom scene" by H. Rand, "Justice in Solomon's Court", *Dor le-dor* 10 (1982), pp. 170-176. The midrash, too, preserves the reminiscence of this fact (cf. the texts mentioned in note 4). With regard to the terms that occur here, cf. the following dictionaries: for *bw'*: F. Zorell, *Lexicon Hebraicum et Aramaicum Veteris Testamenti*, Roma 1968, s.v., 5g (p. 99a); *'md*: *ThWAT* VI, cc. 195f. (H. Ringgren); *dabbēr lipnē*: F. Brown, S.R. Driver, C.A. Briggs, *A Hebrew and English Lexicon of the Old Testament*, Oxford 1906, s.v. 3e (p. 181b), Zorell (*op. cit.*), s.v., 11 (p. 164a); *bw'* hiph'il *ḥaeraeb*: *ThWAT* III, c. 167 (O. Kaiser). With regard to the whole passage cf. now P. Bovati, *Ristabilire la giustizia. Procedure, vocabulario, orientamenti* (AnBib 110), Rome 1986, *passim* (cf. index).

[8] *ThWAT* I, cc. 357f. ("Applikationsbegriff") (S. Wagner).

tinuation of the impasse: "They stood before him" (vs. 16b) and "They spoke before the king" (vs. 22b). This series of actions is interrupted twice two times after one another by the verbum dicendi *'mr* (C-element), which expresses the impasse on a verbal level: the statements of both the women (vs. 17, 22a) and the two pronouncements of the king (vs. 23, 24a).

2. The second half of the story, beginning with the carrying in of the sword, looks like the first one in a formal sense. Here also we find the verbum dicendi *'mr* twice two times (vs. 25, 26a and vs. 26b, 27), now however not first twice a woman speaking, then twice the king (C, C – C′, C′), but in chiastic order: the king, the woman to whom the living child belongs, she again and the king (C′, C – C, C′). The formal similarity goes together with a fundamental difference. The mother of the living child speaks only once, but its announcement by the verbum dicendi *'mr* occurs twice, at the beginning and at the end of the sentence: "Truly, her heart yearned for her son" (vs. 26b). Her last pronouncement gains in significance in the progress of the narrative because of it. Besides, the chiastic pattern of the verbum dicendi which occurs four times directs the attention to the already mentioned sentence in the middle: "Truly, her yeart yearned for her son" (D). This sentence is structurally a pendant of the B-element in vs. 22b, but in terms of its contents it is an antithesis because the emotion does not form a juridical move in the legal case and yet it leads to a breakthrough in the impasse. Consequently, the A- and B-elements do not return after this D-element.

3. Vs. 26b has one verbal pendant, namely in vs. 28b: "Truly, they (all Israel) saw" (D′). The two sentences are related to one another because of their similar beginning (*kî* with the perfect). Thus is the conclusion of the story, that is to say the announcement that Israel saw the wisdom of God at work in king Solomon, in line with what was taking place inside the real mother. The judgement of the king naturally is the immediate cause of Israel's conviction, but in the narrative and verbal structure of the story the latter is primarily connected to the feelings in the motherly heart.

From the above it is apparent that the story has more than one point. Solomon's trick is not the only one, it is even subordinate. What the woman to whom the living child belongs experiences when she is informed about the bogus solution of the king for the legal impasse, forms a climax in the narrative structure which is equal in value to the conclusion which the story embeds in the larger whole of Solomon's succession to the throne, that is to say, that the wisdom of God accompanies the reign of this king.

## II. Death and life

The story is not only directed at the question of how the king will solve this difficult judicial case, in which there are no witnesses (vs. 18), but it gets us also intensely involved in an incident where life, associated with truth, is threatened by death, associated with falsehood.

The topic of life begins with the announcement that both of the women have recently given birth (vs. 17f.). For the time being we are not told whether it concerns a son or a daughter; that new life was created is in itself worthy of attention. Immediately after follows the news of the death of one of the babies, which now appears to have been a son (vs. 19). In this manner the story at once takes us into a sphere where death threatens life.

It is true that life goes on in the person of the other child, but the interchanging of the dead and the living son forms a serious danger for the latter, since his ties with his real mother are broken (vs. 20: "from beside me"). The use of words expresses the threatened situation of the living child in the choice of the root *škb* (hiph'il) for the action "to lay". This verb often means to lie down (qal) in death or to lay down (hiph'il) a dead person[9]. In vs. 20 it is used for laying down the living as well as the dead child. There does not seem to be any difference between the two!

The discovery of the interchange is also narrated in terms which accentuate the opposition between life and death: "I rose in the morning to nurse my child, and behold, it was dead" (vs. 21). Do we read too much into the text when we suspect the suggestion that the real mother "gets up" earlier than the woman who has stolen the living child and therefore forms a threat to it?

The threat to life comes finally to the fore in the most painful manner during the conflict about the possession of the living child (vs. 22), while at this time, three days after its birth, the child asks only for help and care. This dispute is moreover futile, since to begin with the king does not know what to do other than to repeat the precisely identical assertions of the two women, behind which is hidden the dispute about the prevalence of the truth and the future of life (vs. 23).

The threat hanging over the still living child puts him in mortal danger when the king calls for the sword and orders the child to be cut in two (vs. 25). The attention of the readers shifts from the living and the dead child to the question of life and death for the living child. In the immediate context of the terms "alive" and "dead" other words appear which now determine its content: "Give her the living child, and by no means slay it" and "It shall be neither mine or yours; cut (it)" (vs. 26). The concern for life moves the real mother while the false mother chooses for the death of the child, because she begrudges it a mother. It is noticeable that she does not name the child; she asks only for the execution of the sentence – "cut (it)" has no object! –,

[9] qal: Gen. xlvii 30, Deut. xxxi 16, II Sam. vii 12, I Kings i 21, ii 10, Isa. xiv 8, xliii 17, li 20, Ez. xxxi 18, xxxii 27-30, Job iii 12, vii 21, xiv 12, xx 11, Ps. lxxxviii 6, Lam. ii 21; hiph'il: I Kings xvii 19, II Kings iv 21, II Chron. xvi 14.

the real mother uses the affectively loaded term *yālûd*, "the newborn child" (MULDER).

In this paroxism of mortal danger, life prevails after all, and that through the power of a mother's affection (*raḥ$^{a}$mîm*). When the real mother takes the step to give up her son to the other woman, she offers him in fact to life. This gesture is so convincing that the king no longer needs a witness. Motherhood and life bear witness for one another. The ruler can pass judgement: "She is its mother" (vs. 27). This sentence corroborates only the outcome of the struggle between life and death, which is already decided in favour of life.

## III. SIMILAR WOMEN?

The reader brings to the story an appreciation for the two whores that this occupation enjoys in the Bible after all. To be sure, some narrators mention the existence of whoring without expressing their disapproval about it (Gen. xxxviii 15, Jos. ii 1, Judg. xvi 1), but this is not done only because an ethical opinion is not under discussion in the story. In general it is undisputed that whoring defiles the country (Lev. xix 29). The prophets condemn this social phenomenon (Am. ii 7, Jer. v 7) and wisdom warns that whores are deceptive (Prov. vii 10, xxvii 27) and drive men to poverty (Prov. vi 26, xxix 3) and even to death (Prov. vii 27). Finally the fact that whoring in the metaphorical sense has come to mean turning away from YHWH (Ez. xvi 15-34, Hos. iv 11), says enough about the social contempt that has always been its lot (Judg. xi 1).

The question is now, does the narrator allow the reader to keep this contempt for the two women in the course of the story or does he provide information to enable us to judge the whore who turns out to be the mother of the living child differently? To phrase a question in this way is equal to endorsing the second segment of it. The story begins by treating the women equally. They are both whores, their conditions of life and their careers are absolutely identical, since they live in the same house and both give birth to a son. The fact that nobody else was present when the drama of the switch occurred, fulfills a judicial function, since the absence of a witness is necessary in order to place Solomon in an absolute impasse, but is not there at the same time some irony to be heard here? Two women of this kind and yet there was nobody with them at home! The narrator lets us smile for a moment. The similarity of the two women is maintained for long, even down to their squabbling. The chiasm of their assertions in vs. 22 – "No, the living child is mine, and the dead child is yours" and "No, the dead child is yours, and the living child is mine" – brings no differentiation in the appraisal of their personalities, but illustrates the conflict of the two women.

Differentiation between the two women appears only when the king suggests dividing the living child. At that moment one of the women becomes a mother. She realizes that the granting of equal rights in the quantitative sense to the two women would imply the death of her son and therefore she chooses to save the living child, even when this means that she loses it as a son. The other woman chooses to be put in her own right, for at least half, even if this does not mean life but death. As a result of these fundamentally different choices the two identical whores change into diametrically different women. Faced with the choice between life and death they personify wisdom and folly.

The contrast between these two is an unmistakable theme of the chokmatic literature. One can summarise this in the saying: "The wisdom of women builds her house, but folly with her own hands tears it down" (Prov. xiv 1). We see these two women personified at work in various scenes of Prov. i-ix, where lady wisdom invites the people to a behaviour which leads to life, whereas lady folly tries to seduce people to the road which leads to death (i 20-33, ii-iii, v, vi 24-35, vii-ix; cf. Sir. xxvi). The woman in I Kings iii who is willing to give up the child in exchange for the preservation of its life, resembles in more than one way the wise man who by his conduct in whatever area it may be, preserves his own life and that of his descendants. The story forms an illustration for sayings such as the following:

> The mouth of the righteous is a fountain of life, but the mouth of the wicked conceals violence (Prov. x 11)
>
> A tranquil mind gives life to the flesh, but jealousy makes the bones rot (Prov. xiv 30)
>
> A hot-tempered man stirs up strife, but he who is slow to anger quiets contention (Prov. xv 18)
>
> Wisdom is a fountain of life to him who has it, but folly is the chastisement of fools (Prov. xvi 22)
>
> Better is a dry morsel with quiet than a house full of feasting with strife (Prov. xvii 1)
>
> Death and life are in the power of the tongue, and those who live it will eat its fruits (Prov. xviii 21)
>
> It is better to live in a desert land than with a contentious and fretful woman (Prov. xxi 19)
>
> To fear YHWH is the beginning of wisdom; she is created with the faithful in the womb (Sir. i 14)
>
> There is grief of heart and sorrow when a wife is envious of a rival, and a tongue-lashing makes it known to all (Sir. xxvi 6).

The conclusion is obvious. The whore who follows the dictates of her motherly feelings becomes wise as a result of it. Her choice for the life of the child above her right to him terminates a conflict that would have brought about his death. The one who advocates life is mother (Gen. iii 20), and the mother precedes the king in a just verdict. This is illustrated by the series of imperatives in the last scene. The double command of the king, "Cut the living child in two, and give half to the one, and half to the other" (vs. 25) is stripped by the mother of its ostensible wisdom and contradicted: "give to her ... and by no means slay it" (vs. 26a). For cutting is killing and one does not give a dead person as a present. The chiasm "to cut, to give – to give, not to kill" in this way suitably expresses the conflict of values that is hidden behind the words. But while the unreal mother only repeats the command "cut it" and "give" lies beyond her horizon (vs. 26b), the king takes up the words of the real mother literally: "give to her ... and by no means slay it" (vs. 27). Nevertheless, the indirect object "her" refers not to the untrue but to the true mother. The king may have provoked the wisdom, he pursues it in the person of the whore who has become a mother and, as a consequence, has become wise.

## IV. The king

If we suspect that the narrator has no need to set Solomon's trick in a favourable light, it is not because the sword that the king calls for (vs. 24) would function as a horrible threat from the very beginning, as an instrument of blackmail to discover the truth. The sword symbolises in the first place the right and the duty of the king to pass judgement (cf. Deut. xxxii 41f., Isa. xiv 19, xxii 2, xxvii 1, xxxiv 5f., lxvi 16, Jer. xii 12, xlvii 6f., Ez. xxi 1-5, xxxi 17f., xxxii 19f., xxxv 8, Am. ix 1, Zeph. ii 12, Zech. xiii 7f., Ps. xvii 13)[10]. To be sure, it is only brought out when the king has determined that the legal case has been caught up in an impracticable deadlock, but it does not follow from this that it is supposed to be used only as a means of execution. The formulation "bring *me* a sword", whereas it is after all the servants who are ordered to cut the child in two, indicates that the sword has in the first place a forensic meaning. The fact that it is brought out only now could play a narrative role. Whereas the king faces an absolute judicial impasse, he is still determined to do his duty in administering justice, and he is maybe also full of confidence to be able to do this by virtue of the wisdom which YHWH has bestowed upon him (I Kings iii 12)[11]. Under these circumstances, when he cannot expect getting reliable legal indications, he chooses for the only solution that is left to him, almost knowing that here applies *summum ius summa iniuria*.

When scholars have emphasised so strongly and one-sidedly the explanation

[10] *ThWAT* III, cc. 167, 171 (O. Kaiser); *BHH*, c. 1751 (G. Fohrer).

[11] The inner, temporal connection of this story with the preceding account of Solomon's dream is expressed by the opening form in vs. 16: *'āz tābonâ*. Cf. I. Rabinowitz, "*'ĀZ* Followed by Imperfect Verb-Form in Preterite Contexts: A Redactional Device in Biblical Hebrew", *VT* 34 (1984), p. 54: "(The conjunction) *'āz* + imperfect indicates this (i.e. the foregoing) context as approximately the time when, the time or circumstances in the course of which, or the occasion upon which the action designated by the imperfect verb-form went forward"; p. 60: "The time of the episode narrated ... was while the king was as yet at Gibeon".

that this stroke of genius proves the wisdom of the king, then this has perhaps happened under the influence of the theory that the Deuteronomistic historian has transformed a folk legend into evidence that the wisdom of YHWH was at work in Solomon[12]. Now WEINFELD has pointed to the existence of "wisdom substrata" in Deuteronomy and the Deuteronomistic literature[13]. According to him there existed a pre-Deuteronomistic view of Solomon's wisdom, in which the king was described as a shrewd individual in difficult human situations, as a pragmatic ruler, competent in building up a great fortune, who furthermore commanded an extensive knowledge of natural phenomena (I Kings ii 5-9, v 9-14, x 1-10, 14-29). The Deuteronomist would have twisted this point of view into his understanding of Solomon's wisdom as a unique gift from YHWH to the ruler of Israel in order to realise through good jurisdiction a justness and fairness in God's chosen people according to the Tora[14].

This assumption provides indeed an explanatory model for the multilateral plot of the story in I Kings iii 16-28, but at the expense of a certain contradiction between the role of the king in that folktale (vs. 16-27) and the evaluation of him by the Deuteronomist in the final verse (vs. 28). Such inconsistency is in itself indeed possible. It does happen more often that an editor has to accept certain elements in the material transmitted to him and cannot make any changes in it without depriving the *Vorlage* of its intrinsic cohesion.

However, one can apply this explanatory model in another way as well. One variation is the following. The folktale that the Deuteronomist found is not about the clever trick of the king, who is able to use it to find the truth behind two wrangling whores, but about a woman who listens to the dictates of her motherly heart in a matter of life and death, who as a result of it displays wise conduct, finds wise words and thus offers the king, who likewise sees no ways out of the problem, the possibility to nevertheless pronounce a just sentence. Kings often have something with women, for better or for worse. We have already pointed at the contrast between David and Bathsheba on the one hand and Solomon and this whore on the other. But there is also a striking similarity between our story and the tale of the wise woman of Tekoa, who guarded David from blame (II Sam. xiv 13). Thanks to her mastery of the language as an instrument in winning people over and influencing them this woman knew how to prevail upon her king to take the decision that was considered as righteous among the people and which valued life as a higher good than the apparent right of what was called justice, here that of the revenge. Finally,

---

[12] Cf. for this question in general, MULDER, *op. cit.*, pp. 17-22; for this pericope in particular, WÜRTHWEIN, *loc. cit.*

[13] M. WEINFELD, *Deuteronomy and the Deuteronomic School*, Oxford 1972, pp. 244-281.

[14] *Ibid.*, pp. 254-257.

the woman of I Kings iii forms in the life of Solomon the counterpart of the women who seduced the king in his old age into the service of idols and thus undid the theophany in which wisdom had been promised him (cf. I Kings xi 1-10, especially vs. 9).

## Conclusion

The praise given to Solomon's strange manoeuvre in this legal case in the current literature rests on the denial of the fact that the Old Testament presents a number of wise women, in short possesses a typology of the wise woman. In this case "wisdom" implies a particular technical skill (Ex. xxxv 25: in spinning; Jer. ix 16: in complaining) as well as caring for the domestic life (II Kings iv: the Shunammite; Ruth: Naomi; Prov. xxxi 1-9: the mother of king Lemuel; Prov. xxxi 10-31: the worthy woman) and as well the relationship with people and the influencing of public life (I Sam. xxv: Abigail; II Sam. xiv: the woman of Tekoa; xx 14-22: the woman of Abelbeth-maacah)[15]. These women form the opposite of the other types who personify foolishness and who are seducers (Gen. xxxix: the wife of Potiphar; Am. iv 1: "the cows of Bashan"; Prov. ii 16, v. 3, vi 23f., vii 5, 21, xxii 14, xxx 20: "the strange woman"; Job ii 9: the wife of Job, who acts "as a foolish woman"). Here it is noticeable that the foolishness of the second group of women has a pernicious influence precisely because of what they say, just as the wisdom of the first group of women is apparent from their speech.

In my opinion the good whore of I Kings iii may be added to the typology of the wise woman. By listening to the inclinations of her motherly heart she can speak wise words to king Solomon. Thus she creates for him the possibility to judge fairly. The praise of the woman whose value surpasses that of corals is also applicable to her: "She opens her mouth with wisdom, and the teaching of kindness is on her tongue" (Prov. xxxi 26).

This study was inspired by the commentary of Martin Mulder on I Kings iii 16-28. His extensive knowledge of the history and the language of the Scriptures, his balance in method and his habit of reading every text meticulously prove to be productive for others. The fact that he has special attention for the wise woman is a proprium of his exegesis. It probably has something to do with his personal *Sitz im Leben*. This paper is dedicated to the wise woman next to him, Jik, in thankfulness for a close friendship.

---

[15] S. Amsler, "La sagesse de la femme", in: M. Gilbert (ed.), *La Sagesse de l'Ancient Testament* (BEThL 51), Leuven 1979, pp. 112-116; A. Brenner, *The Israelite Woman. Social Role and Literary Type in Biblical Narrative*, Sheffield 1985, pp. 33-46.

# THE KING'S WISDOM IN JUDGEMENT

## *Narration as Example (I Kings iii)*

BY

K.A. DEURLOO

*Amsterdam*

"Solomon's first acts of government" – thus reads the heading wrongly put over the second chapter of I Kings in the Dutch translation of the Old Testament (1951). In his recent commentary, MULDER understands this chapter as the conclusion of the narratives around the Davidic Succession, and more specifically as the confirmation of the acquisition of royal power by Solomon. The latter's first act of government is narrated in the pericope about what is known as the "judgement of Solomon". Consequently, the preceding story about Solomon's dream should be seen as the overture to his future royal action, which will be characterised by wisdom[1].

The complicated beginning of ch. iii connects his marriage to the Egyptian princess with the building of the Temple. This is one of the means used to explain the remarkable fact that Solomon receives the royal gifts out of God's hands in a dream at Gibeon, after having offered sacrifices at the local "chief hill-shrine". The final remarks about Solomon's offerings before the Ark of the Covenant in Jerusalem are probably partly intended as correctives (iii 15). The fact that at the final redaction the high place of Gibeon was not suppressed may well be related to the ambivalence of Solomon's kingship (see already iii 3b), which is dealt with in the concluding chapter (xi). The editorial notes of ch. iii (vv. 1-3, 15), however, aim at putting the dream in an unmistakably positive light.

What Solomon requests and receives is the divine gift for a king *par excellence*: the wisdom to distinguish between *good and evil*. ROSENBERG discusses this contrast as a matter of delicate concern to the Davidic court, especially to David himself as royal judge (II Samuel xiv 17, cf. xiii 22, and xix 35). In the last example the expression is used by Barzillai, who refuses politely to join David and dwell with him at the royal court in Jerusalem. This simple man of the country declares himself too old to distinguish different

[1] M.J. MULDER, *Koningen. Eerste deel* (Commentaar op het Oude Testament), Kampen 1987, p. 115.

tastes. "Barzillai unintentionally states with consummate conciseness and clarity the *reader's* cumulative nausea" with respect to "eating, drinking, leisure, amorous dalliance", of which the reader has been given a taste in the preceding narratives[2]. At the point where this phrase returns in the scene of Solomon's dream, ROSENBERG perceives a new form of historiography. "Whereas the epithet 'speaking/hearing/knowing good and evil' had been applied to David's court as an *ad hoc* characterisation, by indirection, of David's complicated and compromised position as court monarch, Solomon now appropriates it to his own vision of the monarchy, indeed, as its seal and symbol". It now comes to mean: "to proclaim the general good and forget the particular evil. It is the bad faith that sustains all statecraft of a 'cumbersome people'"[3].

Interesting as Rosenberg's observations are, it is highly debatable whether these ideas may be read into the text or indeed behind it. The account of the dream would in that case have to be at least contemporary with the period of Solomon's reign. There are reasons to put the phrase "good and evil" into a wider context. We read e.g. about "Immanuel" (Isaiah vii 16) that the coming events will take place "before the child has learnt to reject evil and choose good", before he has reached adulthood and is able to judge independently (cf. Deuteronomy i 39). This is the plain and common meaning of the phrase, though raised to a high level of pregnancy.

In the "Paradise story" mention is made of two special trees in the garden; the tree of life, which may even provide life *l'lm*, and the tree of the knowledge of good and evil. By eating of the latter one acquired such knowledge as is possessed by God or gods[4]. Although playing a part of their own in Genesis ii and iii, the trees reflect at the same time the two divine gifts which are also attributed to the king as the source of blessing and life and as judicial authority. Whoever curses the king and thereby blocks the sources of blessing, which may for instance result in a drought, is guilty of lese majesty and therefore condemned to death (I Kings xxi 13)[5]. The salutation "May the king live" (I Samuel xvii 55 etc.) or even "Let the king live *l'lm*" (Nehemiah ii 3) is not just a courteous phrase[6]. The gift of a long life is the first to be mentioned after the "understanding heart" of Solomon's request. The latter is the

---

[2] J. ROSENBERG, *King and Kin. Political Allegory in the Hebrew Bible*, Bloomington – Indianapolis 1986, p. 186.

[3] ROSENBERG, *op. cit.*, p. 188.

[4] The plural is more appropriate than the singular (Genesis iii 5, 22). In this context, to eat of the tree of the knowledge of good and evil implies independence in a negative sense: the rupturing of the relationship with YHWH God.

[5] Cf. M.A. BEEK, "De plaatsvervangende koning", in: *Woord en Wereld* (Festschrift Miskotte), Amsterdam 1961, pp. 97ff.

[6] Cf. H. RINGGREN, *TWAT* II (1976), p. 888: "Der König vermittelt ... von Gott geschenktes Leben seinem Volke". (Cf. Lamentations iv 20).

divine gift *par excellence* to be expected in a king: the knowledge of good and evil. Quite characteristically the wise woman of Tekoa says of David: "For your majesty is like the angel of God in discerning good and evil (*lšm' hṭwb whr'*)" (II Samuel xiv 17). Because of this divine gift the king will truly be able to render independent justice. By distinguishing good from evil and subsequently acting in accordance with the understanding thus gained, the king realizes "justice and righteousness" (*mšpṭ wṣdqh*): these two words indicate the outstanding characteristic of the king. He *is* the righteous one in the *active* administration of justice to those who are in distress (*ṣrh*)[7]. This implies an act of liberation (*yš'*) that establishes peace (*šlwm*). Psalm lxxii expresses it both as a gift of God and in its consequences for those without rights, often represented by the widow and the orphan:

> O God, endow the king with thy own *justice*,
> and give thy *righteousness* to a king's son,
> ...
> and deal out justice to the poor and suffering ...

The same pair of words is used to describe David's government in the provisional conclusion found in II Samuel viii 15: "David ruled over the whole of Israel and maintained *justice* and *righteousness* among all his people". It can be approximately equivalent to the throne (Isaiah ix 6, etc.). Mulder points out that in the description of the construction of Solomon's palace the *hapax legomena* "Hall of the Throne" and "Hall of Judgement" relate the throne as the seat of government to the administration of justice by the monarch or in his name (I Kings vii 7)[8]. It is there that the people will proceed in order to receive justice, just as they did to Debora, who "had her seat" under the palm-tree (Judges iv 5). Her activity introduces the justice to be effectuated by the judge Barak in an act of liberation. In the scene which describes Absalom's preparations for the realization of his ambitions, the king's judicial power is called into question. "He would hail every man who had a case (*ryb*) to bring before the king for *judgement* ...". Absalom says: "I can see that you have a very good case, but you will get no *hearing* from the king (*wšm' 'yn lk m't hmlk*) (II Samuel xv 3) – even though this was the very thing one was entitled to expect of a king (*lšm' hṭwb whr'*). The ability to hear and discern thus is indeed deserving of the epithet "wise". It is therefore not surprising that the word 'wisdom' should occur in this semantic field. It is the wise woman of Tekoa who attributes wisdom to David: "Your majesty is as wise as the angel of God and knows all that is going on in the land" (or: "on

---

[7] F.H. Breukelman, "Der König im Tun von Mischpat", *Texte und Kontexte* (1984), pp. 4-12.

[8] Mulder, *op. cit.*, p. 242.

earth'') (II Samuel xiv 20). Proleptically, David said to Salomon on his deathbed: ''Do as your wisdom prompts you'' (I Kings ii 6). The king ought to be married to wisdom. In the case of David, this is literally true. Against Nabal (''Folly''), he was tempted to take the law into his own hands, and not to liberate the one who was oppressed but only himself (*whwš' ydk lk*) (I Samuel xxv 26). In the shape of ''Lady Wisdom'', however, Abigail succeeds in restraining him, thus saving his chances to be a true king[9]. At the end of the story he accordingly marries her. What is supposed to be true ''ideologically'' has taken narrative shape in this chapter. The future monarch and judge in the land may not be tainted with ''having shed innocent blood or given way to anger'' (v. 31). The wisdom which has saved him in this case will also conduct him further, especially in the administration of justice. Of this II Samuel xiv is admittedly a very specific case, though at the same time the outstanding example: the wise woman of Tekoa poses as a widow who comes to the king for justice, for the sake of the life of her only remaining son. In this matter her very existence is at stake: blood avengers ''will stamp out my last live ember and leave my husband no name and no descendant upon earth'' (II Samuel xiv 7).

It is, however, as if the wisdom of Solomon takes shape especially in the building of the temple. The dream at Gibeon is conspicuously confirmed after the dedication of the temple in that YHWH ''appeared to him a second time, as he had appeared to him at Gibeon'' (I Kings ix 2). Though not mentioned explicitly in the passage in question, his wisdom has culminated in the preceding chapters. Hiram, king of Tyre, virtually quotes the divine dream oracle in ch. v: ''Blessed by YHWH today, who has given David a wise son to rule over his great people'' (v 21, cf. iii 8ff.). With Psalm cxi 10 one might say that the construction of the temple is indeed the core of Solomon's wisdom. To rule his great people, however, also implies the administration of justice, which is mentioned first: Israel ''saw that he had wisdom of God within him to administer justice'' (I Kings iii 28). Besides Hiram there is yet another witness among all those who ''came from all peoples to hear the wisdom of Solomon, and from all the kings of the earth, who had heard of his wisdom'' (v 14). The queen of Sheba declares: ''The report which I heard in my own country about you and your wisdom was true ... Blessed be YHWH your God, who has delighted in you and has set you on the throne of Israel; because he loves Israel for ever, he has made you their king to maintain *justice and righteousness*'' (x 6-9). These words return us to the beginning of Solomon's active rule, and draw our attention to the fact that in the preceding dream the subject of Solomon's question is the *administration of justice*.

With reference to iii 7ff., MULDER very aptly speaks of the hyperbole of the

[9] K. BARTH, *KD* IV/2, pp. 481-486.

"little boy" and "the people which cannot be counted", pointing out such stylistic phenomena as "parallel pairs" and "inclusion" [10]. The people which is to be ruled by Solomon is the chosen, the blessed, the "weighty" people. The duty laid on his shoulders is weighty as well as heavy; it is indeed a responsibility which cannot be dealt with without a special gift of God [11]. Irrespective of his age [12] and in spite of his ample experience in state affairs, Solomon appears to be merely a little boy ("een jongetje dat van toeten nog blazen weet", as MULDER translates, not without a sense of humour), for the very reason that Israel is the "uncountable" people of God. His not knowing "how to go out or to come in" has its positive counterpart in "a *discerning* heart, to *judge* thy people and to distinguish between *good and evil*". That is the gift he ought to be granted, for "who is able to *judge* this, thy weighty people?!" To this question the answer can only be that nobody is. We are reminded of the general meaning of the phrase "speaking/hearing/knowing good and evil" (which may for instance be that of "having reached adulthood"); however, to this task no human being is equal in principle. For that, one has to be "like the angel of God in discerning good and evil" or "as wise as the angel of God, knowing all that is going on in the land". What Solomon requests is the only gift he can ask for: a *lb šmʿ*. This term is to be understood in the technical sense of the skill of judicial construction, to be achieved by hearing defendants and witnesses [13]. That explains why the verb *lšpṭ* "to judge", is used repeatedly. Though not always (cf. NEB "so that he may *govern* thy people"), it must here have the meaning of a judicial decision. This decision represents the whole of royal action in a concentrated form, as is also indicated by the vocabulary of the context. Thus, in his reply God summarises the king's words as follows: "Because you have asked ... for discernment in adminis-

---

[10] MULDER, *op. cit.*, pp. 125f.

[11] Cf. C.H.W. BREKELMANS, "Solomon at Gibeon", in: *Von Kanaan bis Kerala* (Festschrift Van der Ploeg), Kevelaer/Neukirchen 1982, pp. 53-59.

[12] Naturally, speculations about Solomon's age arise here: rabbinical tradition sees him as twelve years old; R. KITTEL, *Die Bücher der Könige* (HAT), Göttingen 1900, estimates his age at "ungefähr 18 Jahren" (p. 6); I. BENZINGER, *Die Bücher der Könige* (KHC), Freiburg 1899, at "eher über als unter 20 Jahre" (p. 15). MULDER is quite right in calling such speculations irrelevant to the text (*op. cit.*, p. 125).

[13] To be distinguished from the "wideness of heart" (I Kings v 9), to understand all the phenomena to be observed in the world (cf. x 24). In connection with iii 9, G. VON RAD, *Weisheit in Israel*, Neukirchen 1970, speaks in general terms of "eine 'vernehmende' Vernunft, ein Gespür für die Wahrheit, die von der Welt herkommend den Menschen anspricht" (p. 376). In the same sense, referring to Egyptian sources, M. NOTH, *Könige* (BKAT), Neukirchen-Vluyn 1968, though with a different emphasis, speaks of "die jeweils rechte Eingebung" (p. 51), cf. H. BRUNNER, "Das 'hörende Herz': 1 Kg 3, 14-15 und die Weisheit des Ptaḥḥotep", *ThLZ* 79 (1954), cc. 697-700; contrary J. GRAY, *I and II Kings* (OTL), London 1964, "to hear a case" (p. 126); J.A. MONTGOMERY, *The Book of Kings* (ICC), Edinburgh 1951: "judicial act" (p. 108); H. SCHULT (*THAT* 2, p. 977): "die Fähigkeit zur Urteilsfindung"; F. STOLZ (*THAT* 1, p. 863): "juristisches Abwägen".

tering justice (*lšm' mšpṭ*) . . . I give you a heart so wise and so understanding . . ." (11f.) that you will be unique: we may add, in your administration of justice, as becomes apparent in Solomon's first act of government, which *is* a judgement. Or, to use the queen of Sheba's more general terms: he is maintaining justice and righteousness.

At this point, a minor difference of opinion with MULDER should be discussed, which formally speaking concerns the word *'z*, "then", with which iii 16 begins. MULDER translates this word as *eens* ("once upon a time"), explaining that a narrative thus introduced has a folkloristic rather than a historical character[14]. The latter may readily be conceded to him, without accepting the former in the sense in which he means it. The large number of examples from the world's legendary literature which can be adduced as parallels to this story[15] do not in themselves allow a definite conclusion about its function in this context. The phrase "once upon a time" introduces a fairytale, whereas this story aims at relating an event which is characteristic of Solomon's way of acting. The particle *'z* has a temporal meaning and quite often introduces in Old Testament stories a moment of instantaneous importance. The examples of this use are legion. Within the same context one may refer to viii 1. An attempt will be made below to underline and substantiate another comment made by MULDER: "It is obvious that the story serves to illustrate the wisdom promised to Solomon (v. 12)"[16].

Within the context, this extraordinarily vivid[17] narration is a very conspicuous element. As an isolated anecdote about an event that took place at some time during the Solomonic period, the story is said to have got a more or less accidental place here because of the "wisdom" theme of the dream scene. In itself it would not have been out of place if it had been inserted into the narrative about the visit of the queen of Sheba, as a convincing proof of Solomon's wisdom. There are, however, reasons to think that it aims at giving a fundamental example of the nature of this kingship. We have a similar example of tactful royal behaviour, typical of David, directly after the latter's anointment as king in his modest reaction to the interment of Saul by the men of Jabesh as representatives of the North (II Samuel ii 4b-7).

*Then*, immediately after the bestowal of the divine gift, Solomon's wisdom was put to the test: two women, harlots, brought their case before the king.

---

[14] MULDER, *op. cit.*, p. 133; cf. A. VAN DEN BORN, *Koningen* (De Boeken van het Oude Testament), Roermond – Maaseik 1958, about this particle: "waarmee door de schrijver vaak de in de archiefstukken genoemde (preciese) datum wordt weergegeven" (p. 34).

[15] J.G. FRAZER, *Folklore in the Old Testament*, London 1919, pp. 570f. Th.H. GASTER, *Myth, Legend and Customs in the Old Testament*, New York – Evanston 1969, pp. 491ff.

[16] MULDER, *op. cit.*, p. 133; BENZINGER, *op. cit.*, p. 16: "Die Geschichte ist hier am guten Platz als Beweis für die Erfüllung der göttlichen Zusage v. 12 und als Beispiel für Salomos Weisheit".

[17] With e.g. MONTGOMERY, *op. cit.*, who adds, curiously: "with a genuine feminine strain to it; there is a certain amount of repetitiousness" (p. 109, cf. v. 21, p. 110).

They do not, however, appear as equals. From the very beginning it is really the case of only one of the women. The narrator lets her recount her story in fairly elaborate detail. After an introductory sketch of the spatial situation ("I and this woman dwell in one house"), she starts off with what is for her the most important fact: "I *gave birth*, with her, in the house". She concludes with the same words, redundant in themselves, but stressing the oppressiveness of her situation: "I looked at him closely, and behold, it was not my son, which I had *given birth to*" (iii 21). In between those two moments she delivers her version of what happened: the crucial complicating fact that "on the third day"[18] after she had been delivered, the other woman also gave birth. In a parenthetical nominal clause, the setting is now reduced with juridical precision to the two persons involved: we were together. Then something that is conceivable in her profession is ruled out: there was no stranger with us in the house. This is followed by the redundant addition: only we two were in the house. Nobody else can have played a part: nobody can offer testimony. Then the time is indicated: the night, probably the night after the third day. However, not only the order in which she describes the events is significant, but particularly the information furnished to the reader that a son is involved. The other woman's son died during the night, "because she overlaid it", she adds – leaving any further interpretation to her hearer. This is followed by a very deliberate deed in the middle of the night; according to her reconstruction, "She took my son from my side". She does not fail to mention her own condition: "Your servant was asleep. She laid him in her bosom". Only then do we hear of the dead son. Just as the other woman rose in the night, the mother rose "to feed my son", *in the morning*. This is said twice, "because it could only be discovered in the clear light of dawn that this was not her own child"[19].

The other woman's reply is brief, and equally brief is the first woman's rejoinder. *No* stands against *No*. In retarding deliberation, the king repeats the words of both. This meaningful redundance is underlined in a chiastic construction; twice we hear: "My son is the living one, your son is the dead one; your son is the dead one, my son is the living one". All is centred around that living son of the beginning and the end. After the retardation, achieved by repetitions[20], the king's brusque utterance comes as a shock: "Fetch me a *sword*!" This word, so typical of kings, is used again in the next sentence. Will it likewise be symbolic of the rule of this king? Distantly he orders an

[18] Cf. H. Jagersma, "... *ten derden dage* ...", Kampen 1976.

[19] Mulder, *op. cit.*, p. 136. Because of the intensive reflexive, "close scrutinizing is implied" (J. Gray, *op. cit.*, p. 129).

[20] E. Ruprecht, "Eine vergessene Konjektur von A. Klostermann zu I Reg 3 27", *ZAW* 88 (1976), p. 415: "Die Wiederholung unterstreicht den eigentlichen Streitpunkt und schafft erzählerisch ein die Spannung steigerndes retardierendes Moment".

absurd *iustitia distributiva* to be meted out to "the living *child*". Then the narrator introduces the mother of "the living *son*" with her spontaneous display of compassionate love. Starting just as politely as she had done initially with the interjection *by 'dny* (v. 17), she, too, refers distantly to the "borne one" (*ylwd*) (v. 27). Consequently she gives up her child for the sake of his life and adds, using a *figura etymologica* charged with emotion: "By no means slay it!" In contrast to her, her rival makes her own chilling statement.

Then we hear the royal sentence: "Give *her* ...". Apparently this presents a problem, as it could refer to the last speaker, i.e. the second woman, contrary to the general drift of the narrative. Are we supposed to imagine that meanwhile the king is pointing at the real mother?[21] Possibly inspired by the LXX, BUBER slightly shifts the emphasis in his translation: "Gebt *jener* das lebende Kindlein, – / die mit: Töten, nicht dürft ihr es töten,/ sie ist seine Mutter". Perhaps haplography has caused the omission of *h'mrt*, "she who says"[22]. This possibility deserves consideration, especially in view of *z't 'mrt* in v. 23. However, all these solutions might spoil one's appreciation of the subtle literary game which is played in the words quoted by the king. In v. 23, he repeats meditatively the words of both the women, with a slight shift of emphasis with regard to the first woman, apparently the one who had presented the case: "This is my son, the living one, your son is the dead one". The second woman is quoted verbatim: "No, but your son is the dead one, my son is the living one". Not only does this repetition mark eloquently the theme of the living and the dead sons, one can also observe in the king's words a beginning of discernment. His *no* can only refer to one of the two.

When the king raises his voice for the second time, he is quoting once more, though this time only one of the two women who spoke out under the threat posed by the sword. It has indeed become possible by now to distinguish in the true sense of the word. There was no need for the narrator to add the words "she who says"; he was in fact obliged to omit them, because the woman's words now become the king's in the very form in which she uttered them – which also explains why the woman was made to use the plural form of the imperative. The king can pronounce sentence by quoting the woman verbatim, adding merely: "She is its mother". With her compassionate exclamation she has already passed sentence. The king needed no more than a perceptive ear in order to discern between good and evil. Of the other woman's utterance, only the last word could have been quoted (*gzrw*). Has Salomon not been given a *lb šm'*, a "hearing heart", "to judge thy people and to

[21] BENZINGER, *op. cit.*, p. 16: "Zum Mindesten müsste gesagt sein 'dieser da' mit entsprechender Handbewegung gedacht".

[22] RUPRECHT, *art. cit.*, p. 414; cf. BENZINGER, *op. cit.*, p. 16; MULDER concurs with this opinion.

distinguish between good and evil''? Is this not "discernment in administering justice" and "a heart so wise and so discerning ..."? Referring back to iii 9ff., this terminology, absent in the narrative as such, is indicated in the final paragraph, which gives the narration its exemplary character[23]. "All Israel heard of the *judgement* (*mšpṭ*), which the king had *judged* (*špṭ*); and they feared the king: for they saw that the *wisdom of God* was in him, to do *judgement*" (v. 28). We are as yet given no answer to the question how the case of the two harlots could become an example of the practical application of the divine gift of judging the people of YHWH that Solomon had asked for. In any case the people recognises in this scene the divine nature of the wisdom of Solomon. About the "wisdom of God" MULDER rightly says: "This is less a 'great wisdom' than a 'divine wisdom'. If this were not the case, what would be the sense of the additional remark that the people 'feared the king'? With 'fear' and 'respectful modesty' man approaches people, places, etc. that are associated with God in a special way ..."[24]. Moreover, it is not just an arbitrary case which is described here. At the centre of it is a woman who is concerned about the life of her *son*. This word receives particular emphasis, especially in the repeated chiastic arrangement of vv. 22f., as distinct from *yld*, "child", and *ylwd*, "borne one", in v. 25ff., where incidentally the author mentions once more the "woman of the living son". It is unfortunate if this emphasis is obscured in translation by the use of words like child or baby (thus NEB) on account of the "maternal" situation, since in Israel the birth of a son stands for the promise of a future. That is why for instance in the narrative about the birth of Moses the daughters, the sons, and the *one* son constitute a special theme[25]. No less illustrative are the stories about the Shunnamite woman and her son, who had been dead but was restored to life[26]. One of those furnishes an example of a royal sentence when the woman calls for judicial aid just as Gehazi is telling the king the story about her son, who had been restored to life. It is she who acts, not her husband. This *woman* acts as representative of Israel returning from the exile: after having lived abroad for seven years, she "sought an audience of the king to appeal for the return of her house and land". The story about the prophet induces the king to comply with her request (II Kings viii 1-6).

The lawsuit acted out by the wise woman of Tekoah is just as instructive. She likewise calls in the king's judicial assistance with respect to the life of her

---

[23] A.-M. DUBARLE, 'Le jugement de Salomon: un coeur à l'écoute", *RScPhilT* 63 (1979), pp. 419-427, places too much emphasis on the psychological meaning.

[24] MULDER, *op. cit.*, p. 138; cf. GRAY, *op. cit.*, p. 129 etc.; wrongly KITTEL, *op. cit.*, p. 53: "Gefürchtet von allen Übelwollenden".

[25] J. SIEBERT-HOMMES, "Twelve Women in Exodus 1 and 2", *ACEBT* 9 (1988), pp. 35-46.

[26] A.G. VAN DAALEN, "'Vertel mij toch al het grote dat Elisa gedaan heeft'", *ACEBT* 1 (1980), pp. 51ff.

only remaining son, whose life is threatened by a blood feud. Her husband is dead, so that she has to argue the case as a *woman* and as a *widow*, in mourning because of the fratricide committed by her son[27]. In this narrative a direct connection is established with the existence of Israel. The woman has put her question to the king in order that "he will save me from the man who is seeking to cut off me and my son together from God's own possession" (II Samuel xiv 16). Her living son (her "glowing ember"), however, refers to the king's own son. As she is acting her case, she defends the life of her son, surrounded by the threat of death, but in addition, "Even on the non-fictitious level, she resists death, the punishment *mōt nāmūt*"[28], speaking on behalf of the people. A woman who devotes herself to the sake of her son's life: is that not also the theme of the judgement of Solomon, and might her case not refer metaphorically to Israel? One may object that it is rather unlikely that two harlots should serve this purpose[29]. However, this designation of the two women plays no part beyond the introduction. Moreover, this fact is a narrative necessity for the development of the case which is brought before the king; it is handled as an ethically neutral matter, as is fitting in a juridical case. What other form could one choose for a narrative about two women who live in the same house, without husbands and with their new-born babies? They can hardly be represented as two widows, and must accordingly be introduced as harlots *pour le besoin de la cause*. The example actually asks for a woman whose son must be kept alive. This can serve to illustrate the nature of the justice rendered by a king who should aim at preserving the lives of those who are under threat and have no rights. The judicial procedure used to demonstrate Solomon's wisdom in "maintaining justice and righteousness" (as the queen of Sheba puts it with the words indicating the divine gift in Psalm lxxii) has not been chosen at random. To bear a son and to preserve his life is the outstanding image of the future. Thus this vivid narrative, composed with meticulous care and surprising by its indirect effects, can reach its full impact exactly here, at the moment (*'z*) after the bestowal of the divine gift, as the description of Solomon's first and fundamental royal act. Without God's wisdom, clever though he may be as a politician, he is no more than a little boy, who does not know how to judge the people of YHWH, that is: to ensure the life and future of this chosen and blessed people by administering justice (iii 7ff.). He demonstrates the divine gift of his "hearing heart" in the exemplary decision of the "Judgement of Solomon": the mother is designated and her

[27] Cf. J. Hoftijzer, "David and the Tekoite Woman", *VT* 20 (1970), pp. 419-444, and the discussion with him in J. Fokkelman, *Narrative Art and Poetry in the Books of Samuel*, Vol. 1: *King David*, Assen 1981, pp. 126-147.

[28] Fokkelman, *op. cit.*, p. 142, referring to II Samuel xiv 14.

[29] Many commentators elaborate this aspect fully, while the older exegetical traditions try to blur it. One may simply argue that harlots had access to the throne just like other people.

son's life is entrusted to her hands. Thus the thematic framework of the narrative gives the example its full weight: "*All Israel*" hears the sentence and recognises that this king is to be "feared", as it has become manifest here that in him one finds: the wisdom of God by which he is "able to judge the 'weighty' people of YHWH".

# SOME REMARKS IN CONNECTION WITH THE PESHIṬTA OF KINGS*

BY

P.B. DIRKSEN

*Leiden*

During the period in which Professor M.J. Mulder and I worked together as colleagues in the Theological Faculty of Leiden University his research was directed mainly to the Peshiṭta and to the book of Kings. The most important results of it are his edition of the Peshiṭta text of Ezekiel in the Leiden Peshiṭta (1985) and his commentary on Kings 1-7[1]. It would, therefore, seem appropriate for me on the occasion of his retirement to combine these two subjects and to make some remarks concerning the Peshiṭta of Kings. First a few remarks will be made which directly concern the Peshiṭta of Kings, and next some remarks of a more general nature.

Every user of an edition as the Leiden Peshiṭta has in the edited text and the critical apparatus everything needed for a critical judgement as to the text of the document involved, but this does not mean that such a judgement is always an easy matter. Necessary for such a judgement is firstly an evaluation of the different readings in every single case and secondly an evaluation of the support given to the various readings in the MSS. What is the quality of the various MSS, and what is the value of a certain combination of MSS? For an answer to the second question one has to know what relationships exist between the MSS, as far as these can be ascertained. The following remarks concern this second question.

In recent Peshiṭta research it has become clear that for some books there is a break in the development of the Peshiṭta text in the ninth century. On the one side there are the ancient MSS with 9a1 as the last, on the other side the younger MSS, with the ninth and tenth-century Nestorian MSS in the lead. This holds good for Exodus, Judges, Samuel, Isaiah, and the Dodekapropheton[2]. There is an *a priori* probability that what is true for these books holds

---

* This article was read at a symposium in Leiden on 20 January 1989 on the occasion of Professor M.J. Mulder's retirement from the Faculty of Theology of Leiden University.

[1] M.J. MULDER, *Koningen*, Vol. I, *I Koningen 1-7* (Commentaar op het Oude Testament), Kampen 1987.

[2] M.D. KOSTER, *The Peshiṭta of Exodus. The Development of its Text in the Course of Fifteen Centuries* (Studia Semitica Neerlandica 19), Assen – Amsterdam 1977; P.B. DIRKSEN, "The Rela-

good also for Kings, but this may not be taken for granted. There are cases where the relationships of a MS to other MSS in one book differ from those in another book[3]. For a reliable judgement it will be necessary to establish the place of the individual MSS within the tradition of the text for each book separately. Actually the Book of Kings gives an example of this necessity. What is remarkable in the critical apparatus is that most of the variant readings concern unique readings in the Florentine MS 9a1 (Biblioteca Medicea Laurenziana, Orientali 58), apart from the support of its three seventeenth-century descendants, 17a7, 8, 9. 9a1 is known for its many deviating readings. In Judges 9a1 differs some 140 times from all other MSS up to and including the tenth century. In Kings, however, this number is reached already after the first six chapters, which means that in Kings 9a1 has a text which is highly distinctive. This raises the intriguing question as to how this came to be. Is it a matter of extraordinary carelessness on the part of the copyist or has there been a revision? Or both?[4] But why in one book and not, or at least not to the same extent, in the other? Has perhaps use been made of more than one *Vorlage*?

The bipartition of the text tradition between the ancient and the younger MSS with the break in the ninth century exists also in the Book of Kings, and is likely to be characteristic for the development of the whole O.T. Peshiṭta text. For Kings there are 35 cases in which all ancient MSS (as far as extant) go together against the younger MSS.

> The places are: I i 11 (8h4 has to be added in the critical apparatus after 6h18), 32, 42, 52; ii 42; iii 15; iv 10; vi 17, 20, 32; vii 8, 33 (see note 11), 35 (see note 11); ix 25; xiv 5; II xiv 2, 10, 1 (see note 11), 13; xv 33; xvi 15; xvii 1, 5, 17, 41; xviii 15 (twice), 24, 26; xxi 13; xxii 9; xxiii 18, 36; xxiv 8; xxv 22.

Equally, if not more important, however, is the fact that when the ancient

---

tion between the Ancient and the Younger Peshitta MSS in Judges", in: J.W. VAN HENTEN *et al.* (eds.), *Tradition and Re-Interpretation in Jewish and Christian Literature* (Festschrift J.C.H. Lebram), Leiden 1986, pp. 163-171; *idem*, "The Ancient Peshiṭta MSS of Judges and their Variant Readings", in: P.B. DIRKSEN and M.J. MULDER (eds.), *The Peshiṭta: Its Early Text and History* (Papers Read at the Peshiṭta Symposium held at Leiden 30-31 August 1985) (Monographs of the Peshiṭta Institute, Leiden IV), Leiden 1988, pp. 127-146; *idem*, "10c4 – Judges and 1/II Samuel", Symposium Volume, pp. 270-278; S.P. BROCK, "Text History and Text Division in Peshiṭta Isaiah", Symposium Volume, pp. 49-80, esp. pp. 50-51; A. GELSTON, *The Peshiṭta of the Twelve Prophets*, Oxford 1987, pp. 87-91.

[3] This is true, e.g. for 17a1 and 17a11; see P.B. DIRKSEN, *The Transmission of the Text in the Peshiṭta Manuscripts of the Book of Judges* (Monographs of the Peshiṭta Institute, Leiden I), Leiden 1972, p. xii.

[4] M.P. WEITZMAN maintains that at least in some places 9a1 has an original reading over against all other MSS. See his article "The Originality of Unique Readings in Peshiṭta MS 9a1", in Symposium Volume (note 2), pp. 225-258.

MSS differ among themselves, the younger MSS generally give their support together to one of the two readings, with the exception, of course, of 17a7, 8, 9, which are directly dependent on 9a1. The partition between the ancient MSS is not continued in the younger MSS. The latter differ among themselves in many cases, but these differences have nothing to do with those between the ancient MSS. As against the ancient MSS the younger MSS appear to form one group, with a common type of text.

In the transition from the text of the ancient MSS to that of the younger MSS the ninth- and tenth-century Nestorian MSS have played an important role. Their common text appears to have served as the basis of the later development of the text. This has been established in earlier studies for Exodus and Judges[5] and appears to hold good for Kings as well, as will be indicated in three points[6]. The manuscripts involved are the following:

9c1: Paris, National Library, Syr. 372. Missing: I i 7-41; viii 28-x 24; xviii 39-xx 34; II viii 29-x26; xvii 38-xx 16. Moreover, because of damage to the MS, many smaller portions are missing or illegible.
10c1: New Haven, Conn., Beinecke Rare Book Library, B 47b
10c2: Rome, Vatican Library, Borgiani siriaci 93. Missing: I ii 46-v 28; x 22-xv 29; xx 17-II ii 15; xi 9-xiv 13; xxiii 27-xxv 30. Because of damage some smaller portions are illegible.
10c4: Cambridge, Mass., Houghton Library 137

1. The four early Nestorian MSS have practically the same text. As a rule they go together. In a small number of cases one of them differs from the others, either in a unique reading[7], or in a reading found also in one or more other MSS. In the last case the difference is over small matters and the agreement is accidental.

9c1 has five unique readings (I ii 5; vi 22; vii 18; II xiv 6; xxiii 3), 10c1 seven (I ii 5; vii 51 (+10c4$^{c}$); ix 3; II xvi 14; xvii 5, 29; xxv 30), 10c2 three (I xvii 20; ii xvii 38; xviii 1), and 10c4 four (I v 11; vi 32; xi 22; xvii 18)[8].
9c1 parts company with the others with support elsewhere four times (I ii 42; xvi 7; II xii 13; xv 33)[9], 10c1 three times (I ii 40; vii 38; II iv 30)[10], 10c2

[5] M.D. Koster, *Exodus* ... (note 2), pp. 143ff., 529ff.; P.B. Dirksen, "The Relation ..." (note 2).

[6] For some general remarks concerning the Nestorian MSS in Kings see K.D. Jenner, "10c4 – I/II Kings, Proverbs ...", Symposium Volume (note 2), pp. 279-289, esp. p. 281.

[7] "Unique reading" is used in the sense of "not being shared by one or more MSS of up to and including the tenth century".

[8] For 10c4 see Symposium Volume (note 2), pp. 280-283.

[9] The variant reading *dyqr*]*dyqd* 7a1 9c1 at I xiv 4 in the second apparatus of the edition has to be deleted. In the second apparatus 9c1 has to be deleted at II xviii 15 (twice) and xxv 30.

[10] 10c1 has to be deleted in the second apparatus at II xxi 19.

six times (I xix 14; II vi 24; xviii 17; xix 1; xxii 1; xxv 30), 10c4 three times (I vii 7; x 25; II x 10).

It is clear that these MSS are closely related. Yet none of them can have been the *Vorlage* of any of the others since each of these MSS differs in a number of cases from all the others. The most plausible assumption is that these four MSS have been copied from one and the same *Vorlage*.

2. In Kings, as elsewhere, 8a1 (Paris, National Library, syr. 341) has been corrected by a later hand in about a hundred places[11]. In these corrections the text of 8a1 was apparently adapted to the text as we find it in the early Nestorian MSS. In all cases but two (I vii 37; II xxv 19) the corrected text agrees with these Nestorian MSS. In twenty-two cases[12] 8a1$^{c}$ and these Nestorian MSS differ together from all other ancient MSS. It is clear that 8a1$^{c}$ and the early Nestorian MSS derive from the same source, which does, however, not necessarily mean from the same *Vorlage*. There are some fifty cases in which 8a1 differs from the early Nestorian MSS, without having been corrected. The best way to account for these cases would seem to be the same which was suggested for Judges[13], viz. that 8a1 was carefully corrected on the basis of another MS. This latter MS was, or had already been, copied, by a copyist who introduced some fifty changes, either on purpose or by error. This MS in its turn served as the *Vorlage* of the early Nestorian MSS and so these changes found their way into these later MSS.

3. The text of the early Nestorian MSS is always the same as that of the majority of the post tenth-century MSS. This majority is, of course, an ever changing one, as is the minority. In most cases this minority consists of two or more related MSS. In general the minority reading finds no support among the ancient MSS. In the small number of exceptions there is no pattern whatsoever, and the agreement is to be considered accidental. This means that the minority reading has no ancient roots of its own and can be understood as a deviation from the majority text[14]. Since this majority text is presented in the early Nestorian MSS the conclusion must be that, just as in Exodus and Judges, the text of the early Nestorian MSS lies at the basis of the later text.

---

[11] In the edition no distinction has been made in many cases between 8a1, 8a1*, and 8a1$^{c}$ (8a1$^{1}$). In the following cases 8a1 has to be changed into 8a1*: I iv 10; v 1; vi 32; xii 16 (~); xiii 2; and in I vi 37 into 8a1$^{c}$. 8a1* has to be added at I ii 32; v 22; vii 33 (omnes *minus*), 35; xiii 15, 17 (omnes *minus*); II iv 29 (*pr lamadh*); vii 8 (*lswp'*); ix 2; xiv 11. 8a1 has to be added at I xviii 26 (omnes *minus*); II vii 7 twice (*wrkšhwn* and *wḥmrhwn*), and to be deleted at II xxii 6. 8a1$^{1}$ has to be deleted twice at II iv 8. At II xxi 1 8a1$^{c}$ has to be changed into 8a1* (*vid*) + 8a1$^{c2}$. At I xii 16 *'m'*] *om* 8a1 19g4$^{txt}$.7 has to be deleted, and at II v 14 (*vid*; *dnby*) after 8a1*.

[12] I ii 42; iii 15; iv 10; vi 17, 20, 32; vii 8, 33; ix 25; xix 11; II xiv 2, 11; xvii 1, 5, 17; xvi 15; xviii 15, 24; xxii 9; xxiii 18, 25; xxv 22.

[13] Festschrift Lebram (see note 2), pp. 169f.

[14] This is meant in general, and does not exclude the possibility that in incidental cases a young MS has made use of an ancient MS.

None of them, however, can have been the actual basic MS in view of the places, mentioned above, in which one of these MSS parts company with the others. Most likely, this basic MS is to be found in their common *Vorlage*. This *Vorlage* was just one of the ancient MSS which basically shared their common text, and where these MSS differed among themselves took sides in different combinations. The readings in which this *Vorlage* differed from any or all of the other ancient MSS were transmitted to the later text tradition and so, by sheer accident, became the readings in which the younger MSS together differ from any or all of the ancient MSS.

The conclusion from these observations is the following: The four early Nestorian MSS go back to a common *Vorlage*. This *Vorlage* has also served as the basis for the corrections in 8a1 and was also the basic MS from which the later text tradition developed.

With respect to the last point another opinion has been given by A. GELSTON in his 1987 dissertation on the Peshiṭta of the Twelve Prophets[15]. The actual facts as presented by GELSTON in this study and in his earlier edition of the Peshiṭta text of these books are not different from those for Exodus, Judges, and Samuel: on the one side we have the ancient MSS, with 9a1 as the latest, and on the other side the younger MSS. For the text of the younger MSS GELSTON uses the term "standard text". The problem is well expressed in his words (p. 87): "One of the puzzling features of the transmission of the Peshiṭta is the almost universal diffusion of the standard text from about the ninth century". The bipartition of the text tradition, with the break in the ninth century, is indeed a remarkable fact. From these words of GELSTON it is also clear what in his opinion has happened: there was a "diffusion" of the standard text beginning in the ninth century, not its coming into being. The "standard text" itself existed already much earlier. In short GELSTON's opinion is as follows: There are a number of cases in which all ancient MSS go together against all younger MSS. From this it is clear that the ancient MSS have a type of text of their own. Besides, there are a number of cases in which one or more of the ancient MSS do not agree with the other ancient MSS, but with the (standard text of the) younger MSS. This means that the ancient MSS have in varying degrees been "contaminated" (p. 89) by the standard text. This "contamination" occurs in all ancient MSS, and from this it follows that the standard text was already in existence before the oldest MSS now known were written, and probably antedate the confessional conflict in the fifth century. Although the standard text is older than the oldest MSS, it appears nevertheless to be inferior to the text of the oldest MSS. Moreover, it has not been preserved in any known MS. It emerged only in the ninth century and subse-

---

[15] See note 2.

quently superseded the text of the ancient MSS so as virtually to dominate the later text tradition.

It will be clear that this difference in opinion has its consequences as to the evaluation of the "standard text". In GELSTON's view we have here a very old text form, which even antedates the oldest known MSS, and, consequently, the "standard text" deserves to be treated with all respect due to such an old text. It is true that this "standard text" is inferior to that of the ancient MSS, but this follows from a comparison between the rival readings involved, not from the text history itself. The case is different if the "standard text" is nothing else than the text of a ninth-century (Nestorian) MS. In that case the distinctive readings of the "standard text" in which it differs from the ancient MSS started as unique readings of that basic MS and so stand over against the unanimous witness of all other, and mostly older, ancient MSS.

The view as presented by GELSTON is coherent but one may wonder whether it does not raise more questions than it answers.

In GELSTON's view the standard text came into being as early as the fifth century. How did this bipartition happen? Is it probable that the standard text existed through the four centuries in which the ancient MSS were written and that it exercised its influence on all of these MSS, without even one MS with this standard text having survived? How did this "contamination" actually happen? The most important consideration may be the following: The "standard text" lies at the base of all younger MSS, which must mean that ultimately these younger MSS go back to one MS. If they would derive from two or more MSS then this should be apparent from a possible partition of these younger MSS on the basis of the differences between these basic MSS[16]. What is the date of this basic MS? *A priori* the likelihood is that this new type of text came into being in the time it actually appears, i.e. the ninth century. This date seems indeed the more likely one, since the ninth and tenth-century Nestorian MSS actually have a text which is practically identical with this "standard text", whereas their common *Vorlage* is completely identical with it. There seems to be no reason to carry this text further back to an identical MS of the fifth century[17].

These considerations, finally, lead to the following, more general question: Is it to be commended to speak in this connection of a "textus receptus" or a "standard text"? The first term is used by KOSTER in his study on Exodus, the second, as mentioned above, by GELSTON in his monograph on Dodeka-

---

[16] It is useless to speculate on the theoretical possibility that two or more identical MSS have been in play.

[17] See on this point now also M.D. KOSTER's review of GELSTON's book in *JSS* 33 (1988), pp. 281-285.

propheton. GELSTON says explicitly that he uses "standard text" for what is "textus receptus" for KOSTER (p. 65). Both terms refer to the basic text of the later MSS, beginning with the ninth century, which according to KOSTER actually arose in the ninth century but according to GELSTON some four centuries earlier.

I wonder whether these terms do not suggest too much. In the first place they may easily give the impression that we are dealing here with a text which has received ecclesiastical sanction, and has become more or less normative[18]. We know, however, nothing about an official standardisation of the Peshiṭta text. In the second place the terms may suggest that the younger MSS have a more or less uniform text. As has been indicated above, these MSS have a common basic text, but among themselves they differ very much, and in many cases the differences among themselves are greater than those between their common basic text and that of the ancient MSS. Both terms refer to a text which has been abstracted from the concrete text as it occurs in the MSS. From the point of view of textual history it may serve greater clarity if we speak of this text as what it is: the basic text of the younger MSS, or concretely: the type of text of the ninth- and tenth-century Nestorian MSS.

---

[18] To be sure: neither KOSTER nor GELSTON seems to imply this, although it is not quite clear whether or not GELSTON reckons with this possibility; see p. 88, line 10ff. K.D. JENNER thinks it possible that church-political factors have given rise to a more or less normative text. See his article "Some Introductory Remarks Concerning the Study of 8a1", Symposium Volume (note 2), pp. 200-224.

# PHILOLOGICAL-GRAMMATICAL NOTES ON I KINGS XI 14

BY

J. HOFTIJZER

*Leiden*

Some years ago G. VANONI published an interesting book on chapters xi and xii of I Kings[1] in which I Kings xi 14 is also discussed. In his opinion the verse as we find it in the *textus receptus* is the result of a subsequent redaction of an original text *hdd h'dmy mzr' hmlk*, which served as an introduction to the story of Solomon's troubles with the Edomites[2]. In this article the author will discuss the philological/grammatical problems of this verse anew. In this discussion the arguments of VANONI will also be mentioned.

The text of I Kings xi 14 consists of two clauses: a) a verbal one (*wyqm YHWH śṭn lšlmh 't hdd h'dmy*; b) a nominal one (*mzr' hmlk hw' b'dwm*). The nominal form *śṭn* indicates someone who actively obstructs another person or turns against him. In Ps. cix 4 the verbal form *yśṭnwny* is parallel to *wylḥmwny* in vs. 3[3]. The participle phrase *śṭny npšy* in Ps. lxxi 13 is parallel to *mbqšy r'ty*; the participle form *śṭny* in Ps. cix 20 is parallel to *hdbrym r' 'l npšy*[4]. In I Sam. xxix 4 the text tells us that the princes of the Philistines fear that David may become for them *lśṭn bmlḥmh*. According to the context this means that during the impending battle, he may go over to Saul, turn himself against them and bring Saul the final victory. In II Sam. xix 23 David says to Abishai and his brothers that they may become a *śṭn* for him. Returning after the victory over Absalom, he wants to forgive his enemy Shimei (vs. 22f.; only for the time being, cf. I Kings ii 8f.)[5]. Abishai on the other hand wants to kill Shimei immediately (II Sam. xix 22), which would probably have

[1] G. VANONI, *Literarkritik und Grammatik. Untersuchungen der Wiederholungen und Spannungen in 1 Kon. 11-12* (Arbeiten zu Text und Sprache im Alten Testament, Band 21), St. Ottilien 1984.

[2] VANONI, *op. cit.*, p. 266.

[3] Cf. in the context also vv. 2, 3a, 5. In Ps. xxxviii 21 the subject of the verbal form *yśṭnwny* is *mšlmy r'h tḥt ṭwbh*; the parallels of this subject are *'yby* and *śn'y* (v. 20).

[4] These people are also mentioned in Ps. cix 29. From the beginning of this psalm it is clear that they turn against the poet (vv. 3f.; v. also *supra*).

[5] Cf. M.J. MULDER, *Koningen vertaald en verklaard*, deel I, *1 Koningen 1-7*, Kampen 1987, p. 94, who, referring to David's words in II Sam. xix 23 (especially to *hywm*), rightly speaks of a subtle indication of "stay of execution".

endangered David's reinvestiture[6]; in other words the action proposed by Abishai would have been a danger to David's position[7]. I Kings xi 14 tells that Hadad became a *śṭn* for Solomon; I Kings xi 23, 25 tell that Rezon became a *śṭn* for Solomon and Israel respectively. The last-mentioned text says that he was a *śṭn* for Israel during the whole of Solomon's life *w't hr'h 'šr hdd* (i.e. besides the evil that Hadad did)[8]. Hadad being a *śṭn* (cf. I Kings xi 14) means his being someone who hurt Israel. Moreover Rezon's being a *śṭn* is put on the same level as Hadad doing evil. According to Numb. xxii 22 an angel stood as *śṭn* in the way of Balaam. That he had inimical intentions is clear from vs. 23, 31 (where he says that he intended to kill Balaam). That there was peace and no danger for Solomon is expressed in I Kings v 18 by there being no *śṭn* and no *pg' r'*. In Ps. cix 6 the *śṭn* occurs in a context of a forensic character in the form of the accuser who has to adduce incriminating evidence

---

[6] So e.g. P.L. DAY, "Abishai the *satan* in 2 Samuel 19:17-24", *CBQ* 49 (1987), pp. 543-547 on p. 546.

[7] I do not agree with Miss DAY, art. cit., p. 545 that this text has a "forensic character" and that Abishai wants to be an accuser on David's *behalf* (art. cit., pp. 544f.). In the five other instances where *śṭn l* occurs, *l* always has a negative meaning and not a positive one (Numb. xxii 22; I Sam. xxix 4; I Kings xi 14, 23, 25). Moreover, a "negative" interpretation fits the context.

[8] I take the *w* as being a so-called *waw asseverativum* (cf. also the author, "David and the Tekoite Woman", *VT* 20 (1970), pp. 419-444 on p. 433, n. 4). I take the *hr'h 'šr hdd* as a type of "genitival" construction, more or less equivalent to *r't hdd.* A construction like this is well known from Aramaic (cf. e.g. *DISO*, p. 74, ll. 5 ff.; H. BAUER and P. LEANDER, *Grammatik des Biblisch-Aramäischen*, Halle (Saale) 1927, par. 90), from Punic (J. FRIEDRICH and W. RÖLLIG, *Phönizisch-Punische Grammatik* (Analecta Orientalia 46), Roma 1970, par. 310, 2-3a) and from Akkadian (cf. W. v. SODEN, *Grundriss der akkadischen Grammatik samt Ergänzungsheft zum Grundriss der akkadischen Grammatik* (Analecta Orientalia 33/47), Roma 1969, par. 138. In classical Hebrew this construction is extremely rare. The instances known to me are I Sam. xiii 8, I Kings xi 25, II Kings xxv 10. The fact that this phenomenon is rare, is, in my opinion, insufficient reason to consider it as the (probable) outcome of text corruption (against e.g. H. EWALD, *Ausführliches Lehrbuch der hebräischen Sprache des Alten Bundes*, Göttingen 1870[8], p. 746, n. 1; S.R. DRIVER in F. BROWN, S.R. DRIVER and C.A. BRIGGS, *A Hebrew and English Lexicon of the Old Testament* . . . , Boston – New York 1907, p. 83a). On this point I agree with F.R. KÖNIG, *Historisch-comparative Syntax der hebräischen Sprache*, Leipzig 1897, par. 283b. The *mw'd 'šr šmw'l* (I Sam. xiii 8) is more or less equivalent to *mw'd šmw'l* (the time fixed by Samuel; cf. I Sam. xx 35 *bmw'd dwd*, on the time fixed by an appointment with David, cf. v. 19). The *ḥyl kśdym 'šr rb ṭbḥym* (II Kings xxv 10) is a so-called "expression of the genitive by circumlocution", here the "circumlocution" is used because a construction with *regens* and *rectum* (*kśdy rb* . . .) is impossible (cf. e.g. W. GESENIUS, E. KAUTZSCH, and A.E. COWLEY, *Hebrew Grammar*, Oxford 1910[2], par. 129e). The fact that the parallel text Jer. lii 14 reads *ḥyl kśdym 'šr 't-rb-ṭbḥym* cannot be adduced as an argument that the reading in II Kings xxv 10 *must* be corrupt (against KÖNIG, *op. cit.*, par. 283a). The text II Chr. xxxiv 22 often quoted in the same connection will not be treated here because the *w'šr hmlk* belongs to another grammatical category. In I Kings xi 25 the *r'h 'šr hdd* can be compared with *r't 'bymlk* (Judg. ix 56: the evil done by Abimelek; cf. also Gen. vi 5; Judg. ix 57; I Sam. xxv 39; Jer. vii 12, xi 17, xii 4, xxxii 32; Ps. cvii 34; Eccl. viii 6; Esth. viii 3). For the interpretation of *'t* in I Kings xi 25, cf. Ex. i 14, Lev. xxvi 39 (the *-m* of *'tm* referring to the (sins of the) subject). I do not agree with those authors who consider *w't hr'h 'šr hdd* as a "Randglosse" which does not really belong to its context (against M. NOTH, *Könige* I, Neukirchen/Vluyn 1968, p. 255; E. WÜRTHWEIN, *Das erste Buch der Könige, ein Kommentar*, Würzburg 1979, p. 122; cf. also VANONI, *op. cit.*, p. 97, n. 82).

against the person in question and so (during the process) has to hurt him as much as possible. (Cf. also the parallel *rš'* in vs. 6). One finds a comparable use in Zech. iii 1, 2. In Job i 6, 7, 8, 9, 12; ii 1, 2, 3, 4, 6, 7; I Chr. xxi 1 the *śṭn* indicating a superhuman being has the same characteristics, his aim is to hurt Job and David respectively, which in fact he does as much as possible[9]. In other words in I Kings xi 14 Hadad is described as an adversary, who, instigated by God, has the aim of doing as much harm as possible to Solomon[10]. In the clause *wyqm YHWH śṭn lšlmh 't hdd h'dmy* I take *'t hdd h'dmy* as object and *śṭn* as result object[11]. It is possible to take *śṭn 't hdd d'dmy* as one (interrupted) clause element, as most commentaries do. However, because there is a more or less parallel clause in vs. 23 (on Rezon being a *śṭn* at the same time) it seems better to interpret both clauses in such a way that they share the same verbal form and result object, but have a different object[12]. From the second clause it becomes clear that Hadad was a member of the Edomite royal family[13]. The first element in this clause to be discussed is *mzr' hmlk*. Many commentators have proposed to emend *hmlk hw'* in *hmlwkh* (cf. II Kings xxv 25; Jer. xli 1; Ez. xvii 13; Dan. i 3; cf. also *zr' hmmlkh* in II Kings

---

[9] I do not agree with G. v. RAD, "Die alttestamentliche Satansvorstellung", in: G. KITTEL (ed.), *Theologisches Wörterbuch zum Neuen Testament* II, Stuttgart 1935, pp. 71-74, who takes *śṭn* first of all as belonging to the forensic practice and who wants to interpret all the relevant texts from this standpoint. The material at our disposal rather argues in favour of the *śṭn* being someone who wants to hurt/to attack. A word with this special semantic feature could also be used in a forensic context to indicate the accuser (also against A. BROCK-UTNE, "'Der Feind', die alttestamentliche Satansgestalt im Lichte der sozialen Verhältnisse des Nahen Ostens", *Klio* 28 (1935), pp. 219-227, who interprets Hadad's being a *śṭn* for Solomon as his being a "Verleumder" at the court of the great king at the same time as being the leader of a revolutionary movement (pp. 222f.)). For an interpretation of *śṭn* comparable to the one given here, cf. e.g. G. WANKE, in: E. JENNI and C. WESTERMANN (eds.), *Theologisches Wörterbuch zum Alten Testament* II, München – Zürich 1979, s.v., p. 822.

I will not go into the differences of the *śṭn* in Job and the one in I Chronicles.

[10] This does not mean that Hadad's revolt was a permanent success, cf. e.g. I Kings xxii 48. On this point, cf. e.g. J.R. BARTLETT, "An Adversary Against Solomon, Hadad the Edomite", *ZAW* 88 (1976), pp. 205-226 on p. 225 and A. MALAMAT, "Look at the Kingdom of David and Solomon and its Relations with Egypt", in: T. ISHIDA (ed.), *Studies in the Period of David and Solomon and Other Essays* (Papers read at the International Symposium for Biblical Studies, Tokyo, 5-7 December 1979), Tokyo 1982, pp. 189-204 on p. 201 n. 35.

[11] For this type of construction, cf. e.g. GESENIUS, KAUTZSCH and COWLEY, *op. cit.*, par. 371ii; P. JOÜON, *Grammaire de l'Hébreu biblique*, Rome 1947², par. 125w. For instances where the result-object stands before the object and not after it, cf. e.g. Gen. vi 14; Deut. xxvii 6; II Kings xix 25 (= Is. xxxvii 26). I disagree with VANONI, *op. cit.*, pp. 196ff. that an interpretation of a clause like the first one in I Kings xi 14 is "aus mehreren Grunden zweifelhaft". There is no reason to consider it as a clause where one may suspect "Textwachstum" (*op. cit.*, p. 201). In my opinion, the way in which instances of this clause order (like Judg. iii 9, 15) are characterised as "konstruiert bzw. uneinheitlich" is not free from arbitrariness. That *lšlmh* is not necessarily an apposition to *śṭn* is clear from I Kings xi 23.

[12] One of the few commentators who interpret the clause as I do, is S.J. DE VRIES, *1 Kings* (World Biblical Commentary, Vol. 12), Waco, Texas 1985, p. 145.

[13] On the problem as to whether Edom at the time had a royal family of a dynastic type, cf.

xi 1; II Chr. xxii 10)[14]. This emendation has been rejected (justly in my opinion) as unnecessary[15]. Those who retain the reading of the *textus receptus* mostly interpret *zrʿ hmlk* as the "royal family". It is doubtful whether this is an exact interpretation. If *mlk* is taken in its normal meaning of "king", *zrʿ hmlk* could mean the "offspring/descendants of the king". *Zrʿ* meaning "offspring/descendants" *can* indicate the whole of someone's offspring through all ages (e.g. Gen. iii 15, xii 7, xv 18, etc.), but this is not necessarily so. In some instances *zrʿ* indicates someone's descendants living during his lifetime: his children (and grandchildren). A clear example is Is. liii 10 (*yr'h zrʿ wy'ryk ymym*), where it is said that someone will have a long life and during this time will have the pleasure of seeing descendants (in other words: he will not be childless)[16]. Cf. also the following texts: a) Gen. xlvi 7 (Jacob takes with him his sons and grandsons, his daughters and granddaughters *wkl zrʿw*: namely all his descendants)[17]; b) Gen. xlviii 11 (speaks of Jacob's joy to be able to see not only Joseph, but also Joseph's *zrʿ* (*zrʿk*). Here *zrʿ* clearly refers to Joseph's sons Ephraim and Manasseh (cf. vs. 1, 8ff.; cf. also vs. 13ff.)); c) Lev. xx 2 (speaks about someone sacrificing *mzrʿw* to the Molekh (cf. Lev. xviii 21, xx 3, 4))[18]; d) Lev. xxii 13 (the verse discusses the possibility that a priest's daughter gets into a difficult position if she has no *zrʿ*); e) I Sam. ii 20 (After Elkana and Hannah have brought Samuel to Eli, the last-mentioned blesses them and prays that Elkana may get *zrʿ* from Hannah instead of the son they have renounced; here clearly "children, sons" are meant). The word *zrʿ* referring to "descendants/children" is probably also found in Jer. xxxvi 31, xlix 10[19]. Therefore it would be quite possible to interpret *zrʿ hmlk* in I Kings xi 14 as "descendants/children" of the Edomite king. That here "children, sons" are meant, becomes probable from the *'byw* in vs. 17: Hadad,

---

e.g. J.R. Bartlett, "The Edomite King-List of Genesis xxxvi 31-39 and 1 Chron. i 43-50", *JThSt* 16 (1965), pp. 301-314 on p. 313, and the same author, art. cit., *ZAW* 88 (1976), pp. 206f.

[14] Basing themselves on the LXX; cf. e.g. A. Klostermann, *Die Bücher Samuelis und der Könige ausgelegt*, Nordlingen 1887, a.l.; I. Benzinger, *Die Bücher der Könige erklärt*, Freiburg i.B. – Leipzig – Tübingen 1899, p. 78; C.E. Burney, *Notes on the Hebrew Text of the Book of Kings*, Oxford 1903, p. 160; E. Meyer, *Die Israeliten und ihre Nachbarstämme*, Halle a.S. 1906, p. 359, n. 3; A.B. Ehrlich, *Randglossen zur hebräischen Bibel. Textkritisches, Sprachliches und Sachliches* VII, Leipzig 1914, p. 241.

[15] Cf. J.A. Montgomery and Gehman, *A Critical and Exegetical Commentary on the Book of Kings*, Edinburgh 1951, p. 245.

[16] A well-known way to indicate a blessed life, cf. e.g. H. Tawil, "Some Literary Elements in the Opening Sections of the Hadad, Zakir, and the Nerab II Inscriptions in the Light of East and West Semitic Royal Inscriptions", *Orientalia* 43 (1974), pp. 40-65 on p. 63ff.

[17] I take the *w* before *kl* as *waw explicativum*.

[18] Cf. also II Kings xxiii 10, where someone is said to sacrifice *bnw* or *btw* to the Molekh (cf. also Jer. xxxii 35).

[19] For *zrʿ* referring to a single child, cf. Gen. iv 25; I Sam. i 11; II Sam. vii 12 (cf. the parallel text I Chr. xvii 11, where instead of *'t-zrʿk 'ḥryk 'šr yṣ' mmʿyk* one finds *'t-zrʿk 'ḥryk 'šr yhyh mbnyk*). Cf. possibly also Jer. xxxiii 26 (I take the *w* before *dwd* as *waw explicativum*).

one of the sons of the king, is saved by servants of his father who bring him to Egypt[20]. This is not meant to deny that words for "kingship" like *mlwkh* are interchangeable in certain context types with a noun like *mlk* as VANONI has argued[21]. But contextually the interpretation of *zr' hmlk* as "sons of the king" which is also possible, is in my opinion preferable, especially in view of the *'byw* of vs. 17. Some authors (VANONI among them) consider the *b'dwm* or *hw' b'dwm* at the end of the second clause as a later gloss[22] (a gloss on either *hmlk* or on the difficult *'t-'dwm* in vs. 15). In my opinion, however, there is no reason why (*hw'*) *b'dwm* would not fit the context. In the nominal clause *mzr' hmlk hw' b'dwm*, *hw'*, being one of the two core elements, is an essential constituent. The *b'dwm* gives no reason to consider it as a strange element in the clause. For the use of a prepositional phrase consisting of the preposition *b* and a *nomen geographicum* in a comparable clause type one may compare the following instances (I give here as examples nominal clauses and *hyh*-clauses telling which function/social status someone has): Gen. xxxvi 16 (*'lh 'lwpy 'lypz b'rṣ 'dwm*; cf. Gen. xxxvi 17, 21), Numb. xxv 15 (*r'š 'mwt byt 'b bmdyn hw'*), Deut. vi 21 (*'bdym hyynw lpr'h bmṣrym*), I Sam. xiv 3 (*w'ḥyh . . . khn YHWH bšlw*), Zech. ix 7 (*whyh k'lp byhwdh*); cf. also Judg. xviii 19 (*hywtk khn lšbṭ wlmšpḥh byśr'l*). These texts tell that certain people have a certain function/social status within a country or locality (i.e. within the framework of the society living in that country or locality). Cf. also I Kings xviii 36 (*'th 'lhym byśr'l*), words used in a context in which Elijah underlines the power of God and describing a situation in which the Israelites have to decide whom they have to serve, God or the Baal (cf. e.g. vs. 24, 39). Elijah says here that God has the supreme (divine) authority within Israel[23]. The second clause of I Kings xi 14 tells which place Hadad occupied within Edomite society: he was one of the king's sons[24]. There is no reason whatsoever to consider (*hw'*) *b'dwm* as a *Fremdkörper* in this clause[25]. The last point

[20] For this reason it is also unnecessary, in my opinion, to vocalise *mlk* as *molek* meaning "kingship", a solution possible in itself, proposed by M. WEIPPERT, *Edom. Studien und Materialien zur Geschichte der Edomiter auf Grund schriftlicher und archäologischer Quellen*, Tübingen 1971, p. 297.

[21] VANONI, *op. cit.*, p. 158 (n. 492).

[22] Cf. e.g. MONTGOMERY and GEHMAN, *op. cit.*, p. 245; BARTLETT, art. cit., *ZAW* 88 (1976), p. 206; VANONI, *op. cit.*, p. 266; cf. also A. JEPSEN in the *Biblia Hebraica Stuttgartensia*, Stuttgart 1977.

[23] Cf. also Eccl. i 12 (*'ny qhlt hyyty mlk 'l yśr'l byrwšlm*) where *byrwšlm* indicates that Solomon exercises his royal power over Israel in the centre of the country, the capital.

[24] One may also compare nominal and *hyh*-clauses which tell of which quality someone has and where a comparable prepositional phrase functions as constituent on clause level: Ex. xi 3 (*h'yš mšh gdwl m'd b'rṣ mṣrym*); Judg. vi 15 (*'lpy hdl bmnšh*); II Sam. xiii 13 (*w'th thyh k'ḥd hnblym byśr'l*), etc. Cf. also (said of God): Ez. xxxix 7 (*'ny YHWH qdwš byśr'l*); Ps. xcix 2 (*YHWH bṣywn gdwl*), cf. Ps. lxxvi 2.

[25] On this point I agree with the majority of commentators, cf. e.g. R. KITTEL, *Die Bücher der*

I want to tackle is the clause order in both clauses and the relation between them.

W. RICHTER has justly concluded that in a clause of the type of the first one in I Kings xi 14 (*wyqm YHWH śṭn lšlmh 't hdd h'dmy*) the relation between the object and the result object is the same as in a nominal clause where both elements are clause cores[26]. In our case the corresponding nominal clause would have as core elements a definite element (*hdd h'dmy*) and an indefinite one (*śṭn* [*lšlmh*]). In such a nominal clause two sequences are possible: *hdd h'dmy śṭn* and *śṭn hdd h'dmy*. One can describe the function of a nominal clause (as far as the core elements are concerned) in two ways: 1) by basing oneself on the morphological character of the core elements; 2) by basing oneself on the order of the core elements[27]. In clauses like *hdd h'dmy śṭn* and *śṭn hdd h'dmy* Hadad is classified as a *śṭn*[28]. The clause with the order *śṭn hdd h'dmy* is functionally marked in such a way that the order of the core elements indicates that the focus is on Hadad's classification as a *śṭn*[29]. The clause with the order *hdd h'dmy śṭn* is functionally unmarked as far as this function is concerned[30]. In the first clause of I Kings xi 14 (the result object preceding the object), the word order used is not one commonly found in comparable

---

*Könige übersetzt und erklärt*, Göttingen 1900, p. 97; J. GRAY, *I & II Kings, A Commentary*, London 1970, p. 281; E. WÜRTHWEIN, *op. cit.*, p. 135.

[26] W. RICHTER, *Grundlagen einer althebräischen Grammatik* III (Arbeiten zu Text und Sprache im Alten Testament, Band 13), St. Ottilien 1980, pp. 100f. (cf. also VANONI, *op. cit.*, pp. 196ff.). Cf. already P. JOÜON, *op. cit.*, par. 125v.

[27] In my opinion it would be wrong to choose between both approaches: one has to use them both.

[28] Cf. e.g. F.I. ANDERSEN, *The Hebrew Verbless Clause in the Pentateuch* (Journal of Biblical Literature Monograph Series XIV, ed. R.A. KRAFT), Nashville – New York 1970, p. 32; W. RICHTER, *op. cit.*, pp. 86ff.; R. CONTINI, *Tipologia della frase nominale nel semitico nordoccidentale del I millennio A.C.*, Pisa 1982, p. 43; R. BARTELMUS, *HYH. Bedeutung und Funktion eines hebräischen "Allerweltwortes"* (Arbeiten zu Text und Sprache im Alten Testament, Band 17), St. Ottilien 1982, p. 100. In this article I will not go into the differences of opinion and approach between these authors. My quoting them does not mean that I agree with all their conclusions on the different morphological types of nominal clauses.

[29] Cf. the author's "The Nominal Clause Reconsidered", *VT* 23 (1973), pp. 446-510 on pp. 496 ff. Here I have avoided using the term "contrastive" I used in this article (cf. pp. 492f.), because I agree with those authors who have argued that the interpretation of the function of this word order as indicating that it is of importance that *this* indefinite core element is used *and not another one*, lays too much stress on the characteristics of this core element *as to be distinguished* from other possible characteristics (cf. e.g. CONTINI, *op. cit.*, p. 17; T. MURAOKA, *Emphatic Words and Structures in Biblical Hebrew*, Jerusalem – Leiden 1985, pp. 12f., 16). For the interpretation given in the present article, cf. also MURAOKA, *op. cit.*, p. 8, according to whose very helpful approach the clause *śṭn hdd h'dmy* can be interpreted as an answer to the question "what is Hadad?". I myself have avoided the use of the term *emphasis* because, in my opinion, emphasis is a formal phenomenon and (to avoid misunderstanding) ought not to be used to indicate functional phenomena (cf. also the author, art. cit., *VT* 23 (1973), pp. 492f., n. 1).

[30] Cf. the author, art. cit., *VT* 23 (1973), p. 500. A comparable conclusion is proposed by MURAOKA, *op. cit.*, p. 7. He says that the P-S pattern (except where the predicate is a preposi-

instances[31]. Whereas clauses like *wyqm YHWH . . . 't hdd h'dmy śṭn* and *wyqm YHWH śṭn . . . 't hdd h'dmy* correspond to nominal clauses with *hdd h'dmy* and *śṭn* as core elements, it is most likely that, whereas the order of core elements in the relevant nominal clauses has a certain function, the order of object and result object in the corresponding verbal clauses also has a function, probably a corresponding one. This would mean that in e.g. I Kings xi 14, 23 the result object preceding the object means that the focus is on Hadad and Rezon, respectively, being a *śṭn*[32]. This would fit the context very well, the idea being that Solomon has to be punished for his sins, this happening by God's opposing against him two dangerous/aggressive enemies[33]. In the second clause of I Kings xi 14 the order of the core elements *mzr' hmlk* and *hw'* indicates that the focus is on the "he" being one of the king's sons[34]. It is not only the word order of this clause which is of interest, but also its being asyndetic. Asyndetic nominal clauses of which the second one of the core elements is an independent personal pronoun of the third person have a special function. They give information which contributes to a better understanding of the context (sc. of what is told in the preceding or following clause(s))[35]. To give some examples: 1) Lev. iv 21 (*hṭ't hqhl hw'*; that the bullock has to be burnt becomes understandable when one knows that it is a sin-offering, cf. vs. 14; cf. also Ex. xxix 14, 18, 25; Lev. i 13, 17, etc.); 2) Ex. xii 2 (the clause

---

tional or adverbial phrase) has a function "description" and that the S-P pattern has as function "description" or "identification". This means that the one pattern is functionally marked (functional indication: description) and that the other is unmarked as to that functional indication. The author avoids using the terms *subject* and *predicate* in this connection for practical reasons (cf. art. cit., *VT* 23 (1973), pp. 487f.; cf. also the author's "A Grammatical Note on the Yavne-Yam ostracon", in: J.W. v. HENTEN *et al.* (eds.), *Tradition and Re-Interpretation in Jewish and Early Christian Literature . . .* (Studia Postbiblica 36), Leiden 1986, pp. 1-6, on p. 4 n. 15). I do not agree with BARTELMUS, *op. cit.*, p. 116 that the order of core elements in a nominal clause is "allenfalls von stilistischem Belang".

[31] Cf. also VANONI, *op. cit.*, pp. 196f.

[32] This solution would fit the instances quoted in n. 11. In Gen. vi 14 (*qnym t'śh 't-htbh*) it would fit the context telling *how* the ark had to be made. The order to make the ark itself being already given in the preceding clause. In Deut. xxvii 6 (*'bnym šlmwt tbnh 't-mzbḥ YHWH*) it would fit the context telling *how* the altar had to be made, the order to make the altar itself already being given in v. 5. In Judg. iii 9 it would fit the context if the focus was on the coming of a *saviour*, whereas v. 8 already says that the Israelites were in the power of a foreign oppressor (the same is true for Judg. iii 15, cf. the description of the bad situation in v. 14). In II Kings xix 25 it would fit the context if the focus was on *what* happened to the fortified cities during God's punishment (cf. Is. xxxvii 26). Self-evidently a study of the whole relevant material will be necessary.

[33] For the structure of the chapter, cf. also B. PORTEN, "The Structure and Theme of the Solomon Narrative (1 Kings 3-11)", *HUCA* 38 (1967), pp. 93-128 on pp. 113, 128.

[34] Cf. the author, art. cit., *VT* 23 (1973), pp. 505ff. Here also I have adjusted my terminology, cf. n. 29.

[35] This rule is only valid when another clause precedes in that special part of the context to which the nominal clause in question belongs. Also main clauses of this type used as *apodosis* are to be excluded (cf. e.g. Lev. xi 37, 38).

*r'šwn hw' lkm* . . . explains why the month in question is the most important one); 3) Ex. xii 11 (the clause *psḥ hw' lYHWH* explains why the meat has to be eaten in haste); 4) Ex. xxxiv 14 (the clause *'l qn' hw'* is used to explain why God is called *qannā*; 5) Lev. v 19 (the clause *'šm hw'* explains why one has to act as described in the preceding verses to be forgiven; cf. Lev. vii 5); 6) Lev. vi 18 (the clause *qdš qdšym hw'* explains why the sin-offering has to be handled as described in this verse; in Lev. vi 22 the same clause explains why only male priests eat the meat of the sin-offering; cf. Lev. vii 6, xiv 13; Numb. vi 20, cf. also Ex. xlv 1, 4; compare Lev. x 12, 17, where a *ky*-clause is used); 7) Lev. xi 4 (the clause *ṭm' hw' lkm* explains why a certain type of food is forbidden; cf. Lev. xi 5, 6, 7, 8, 13; Dt. xiv 7, 10; cf. also Lev. xi 28, 35; compare Lev. xi 42, where a *ky*-clause is used); 8) Lev. xiii 6 (the clause *mspḥt hw'* makes it understandable why a priest declares a certain person clean, cf. Lev. xiii 8, xiii 13, 17, 20, etc.; compare Lev. xiii 28, where a *ky*-clause is used; 9) Lev. xiii 3 (the clause *ng' ṣr't hw'* makes the condition of the skin understandable; cf. Lev. xiii 43, 44); 10) Lev. xiii 46 (the clause *ṭm' hw'* explains why the person in question is treated as unclean; cf. Lev. xv 25; Numb. xix 20; cf. Lev. xiii 52, where a *ky*-clause is used); 11) Lev. xvi 4 (the clause *bgdy qdš hm* explains why the priests wear certain clothes); 12) Lev. xvi 31 (the clause *šbt šbtwn hy' lkm* explains why the Israelites have to act on a certain day as prescribed; cf. Lev. xxiii 3, 32, 36); 13) Lev. xviii 17 (the clauses *š'rh hnh* and *zmh hw'* explain why certain sexual acts are forbidden; cf. Lev. xviii 22, 23, xx 14, 21); 14) Lev. xxv 55 (the clause *'bdy hm 'šr* . . . explains why the Israelites are God's slaves; cf. Numb. iii 9); 15) Numb. i 16 (the clause *r'šy 'lpy yśr'l hm* explains why these people represented Israel in the congregation; cf. Numb. vii 2); 16) Numb. xviii 19 (the clause *bryt mlḥ 'wlm hw'* . . . explains why God gave certain parts of the offerings to the priests); 17) Ex. xiii 2 (the clause *ly hw'* explains why God can ask the Israelites to sanctify all first-born sons to him); 18) Josh. xiv 15 (*h'dm hgdwl b'nqym hw'*; here the former name of the city (Qiryat-Arba) is explained by the fact that it was named after a certain Arba, one of the biggest men among the giants); 19) II Sam. xiii 20 (*'ḥyk hw'*; Absalom asking Tamar to keep quiet is made understandable by the fact that Amnon is her brother; cf. Lev. xiii 7, 8, 11, 12, 14, 15, 16; in Lev. xiii 13 a *ky*-clause is used); 20) Is. i 13 (the clause *tw'bh hy' ly* explains why God refuses certain offerings); 21) Jer. iv 22 (the clause *bnym sklym hmh* explains why the Israelites act so foolishly; cf. Jer. x 15, li 18); 22) Jer. xxiii 16 (the clause *mhblym hmh 'tkm* explains why the people must not listen to certain prophets); 23) Ez. iv 3 (the clause *'wt hy' lbyt yśr'l* explains why the prophet has to act as described in the preceding clauses); 24) Ps. xxxiii 20 (the clause *'zrnw wmgnnw hw'* explains why people wait for the Lord; cf. also Ps. cxv 9, 10, 11 where the clause *'zrm wmgnm hw'* gives the necessary background for the exhortation to trust the Lord; cf. Ps. xcix 3, 5, cf. also Ps. cxlix 9;

Prov. xxx 5)[36]. So the second clause of I Kings xi 14 is a clause meant to give a better understanding of the context (i.c. of what is told in the first clause). That Hadad could become a dangerous enemy for Solomon becomes more understandable if we know that he was a son of the king who having survived the massacre (cf. vs. 15f.), could aim to restore the royal house in Edom[37]. Whatever reasons can be adduced for presupposing that the present introduction to the tale of Hadad's return (I Kings xi 14) is not the original text, but the result of a redaction, in my opinion, grammatical reasons cannot be adduced[38].

---

[36] In these instances the other core element can be of different types morphologically: definite noun/indefinite noun/prepositional phrase.

[37] Cf. also Numb. xxv 15. The clause *r'š 'mwt byt-'b bmdyn* ... does not merely contain additional information. It underlines the purport of the statement that the woman killed was the daughter of Zur, namely that the daughter of an important man was killed. (Cf. also the statement in v. 14 that the Israelite killed was an important man too). So in the clause *bn-'šh 'lmnh hw' mmṭh nptly* (I Kings vii 14) also contains no mere additional information. It makes it more understandable why Solomon, who was looking for help in Phoenicia, sent for him. The clause *mg'lnw hw'* in Ruth ii 20 indicates the purport of the statement made in the preceding clause, that Boaz was one of the next of kin. The clause *'ym wnwr' hw'* (Hab. i 7) indicates that it means that the Babylonians will come (cf. vs. 6). The clause *ṣdyq wnwš' hw'* (Zech. ix 9) indicates what it means that the king will come: not a mere king, but a righteous one. Cf. also Jer. v 15, vi 23.

[38] Against VANONI, see above.

# ZUR GESCHICHTE DER GRENZE ZWISCHEN JUDA UND ISRAEL

VON

A.S. VAN DER WOUDE

*Groningen*

Mehrfach reden die Königs- und Chronikbücher von Bruderkriegen zwischen Juda und Israel, die seit dem tragischen Auseinanderbrechen Großisraels fast ausnahmslos auf benjaminitischem Territorium nördlich von Jerusalem ausgetragen wurden[1]. Es herrschte laut I Reg. xiv 30 allezeit Krieg zwischen Rehabeam und Jerobeam[2]. I Reg. xv 7 berichtet, daß Abija und Jerobeam sich bekämpften, und nach II Chr. xiii 19 hätte der judäische König dem Nordreich sogar die Städte Betel, Jeschana und Efron weggenommen[3]. I Reg. xv 16 erwähnt, daß es zwischen Asa und Bascha "während ihrer ganzen Lebenszeit" Krieg gab. Letzterem gelang es nach Süden vorzustoßen, die Stadt Rama (*er-rām*) zu erobern und diese als Festung auszubauen. Erst ein vom judäischen König veranlasster Ablenkungsangriff Benhadads, des Königs von Aram, zwang Bascha die Stadt wieder aufzugeben. Das von ihm zur Befesti-

---

[1] In I Reg. xiv 30 wird allerdings nicht ausdrücklich erwähnt, daß der Krieg zwischen Rehabeam und Jerobeam auf benjaminitischem Gebiet geführt wurde. Daß dies aber vorwiegend der Fall gewesen sein muß, geht aus den Kämpfen zwischen Abija und Jerobeam und zwischen Asa und Bascha mit aller Wahrscheinlichkeit hervor. Daß im Festungssystem Rehabeams (II Chr. xi 5-12) keine benjaminitischen Städte nördlich von Jerusalem begegnen, dürfte sich daraus erklären, daß es Rehabeam nicht gelang, das Vorfeld von Jerusalem fest in seine Hand zu bekommen. Zur Zeit des israelitischen Königs Joasch und des judäischen Königs Amazja wurde bei Bet-Schemesch Schlacht geliefert, vgl. II Reg. xiv 11ff.

[2] I Reg. xv 6 ist Zusatz aus xiv 30.

[3] Ob dieser Bericht historisch zuverlässig ist, ist umstritten. W. RUDOLPH (*Chronikbücher* (HAT I/21), Tübingen 1955, S. 235) urteilt, daß die Nachricht, daß Betel, Jeschana und Efron dem König Asa als Frucht seines Sieges über Jerobeam in den Schoß fielen, nicht erfunden sein kann; vgl. auch K.-D. SCHUNCK, *Benjamin* (BZAW 86), Berlin 1963, S. 154, der von einer "durchaus glaubwürdigen Überlieferung" spricht, ähnlich wie J.M. MYERS, *II Chronicles* (The Anchor Bible), Garden City, NY 1965, S. 81 ("Verse 19 is certainly based on authentic information") und J. BRIGHT, *A History of Israel*, Philadelphia 1974[3], S. 230 ("The incident is certainly historical"). R.W. KLEIN ("Abijah's Campaign Against the North (II Chr. 13) – What Were the Chronicler's Sources?", *ZAW* 95 (1983), S. 210-217, kommt aber zum Ergebnis, daß die chronistische Quelle "for the geographical information dealing with Abijah's Benjaminite expansion was a list of cities now present in Jos. 18, 21-24. The Chronicler knew this list in a form older than that preserved in either the MT or LXX of Joshua". Er verneint also die Historizität der Nachricht. Dasselbe tut P. WELTEN, *Geschichte und Geschichtsdarstellung in den Chronikbüchern* (WMANT 42), Neukirchen 1973, S. 116-129, aufgrund einer ausführlichen Analyse von II Chr. xiii 3-20. Nach ihm handelt es sich in diesem Textabschnitt um eine Komposition des Chronisten *ohne Verwendung älterer Quellen*.

gung Ramas herbeigeschaffene Baumaterial verwendete Asa daraufhin zum Ausbau von Geba (*dscheba'*) und Mizpa (*tell en-naṣbe*), vgl. I Reg. xv 22; II Chr. xvi 6. Damit war wohl die Grenze zwischen Juda und Israel für längere Zeit festgelegt: vom benjaminitischem Stammesgebiet gehörte das Vorfeld von Jerusalem zum Südreich; dagegen wurden der östliche Teil sowie die nördlich und östlich des *wādi eṣ-ṣuwēnīṭ* gelegenen Ortschaften vom Nordreich beherrscht. Daß dieser Grenzverlauf sich zur Zeit Joschafats und der Omriden nicht geändert hat, dürfte aus der Notiz von II Chr. xvii 1b-2 hervorgeben, wo es heißt, daß Joschafat "sich stark über Israel erwies"[4] und "Truppen in alle befestigten Städte Judas brachte und eine Besatzung in das Land Juda und in die Städte Efraims, die sein Vater Asa erobert hatte, legte". Mit "Israel" muß hier wie in II Chr. xxi 2, 4 das Südreich und mit "Efraim" das Nordreich gemeint sein, denn die von Asa eroberten Städte lagen auf benjaminitischem Gebiet (II Chr. xvi 6). Weil in II Chr. xvii 4 gleich nach dem zitierten Textpassus das Nordreich dem Sprachgebrauch des Chronisten gemäß wiederum Israel und das Südreich in xvii 5a, 6b Juda genannt wird, liegt offenbar in v. 1b-2 eine Notiz vor, die der Chronist einer ihm zur Verfügung stehenden Quelle entnommen hat (RUDOLPH)[5]. Wenn das zutrifft, bestätigt der Vermerk, daß auch zu Lebzeiten Joschafats die Grenze, die Asa festgelegt hatte, unverändert blieb. Die Omriden haben sich offenbar mit dem von Asa geschaffenen Status quo zufrieden gegeben, weil die damaligen Machtverhältnisse es mit sich brachten, daß der kleinere Staat Juda im Gefolge des von ihnen geführten Staates Israel erschien. Joschafat verbündete sich bei einem kriegerischen Unternehmen um den Besitz von Ramot in Gilead (I Reg. xxii) mit Ahab und mit dessen Sohn Joram bei einem Feldzug gegen Moab (II Reg. iii 4-27). Mit diesem König zog Ahasja von Juda, der Enkel Joschafats, in den Krieg gegen die Aramäer (II Reg. viii 28). Die friedlichen Verhältnisse zwischen beiden Staaten wurden sogar durch Verschwägerung der Königshäuser besiegelt: Joschafats Sohn Joram heiratete die israelitische Königstochter Atalja (II Reg. viii 18, 26).

Zu erneutem Kampf zwischen dem Süd- und dem Nordreich ist es dann wieder im Anfang des 8. Jahrhunderts gekommen. In II Reg. xiv wird in einer nordisraelitischen Überlieferung mitgeteilt, daß Amazja von Juda einen Krieg gegen Joasch von Israel anzettelte, der zu der demütigenden Niederlage von Amazja führte. Die siegreichen Israeliten plünderten daraufhin die Tempel- und Palastschätze Jerusalems und schleiften einen Teil der Nordmauer der Stadt. Ob Joasch damals auch das benjaminitische Territorium im Vorfeld von Jerusalem annektiert hat, bleibt in den Königs- und Chronikbüchern unerwähnt, aber die Möglichkeit, daß er die Grenze des Nordreichs nach Süden

---

[4] Für diese Übersetzung vgl. W. RUDOLPH, *a.a.O.* (Anm. 3), S. 249.

[5] Ebenda.

vorgeschoben hat, besteht durchaus, wenn man bedenkt, daß das Niederreißen der Nordmauer Jerusalems wohl nur dann politisch-militärisch sinnvoll war, wenn auch das Vorgelände der Stadt vom israelitischen König beherrscht wurde.

Wenigstens in der frühesten Regierungszeit von Josia befand sich das benjaminitische Vorfeld von Jerusalem wieder in judäischen Händen: in II Reg. xxiii 8 erscheint in der Redewendung "von Geba bis Beerscheba" Geba als nördliche Stadt von Juda. Offenbar konnte Josia auch die in der als benjaminitisch bezeichneten Ortsliste von Jos. xviii 21 ff. vorkommenden Städte, die vorher dem Südreich nicht oder allenfalls nur vorübergehend[6] gehört hatten, zu Juda schlagen. Diese Gebietserweiterung nach Norden wird durch die Angaben von Esra ii und Nehemia vii bestätigt: Anzunehmen ist, daß die Babylonier und die Perser die Grenze zwischen Juda und der Provinz Samaria so beibehielten, wie sie sie vorfanden. Es kann daher nicht wundernehmen, daß der Statthalter Gedalja nach der Zerstörung Jerusalems seinen Amtssitz in Mizpa hatte.

Aus der Tatsache, daß die Nordgrenze von Juda in der frühesten Regierungszeit von Josia bis zu Geba reichte (II Reg. xxiii 8), hat man öfters geschlossen, daß sie sich seit den Tagen Asas nicht oder nur geringfügig geändert habe[7]. Für diese These pflegt man sich jedoch ausschießlich auf die Angaben der Königs- und der Chronikbücher zu stützen, ohne diejenigen der prophetischen Schriften zu berücksichtigen. Doch sollten auch die in ihnen enthaltenen, sich auf das 8. Jahrhundert beziehenden Daten in Betracht gezogen werden, vor allem zur Beantwortung der Frage, ob Joasch von Israel nach der Niederlage von Amazja von Juda tatsächlich das benjaminitische Territorium nördlich von Jerusalem annektiert hat.

Bevor wir uns den einschlägigen Texten aus der prophetischen Literatur des 8. Jahrhunderts zuwenden, soll zunächst das umstrittene Problem, wem das Stammesgebiet von Benjamin nach dem Auseinanderbrechen Großisraels rechtens zugehörte, in aller Kürze behandelt werden. Trotz gegenteiliger Meinung einer Anzahl von Forschern[8] muß u.E. daran festgehalten werden, daß

---

[6] Wenn nämlich II Chr. xiii 19 glaubwürdige Überlieferung enthalten sollte.

[7] So z.B. M. Noth, *Geschichte Israels*, Göttingen 1959[4], S. 215 ("anscheinend"); P. Welten, *a.a.O.* (Anm. 3), S. 126 (Mizpa wurde in Asas Tagen zur judäischen Grenzfestung und "blieb es auch bis in die Zeit Josias"); J.H. Hayes and J. Maxwell Miller, *Israelite & Judaean History* (Old Testament Library), London 1977, S. 391 ("Henceforth the boundary across the mountains between the two kingdoms remained basically unchanged"); Y. Aharoni, *Das Land der Bibel. Eine historische Geographie*, Neukirchen 1984, S. 331 (Der Grenzverlauf "blieb unverändert bis zum Ende des nördlichen Königreiches bestehen und wurde dann die Grenze der assyrischen Provinz Samaria"); vgl. ders., "The Northern Boundary of Judah", *PEQ* 90 (1958), S. 27-31.

[8] Vgl. K.-D. Schunck, *a.a.O.* (Anm. 3), S. 149ff. (vornehmlich aufgrund der Grenzliste von Jos. xvi 1-3); Y. Aharoni, *a.a.O.* (Anm. 7), S. 329; S. Herrmann, *Geschichte Israels in alttestamentlicher Zeit*, München 1980, S. 249f.; H. Weippert, "Die Ätiologie des Nordreichs und seines Königshauses (I Reg 11 29-40)", *ZAW* 95 (1983), S. 344-375.

der Stamm Benjamin, der traditionellerweise zu den zehn Nordstämmen zählte[9], sich bei der sogenannten Reichstrennung zum Nordreich geschlagen hat[10]. Dies geht schon mit ziemlicher Sicherheit aus der Ahija-Geschichte von I Reg. xi 29ff. hervor, in der erzählt wird, daß an Jerobeam zehn Stämme zugewiesen wurden. Wie immer man auch die Textperikope zu erklären gedenkt[11], zu diesen zehn muß auch Benjamin gehören[12]. I Reg. xii 20 bestätigt diese Erklärung. Wenn es dort heißt, daß die Israeliten Jerobeam zum König über "ganz Israel" machten, beinhaltet eben diese Wendung nach Ausweis von I Sam. xviii 16; II Sam. iii 12, 21; v 5, 17 und besonders II Sam. ii 9, daß Benjamin in den zehn Stämmen einbegriffen war. Weiter sollte man bedenken, daß von einer "Reichsteilung" im üblichen Sinne nicht gesprochen werden kann, weil es sich um die Nichterneuerung der Personalunion, die unter David und Salomo bestanden hatte, handelte. Bei dieser Personalunion gehörte Benjamin zu den Nordstämmen. Schließlich ist es kaum denkbar, daß, nachdem der große Aufstand gegen David, von dem II Sam. xx berichtet, von einem Benjaminiten namens Scheba angeführt worden war, der Stamm sich beim Auseinanderbrechen der Personalunion auf einmal auf der Seite Judas gegen die neun Bruderstämme wandte[13]. Alle diese Daten lassen nur eine Schlußfolgerung zu: Benjamin hielt bei der sogenannten Reichstrennung den übrigen Nordstämmen die Treue. Die Könige des Nordreichs mußten also das ganze Territorium Benjamins beanspruchen. Dem entspricht auch, daß das benjaminitische Stammesgebiet nördlich und östlich des *wādi eṣ-ṣuwēnīṭ* bis zum Fall Samarias stets israelitisch gewesen ist, wie aus I Reg. xvi 34, wo von der Neubesiedlung Jerichos von einem aus Betel herrührenden Efraimiten die Rede ist, und aus den Elia-Elischa-Geschichten (II Reg. ii 4ff., 15ff.; vgl. auch Gilgal: II Reg. ii 1; iv 38) hervorgeht. Andererseits konnten die Könige des Südreichs aus Sicherheitsgründen nicht auf ein von ihnen beherrschtes Vorfeld ihrer Residenz, die nach der Reichstrennung an den Rand von Juda geraten war und unmittelbar benjaminitisches Territorium berührte, verzichten. So läßt sich leicht erklären, daß schon Rehabeam den Besitz dieses Vorgelän-

---

[9] Vgl. H. Weippert, "Das geographische System der Stämme Israels", *VT* 23 (1973), S. 76-89.

[10] J. Debus, *Die Sünde Jerobeams* (FRLANT 93), Göttingen 1967, S. 15ff.; J.H. Hayes and J. Maxwell Miller, *a.a.O.* (Anm. 7), S. 390; J. Bright, *a.a.O.* (Anm. 3), S. 229 ("very possibly"); H. Jagersma, *Geschiedenis van Israel in het oudtestamentisch tijdvak*, Kampen 1984, S. 185f.; H. Donner, *Geschichte des Volkes Israel und seiner Nachbarn in Grundzügen* 2, Göttingen 1986, S. 244.

[11] Vgl. jetzt H. Weippert, "Die Ätiologie des Nordreichs und seines Königshauses", *ZAW* 95 (1983), S. 344-375 und die dort erwähnte Literatur.

[12] M. Noth, *Könige* (BK XI/4), Neukirchen 1968, S. 259f. und H. Donner, *a.a.O.* (Anm. 10), S. 234 halten dafür, daß in der Ahija-Geschichte Juda als Herrschaftsgebiet der Davididen nicht beachtet und Levi und Simeon nicht mitgezählt werden. Für eine andere Lösung der anstehenden Problematik s. C.H.J. de Geus, *The Tribes of Israel* (Studia Semitica Neerlandica 18), Assen 1976, S. 116ff.

[13] J. Debus, *a.a.O.* (Anm. 10), S. 16.

des von Jerusalem anstrebte und folglich Grenzstreitigkeiten zwischen Juda und Israel auslöste, die bis zur Zeit Asas andauerten. Eben weil die Könige des Südreichs benjaminitisches Gebiet rechtens nicht beanspruchen konnten, mittlerweile aber notgedrungen eine Pufferzone für Jerusalem brauchten, ist es verständlich, daß die Feindseligkeiten zwischen Juda und Israel just im Vorfeld Jerusalems und nicht etwa im südlichen Jordangraben ausgetragen wurden. Es gelang den Königen des Südreichs tatsächlich, ihr Vorhaben zu realisieren. Ob allerdings die Könige des Nordreichs bereit waren, diese Okkupation eines Teils ihres Reiches auf Dauer hinzunehmen, läßt sich mit Recht bezweifeln. Hinsichtlich dieser Frage geben uns die Königs- und Chronikbücher keine Auskünfte, aber eine Analyse der für dieses Problem einschlägigen Stellen in den Schriften Hoseas und Michas dürfte dazu geeignet sein uns genauer über den Grenzverlauf zwischen Juda und Israel im 8. Jahrhundert zu unterrichten.

In Hosea v 1-2 wird den Führungskreisen Israels vorgeworfen, daß sie das Recht nicht gewahrt haben und folglich eine Falle für Mizpa und zum ausgespannten Netz über Tabor sowie zur tiefen Fanggrube in Schittim[14] geworden sind. Mit dem hier erwähnten Mizpa ist vermutlich nicht das Mizpa in Gilead (vgl. Jud. xi 11, 29), sondern die etwa 10 km nördlich von Jerusalem liegende Stadt (heute *tell en-naṣbe*) gemeint. Wenn diese Identifizierung zutrifft, muß Mizpa zur Zeit des Propheten Hosea israelitisch gewesen sein. Dann wäre die Grenze des Nordreichs, die seit Asa nördlich der Stadt verlief, mittlerweise nach Süden vorgeschoben worden. Daß dies tatsächlich der Fall gewesen sein muß, stellt sich heraus, wenn man Hosea x 9 heranzieht. In diesem Text hält der Prophet Israel vor, daß die alte Schuld von Gibea gegenwärtige Schuld ist und daß deswegen die alte Katastrophe von Gibea als eine neue über die Stadt kommen wird. Daß in diesem Text mit Gibea das heutige *tell el-fūl*, etwa 5 km nördlich von Jerusalem, gemeint ist, geht aus dem Kontext unmißverständlich hervor: der Prophet spielt auf die ungeheure Untat gegen den levitischen Fremdling (Jud. xix) und den diesem Verbrechen folgenden Krieg zwischen Benjamin und den anderen israelitischen Stämmen (Jud. xx) an. Wenn nun aber ausdrücklich gesagt wird, daß Israel "in Gibea[15] Krieg erreichen wird der Frevler wegen", läßt sich die Schlußfolgerung wohl nicht umgehen, daß Gibea zur Zeit Hoseas zum Territorium des Nordreichs gehörte, offenbar auch nach dem syrisch-efraimitischen Krieg, wenn man wenigstens mit Wolff[16] und Jeremias[17] den Abschnitt Hosea x 9ff. um etwa 727 ansetzt.

---

[14] Zum Text s. die Kommentare.

[15] Die Auffassung von J. Jeremias, *Der Prophet Hosea* (ATD 24/1), Göttingen 1983, S. 132, daß "wie in Gibea" zu deuten sei, läßt sich u.E. nicht aufrechterhalten. In dem Falle müßte es *kaggib'ā* heißen (so ändert W. Rudolph, *Hosea* (KAT XIII/1), Gütersloh 1966, S. 199 den Text), vgl. Gesenius – Kautzsch, § 118 s-w.

[16] H.W. Wolff, *Dodekapropheton 1. Hosea* (BK XIV/1), Neukirchen 1961, S. 237.

[17] J. Jeremias, *a.a.O.* (Anm. 15), S. 133.

Das, was wir hinsichtlich II Reg. xiv 13 vorhin schon vermuteten, scheint tatsächlich der Fall gewesen zu sein: als Joasch von Israel die Nordmauer Jerusalems schleifte, annektierte er auch das benjaminitische Vorgelände der Stadt, das seit Asa in judäischen Händen gewesen war.

Wenn diese Überlegungen zutreffen, dann steht die Deutung von Hosea v 8f., die Albrecht ALT in seinem glänzenden und epochemachenden Aufsatz von 1919 zu Hosea v 8 – vi 6 ("Ein Krieg und seine Folgen in prophetischer Beleuchtung")[18] gegeben hat, auf schwachen Füßen. ALT hatte angenommen, daß der Passus auf dem Hintergrund des syrisch-efraimitischen Krieges zu deuten sei. Seiner Meinung nach habe das aramäisch-israelitische Heer das "bis dahin von Juda behauptete Grenzgebiet mit Gibea und Rama, das nördliche Glacis sozusagen der judäischen Festung" (Jerusalem) besetzt. Diese politisch-geographische Situation habe dann den Propheten Hosea veranlasst, einen Gegenangriff vom Süden her in Aussicht zu stellen, der über das Grenzgebiet hinweg in unumstrittenes israelitisches Land einbrechen sollte. Was Hosea erwarte, sei "ein Rückschlag im Kriege, ein Gegenstoß der Judäer gegen den Vorstoß der Israeliten und Aramäer" gewesen. Daher habe er Gibea, Rama und auch Betel alarmiert. In Hosea v 10 sei dieser Übergriff der Judäer auf israelitisches Land vorausgesetzt. Die Aussage, daß sich die Fürsten Judas wie Grenzverrücker benommen hatten, bedeute, daß sie nicht nur das Grenzgebiet, das früher zu Juda gehörte, wieder zu ihrem Reiche geschlagen, sondern auch von einem bisherigen israelitischen Landstreifen Besitz ergriffen und so die alten territorialen Rechte des Nachbarreiches verletzt hätten. Dieser Deutung von Hosea v 8ff. sind inzwischen fast alle Kommentatoren gefolgt, wenn auch gelegentlich mit Einschränkungen. So findet WOLFF[19], daß die drei genannten Siedlungen (Gibea, Rama, Bet-Awän/Betel) im 8. Jahrhundert vielleicht seit dem erfolgreichen Angriff des Königs Joasch von Israel auf Jerusalem alle zum Nordreich gehört haben und daß die Alarmierung der genannten Orte vom Nordreich her unter dieser Voraussetzung besser einleuchte, als wenn sie erst in den letzten Wochen beim Vormarsch des syrisch-efraimitischen Heeres auf Jerusalem eingenommen worden wären, wie dies ALT angenommen hatte. Vor WOLFF hatte schon JEPSEN[20] hervorgehoben, daß, wenn der Prophet in v 8f. auch Gibea und Rama vor einer Grenzverletzung Judas warnt, dies kaum einen Sinn habe, wenn diese Orte eigentlich zu Juda gehörten und nur eben vorher von Pekach zu Israel geschlagen waren.

Inzwischen bereitet die Erklärung, die ALT von Hosea v 8-9, 10 gegeben hat, nicht nur Schwierigkeiten, weil er voraussetzte, daß das Vorfeld Jerusa-

---

[18] A. ALT, "Hosea 5, 8-6, 6. Ein Krieg und seine Folgen in prophetischer Beleuchtung", *Neue Kirchliche Zeitschrift* 30 (1919), S. 537-568 = *KS* II, S. 163-187.

[19] *A.a.O.* (Anm. 16), S. 143. Auch O. PROCKSCH, *Jesaja* I (KAT IX), Leipzig 1930, S. 176, stellte fest: "Zu Hoseas Zeit (c. 735) gehörte Gibea noch zum Nordreich (Hosea 5:8)".

[20] A. JEPSEN, *Die Quellen des Königsbuches*, Halle (Saale) 1956², S. 97.

lems vor dem syrisch-efraimitischen Krieg in judäischen Händen war. Wir wissen nichts über einen Vorstoß judäischer Truppen unter Führung von Ahas in benjaminitisches und efraimitisches Gebiet, nachdem Rezin und Pekach sich entschließen mußten, die Belagerung Jerusalems aufzugeben. Es erscheint im Hinblick auf II Chr. xxviii 5ff. unwahrscheinlich, daß Ahas zu einem solchen Feldzug imstande war, und es ist fraglich, ob der assyrische König seinem Vasallen damals erlaubte, in israelitisches Territorium einzudringen. Jedenfalls widerspräche eine judäische Besetzung des benjaminitischen Vorgeländes von Jerusalem unserer vorhin aus Hosea x 9 gezogenen Schlußfolgerung, daß sogar Gibea, das in unmittelbarer Nähe der judäischen Residenz lag, bis zum Fall Samarias israelitisch blieb, nachdem Joasch von Israel das Vorgelände Jerusalems im Anfang des 8. Jahrhunderts annektiert hatte. Daß der Prophet in Hosea v 8 Gibea, Rama und Betel alarmiert, braucht (wegen der Reihenfolge der Städte) nicht auf eine Marschroute eines von Süden her heranrückenden Heeres hinzuweisen. Die Wahl dieser Ortschaften läßt sich auch so erklären, daß sie zum Heimatland des Propheten gehörten. In dem Fall wären die Städte nicht alarmiert worden, weil *Juda* im Begriff war, sie in einem Gegenstoß wieder zu erobern bzw. von einem bisherigen israelitischen Landstreifen Besitz zu ergreifen, sondern weil Hosea die Unterjochung des ganzen Nordreichs *bis zum äußersten Süden des Staates* erwartete. Anscheinend ist daher nicht der syrisch-efraimitische Krieg vorausgesetzt, sondern, wie auch der Wortlaut von v. 9 nahelegt ("Efraim wird verwüstet am Tage der Züchtigung. In Israels Stämmen verkündige ich, was feststeht"), ein bevorstehender Angriff der Assyrer. Dann aber stammen Hosea v 8-9 und 10 aus der Zeit *vor* dem syrisch-efraimitischen Krieg! Wenn die Fürsten von Juda (so der überlieferte Text) mit Grenzverrückern *verglichen* werden, liegt es auf der Hand nicht an Grenzänderungen zu denken, sondern an eine geistige Einstellung, die kennzeichnend ist für diejenigen, die Ackergrenzen ändern. Es handelt sich offenbar um Leute, die ihren Besitz ohne Rücksicht auf das Gottesrecht zu nehmen, vergrößern, die Armen unterdrücken und um ihre Habe bringen. Inzwischen muß bezweifelt werden, ob im ursprünglichen Text von v. 10 von den Fürsten *Judas* die Rede gewesen ist. Es will mir scheinen, daß die älteren Kommentatoren durchaus recht hatten bei der Behauptung, daß in Hosea v 8 – vi 6 ein parallel mit "Efraim" verwendetes "Israel" im nachhinein redaktionell durch "Juda" ersetzt worden ist[21], vgl. besonders Hosea v 13 und xii 4. Wir können dieser These hier nicht weiter nachgehen. Es mag im Zusammenhang unserer Fragestellung genügen, die Schlußfolgerung zu

---

[21] So z.B. K. Marti, *Das Dodekapropheton* (Kurzer Hand-Commentar zum Alten Testament XIII), Tübingen 1904, S. 49f.; L.H.K. Bleeker, *De kleine profeten* I. *Hosea, Amos* (Tekst en Uitleg), Groningen 1932, S. 187; W.R. Harper, *A Critical and Exegetical Commentary on Amos and Hosea* (ICC), Edinburgh 1936, S. 275.

ziehen, daß nichts in Hosea v 8ff. uns zwingt, der Erklärung ALTS beizupflichten. Hosea v 8 bestätigt vielmehr, was sich aus unserer Analyse von v 1-2 und x 9 ergab und was schon von JEPSEN und WOLFF vermutet wurde: das benjaminitische Territorium nördlich von Jerusalem befand sich zur Zeit des Propheten Hosea in israelitischen Händen und es blieb israelitisch bis zum Fall Samarias[22].

Dieses aufgrund der Erklärung hoseanischer Stellen zutage geförderte Ergebnis wird u.E. auch durch Micha i und Psalm lxxx bestätigt. Vor ungefähr 15 Jahren haben wir die doppelte These vertreten, daß a) Micha i eine literarische Einheit bildet und daher wegen i 6ff., wo der Fall Samarias vorausgesagt wird, vor 722 anzusetzen ist, und b) daß die in Micha i 10-12 erwähnten Ortschaften im Gegensatz zu denen von i 13-16 deswegen nicht von uns identifiziert werden können, weil es sich um Weiler in nächster Nähe von Jerusalem handelt, die darum vom Propheten, der einen Angriff der Assyrer von Norden her erwartete, genannt werden, weil es nach Norden und Osten der Stadt hin keine größeren Städte gab, die zum Gebiet des Südreichs gehörten[23]. So wird auch verständlich, daß Micha i 9 (vgl. i 12) Jerusalem als "Tor" seines Volkes bezeichnet und nicht etwa Mizpa oder Rama, was doch naheliegend gewesen wäre, wenn diese Ortschaften damals zu Juda gehört hätten.

Psalm lxxx, ein Klagelied des Volkes, stammt, wie O. EISSFELDT[23a] überzeugend nachgewiesen hat, aus der Zeit des Rumpfstaates Efraim, also aus dem Jahrzehnt zwischen 732 und 722 v. Chr. Wenn im dritten Vers dieses Psalms YHWH, der Kerubenthroner, flehentlich gebeten wird, vor Efraim und Benjamin und Manasse zu "erscheinen", handelt es sich bei Benjamin wohl nicht um einen *Teil* seines Territoriums, sondern um das ganze Gebiet des Stammes. Dann aber bestätigt auch Ps. lxxx, daß Benjamin bis zum Fall Samarias israelitisch war, seitdem Joash von Israel es zum Nordreich geschlagen hatte.

Wie schon erwähnt, erscheint Geba in II Reg. xxiii 8 zur Zeit des judäischen Königs Josia als nördliche Grenzstadt. Man gewinnt aus diesem Text den Eindruck, daß das schon längere Zeit der Fall war, m.a.W. daß das Vorfeld von

---

[22] Wenn unsere These, daß das benjaminitische Vorfeld von Jerusalem seit dem Anfang des 8. Jahrhunderts v. Chr. zum Nordreich gehörte, zutrifft, kann die auf Verwaltungsunterlagen beruhende judäische Städteliste Jos. xv 21-62, zu der AHARONI Jos. xviii 25-28 als wesentlichen Bestandteil hinzufügt (Y. AHARONI, "The Province-List of Judah", *VT* 9 (1959), S. 225-246; ders., *Das Land der Bibel*, Neukirchen 1984, S. 359-371), *in dieser Gestalt* nicht aus der Zeit Usijas stammen (so AHARONI). Z. KALLAI, *The Historical Geography of the Bible*, Jerusalem 1986, S. 398-404, trennt die benjaminitische Städteliste (Jos. xviii 21-28) völlig von der judäischen (Jos. xv 21-62) und setzt jene aufgrund von II Chr. xiii 19 (zu diesem Text s. jedoch Anm. 3) in der Zeit Abijas an.

[23] A.S. VAN DER WOUDE, *Micha* (De prediking van het Oude Testament), Nijkerk 1976 (= 1985³), S. 19f., 40f.

[23a] O. EISSFELDT, "Psalm 80", in: *Geschichte und Altes Testament* (Festschrift A. Alt), Tübingen 1953, S. 65-78 = *KS* III, S. 221-232.

Jerusalem, das, seit Joasch dies annektiert hatte, bis zum Fall Samarias israelitisch war, schon vor Josia wieder judäischer Besitz wurde. Wann das geschah, läßt sich weder aus den Königs- und Chronikbüchern noch aus der prophetischen Literatur ausfindig machen. Dagegen dürften die königlichen Siegelabdrücke, die auf Vorratskrüge gestempelt wurden und in großer Zahl auf verschiedenen judäischen *tulul* gefunden worden sind[24], uns einen Anhaltspunkt für die Beantwortung der Frage, wann Juda das Vorgelände Jerusalems zurückgewann, bieten. Die besagten Siegelabdrücke sind vor allem in der Schefela und im Gebiet von Jerusalem, aber auch sonstwo im judäischen Bereich zutage gefördert worden. Augenblicklich wird mit guten Gründen angenommen, daß sie nur während einer beschränkten Zeit unter Hiskija, vornehmlich vor Sanheribs Feldzug gegen Jerusalem im Jahre 701, verwendet wurden. Ihre Verbreitung nach Norden hin reicht bis Mizpa; im ehemaligen Nordreich wurden sie nicht gefunden, auch nicht in Betel, so daß eine Datierung der Siegelabdrücke auf die Zeit Josias ausscheidet. Das heißt für unsere Fragestellung, daß es Hiskija gelungen sein muß, das benjaminitische Vorgelände von Jerusalem wieder zu Juda zu schlagen. Ob diese Wiedergewinnung des Territoriums der Großmütigkeit seines assyrischen Oberherrn zu verdanken ist oder ob Hiskija es im Laufe seiner Regierung einfach annektiert hat, läßt sich nicht mehr entscheiden. Im Hinblick auf die vom König betriebene Expansionspolitik, die im Westen zur Ausweitung der Grenzen Judas auf Kosten der philistäischen Städte (II Reg. xviii 8) und offenbar im Süden zu einem Vorstoß in das Gebirge Seir führte (vgl. I Chr. iv 42f.), ist die zweite Möglichkeit nicht auszuschließen.

In diesem Zusammenhang empfiehlt sich schließlich eine kurze Erörterung von Jesaja x 27b-32, jenem merkwürdigen Abschnitt, in welchem der Vormarsch eines Feindes vom Norden her in Richtung Jerusalems geschildert wird:

Er zieht von Samaria hinauf (?),
rückt gegen Ajat vor,
zieht durch Migron,
Michmas vertraut er seinen Troß an.
Sie passieren die Schlucht:
"Geba sei unser Nachtquartier!"
Rama erschrickt,
Gibea Sauls flieht.
Laß deine Stimme gellen, Tochter Gallim!
Horch auf, Laischa!

[24] Zu den königlichen Siegelabdrücken und ihrer Datierung vgl. P. Welten, *Die Königs-Stempel*, Wiesbaden 1969; Y. Aharoni, *a.a.O.* (Anm. 7), S. 404ff.; A. Na'aman, "Sennacherib's Campaign to Judah and the Date of the *lmlk* Stamps", *VT* 29 (1979), S. 61-86.

Gib ihr Antwort, Anatot!
Madmena macht sich davon,
die Bewohner von Gebim bringen sich in Sicherheit.
Heute noch bezieht er Stellung in Nob,
schwingt er seine Hand gegen den Berg der Tochter Zion,
gegen die Höhe Jerusalems[25].

Wer der Gegner ist, der die Stadt Jerusalem von Norden her in seine Gewalt zu bringen versuchte, wird in diesem Textabschnitt nicht ausdrücklich gesagt, aber der jesajanische Kontext legt nahe, an die Assyrer zu denken. BARTH[26] hat mit Recht darauf hingewiesen, daß die aufgezählten Orte nur bis Geba eine fortlaufende Marschroute ergeben; nach der Erwähnung dieser Stadt werden Angst- und Fluchtreaktionen judäischer Ortschaften geschildert. Der zeitliche Standort des Spruches ist also "in der Nacht oder – wahrscheinlich – am Morgen nach der Nacht des Lagers von Geba": "heute noch" wird der Feind vor Jerusalem stehen. Was uns in diesem Zusammenhang besonders interessiert, ist, daß die Marschroute auf Geba hinausläuft: die Stadt erscheint offenbar als Grenzort Judas. Dann aber muß der Versuch von DONNER[27] das Gedicht aus einer bestimmten Phase des syrisch-efraimitischen Krieges heraus zu deuten, abgelehnt werden: Abgesehen davon, daß unser Text in keiner Weise suggeriert, daß der Feind aus zwei verbündeten Völkern (Aramäern und Israeliten) bestand, und daß der Redaktor, der die Perikope nach den Assurstücken von Kap. x einordnete, den Gegner gewiß mit den Assyrern identifizierte, muß nach unseren bisherigen Überlegungen festgestellt werden, daß zur Zeit des syrisch-efraimitischen Krieges die Grenze zwischen Israel und Juda unmittelbar nördlich von Jerusalem verlief. Andere Kommentatoren haben an den Angriff von Sanherib gegen Jerusalem im Jahre 701 gedacht, aber dieser erfolgte nicht von Norden her, sondern von Südwesten. WILDBERGER[28] möchte daher eher an die Episode des sich etwa zehn Jahre früher ereigneten asdoditischen Aufstands denken. Aber auch gegen diese Deutung erheben sich schwere Bedenken, weil wir von einem assyrischen Übergriff auf Juda zu jener Zeit nichts wissen. WILDBERGER gesteht selber, daß sich kein Versuch historischer Einordnung zu unbezweifelbarer Gewißheit erheben läßt. Unserer Mei-

---

[25] Zu den schwierigen textkritischen Problemen des Textes s. die Kommentare und D.L. CHRISTENSEN, "The March of Conquest in Isaiah x 27c-34", *VT* 26 (1976), S. 385-399. Vgl. auch H. BARTH, *Die Jesaja-Worte in der Josiazeit* (WMANT 48), Neukirchen 1977, S. 54ff.

[26] *A.a.O.* (Anm. 25), S. 54-76, bes. S. 65.

[27] H. DONNER, *Israel unter den Völkern. Die Stellung der klassischen Propheten des 8. Jahrhunderts v. Chr. zur Außenpolitik von Israel und Juda* (SVT 11), Leiden 1964, S. 30-38.

[28] H. WILDBERGER, *Jesaja* I (BK X/1), Neukirchen 1972, S. 428. Vgl. auch O. PROCKSCH, *a.a.O.* (Anm. 19), S. 175; J. VERMEYLEN, *Du prophète Isaïe à l'apocalyptique* I, Paris 1977, S. 267 ("vraisembablement"); R.E. CLEMENTS, *Isaiah 1-39* (The New Century Bible Commentary), Grand Rapids – London 1980, S. 118f.

nung nach sollte man eine derartige Einordnung auch nicht versuchen. Der Verfasser des Textes erwartete, ähnlich wie damals Micha, einen Verstoß der Assyrer von Norden her gegen Jerusalem. Historisch ereignet hat sich jedoch ein solcher Angriff von Samaria her nicht, ebensowenig wie die Prophetie Michas, die uns in Kapitel i 8ff. des nach ihm genannten Buches überliefert worden ist, buchstäblich in Erfüllung ging. Inzwischen steht nichts im Wege, die jesajanische Herkunft des Textes anzunehmen. Wie wir gesehen haben, gelang es Hiskija, das benjaminitische Vorfeld von Jerusalem, das seit Joasch von Israel Juda entrissen worden war, wiederzugewinnen, so daß der Prophet Geba als nördliche Grenzstadt Judas bezeichnen konnte.

Später hat Josia die Nordgrenze Judas noch weiter nach Norden vorschieben und das Gebiet Jerichos und Betels seinem Reich einverleiben können. Aufgrund dieser späteren Situation setzt die deuteronomistische Redaktion der Königsbücher einmal, der Chronist aber ständig voraus, daß Benjamin seit den Tagen Jerobeams I. zum Südreich gehörte[29].

Obige Zeilen sind in Ehrerbietung dem Freund und Kollegen Martin J. Mulder gewidmet, der sich nicht nur um die Auslegung der Bücher der Könige verdient gemacht, sondern auch durch seine hervorragende Kenntnisse vieler anderer Gebiete der alttestamentlichen und der frühjüdischen Literatur und Geschichte sowie durch seine Peshiṭta-Arbeiten als namhafter Gelehrter ausgezeichnet hat. Auch nach seiner Emeritierung wünschen wir ihm und seiner Familie noch manche glückliche Jahre, in denen er uns hoffentlich weiterhin die Ergebnisse seiner tiefschürfenden Untersuchungen bescheren wird.

---

[29] Deuteronomistisch: I Reg. xii 21-24; chronistisch: II Chr. xi 1, 3, 10, 12, 23; xiv 7; xv 2, 8, 9; xvii 17; xxv 5; xxxi 1 (xxxiv 9, 32).

# SOLOMON'S TEMPLE AND YHWH'S EXCLUSIVITY

BY

M.J. MULDER

*Badhoevedorp/Leiden*

"There is no god like Yahweh and Israel is his prophet". Thus the typification runs that, about a century ago, Julius WELLHAUSEN gave of Deutero-Isaiah's message to his people in the Babylonian Exile[1*]. A "credo" such as this in the context of the sixth century B.C. is acceptable to a group of exiles and to us. But when one, within the framework of scholarly research and teaching, has pursued in recent years the study of the literary data pertaining to the building of Solomon's temple in Jerusalem – data available in the Old Testament books of Kings as we have it –, one cannot escape having doubts: Was the temple Solomon had built – or rebuilt[2] – really intended for the exclusive use of the cult of Israel's God YHWH? Indeed there are quite a few details in the transmitted description of this temple that are hard to explain from or to be made consistent with the cult of YHWH as it was practiced later on. So, e.g., the pillars Jachin and Boaz, standing, according to I Kings vii, before the entrance to the temple building, definitely formed no part of the Jahwistic heritage; they were cultic symbols, clearly derived and intentionally adopted from Canaanite-Jebusitic cult practices[3]. The same goes for the "sea of cast metal" and the "trolleys of bronze" described in detail in the same chapter. It is, therefore, not surprising that in the later literature of ancient Israel these cultic paraphernalia either were not mentioned at all or recurred in a form strongly adapted to the later cult of YHWH. For all that, however, the author(s) of Kings deserve(s) our gratitude for having incorporated evidently very old details of the temple built – or rebuilt – by Solomon in Jeru-

---

[1] J. WELLHAUSEN, *Israelitische und jüdische Geschichte*, Berlin 1958[9], p. 152: "Es gibt keinen Gott als Jahve und Israel ist sein (Knecht d.h.) Prophet – so lautet das triumphierende Credo".

* This article is a translation of the valedictory lecture on 20 January 1989 at the State University, Leiden. Mrs. T.C.M. HEESTERMAN-VISSER has taken care of the translation into English, for which I owe her my thanks.

[2] See K. RUPPRECHT, *Der Tempel von Jerusalem. Gründung Salomos oder jebusitisches Erbe?* (BZAW 144), Berlin 1977; *idem*, "Die Zuverlässigkeit der Überlieferung von Salomons Tempelgründung", *ZAW* 89 (1977), pp. 205-214.

[3] See my commentary *Koningen i-vii*, Kampen 1986, p. 264; and also my "Die Bedeutung von Jachin und Boaz in 1 Kön. 7:21 (2 Chr. 3:17)", in: *Tradition and Reinterpretation in Jewish Early Christian Literature* (Festschrift J.C.H. Lebram), Leiden 1986, pp. 19-26.

salem, probably originating from age-old archives[4]. However hard to interpret some parts of I Kings vi and vii may be – because of the tattered state of the text –, so much is clear that between the redactional (Deuteronomistic) rubble we can discern valuable building bricks useful for a, to a certain extent, reliable reconstruction of the *oldest* model of Solomon's temple. In passing, we can also glean from these fragments that to be so highly extolled later on, the temple of Solomon in its original design can not have been such a particularly magnificent building. What we see emerging from the available data is rather the picture of a private or court chapel[5] that in the course of the centuries must have been restored several times, altered and, in view of an increasing number of priests and its growing national significance, considerably added to[6]. It is, therefore, clear that the temple design in Ezekiel xl-xlii, for instance, can not as a matter of course be traced back to an *originally* Solomonic temple. There is even less justification for overlaying the model of the Solomonic temple with the description of the so-called Tabernacle – the tent, used as a desert sanctuary by the Israelites during their exodus from Egypt to the "Promised Land", and described in Ex. xxv ff. and xxxvi ff., texts ascribed to P, the Priestly Code since KUENEN, WELLHAUSEN and other scholars from the last century –, as though the Tabernacle had been the blueprint of the Solomonic temple. If the Tabernacle did at all have a model other than that shown by YHWH to Moses on the Mount, as an old tradition has it[7], it will have been the so-called second temple of Jerusalem, rebuilt after the Exile, to which undoubtedly the then leading priests were a party[8]. All of these considerations lead us to the question already put in our opening words: To what extent was the Solomonic temple exclusively a YHWH temple? And if at the time it was not yet (fully) so, when did it become that?

These questions are inextricably linked up with the ever fascinating problem of the religious and the profane history of Israel. It can safely be stated that gradually a *communis opinio* has come into being concerning the view that the Old Testament is not a book of history in which – even in those books we call

---

[4] Cf. i.a. M. NOTH, *Könige* (BK IX/1), Neukirchen/Vluyn 1968, p. 106: "Der Grundbestand des Kapitels [i.e. chapter vi, MJM] geht sicher auf amtliche Aufzeichnungen der königlichen Verwaltung in Jerusalem zurück".

[5] Cf. i.a. K. MÖHLENBRINK, *Der Tempel Salomos. Eine Untersuchung seiner Stellung in der Sakralarchitektur des Alten Orients* (BWANT 59), Stuttgart 1932, p. 50; A. ALT, *Kleine Schriften zur Geschichte des Volkes Israel* II, München 1953, p. 46; H. VORLÄNDER, *Mein Gott. Die Vorstellungen vom persönlichen Gott im Alten Orient und im Alten Testament* (AOAT 23), Neukirchen/Vluyn 1975, pp. 240-244.

[6] See e.g. II Kings xxiii 11f., where as a result of Josiah's reformation the temple was restored.

[7] Hebr. viii 5; cf. Ex. xxv 9, 40; cf. also R. SCHMITT, *Zelt und Lade als Thema alttestamentlicher Wissenschaft, Eine kritische forschungsgeschichtliche Darstellung*, Gütersloh 1972, pp. 244-249.

[8] Cf. also A. KUENEN, *De Godsdienst van Israël tot den ondergang van den joodschen staat* I, Haarlem 1869, p. 333.

historical – an authentic report is given of the course the history of the states of Israel and Judah has taken. At present, an issue among scholars is, therefore, in particular the question whether the Old Testament actually does give historically reliable information in our sense of the word, and if so, how we are to localise, evaluate and subsequently to incorporate it into our description of the profane and religious history of Israel[9]. The Danish Old Testament scholar N.P. LEMCHE, in a book on *Ancient Israel* published of late, discusses the history of the society of ancient Israel[10]. In his book, he defends the thesis that the notion "Israel" was the result of a social development among the Canaanite population of Palestine in the second half of the second millennium B.C. He is, moreover, of the opinion that the Old Testament contains hardly any historically reliable information, in our sense of the word, reaching back to the period before the seventh century B.C. It is especially the results of archaeological finds and extrabiblical data that can and must – according to LEMCHE – contribute to the reconstruction of Israel's early history. The Old Testament itself has scarcely anything of value to offer in aid of such a reconstruction. Where Israel's religious history is concerned, this signifies, among other things, that the Israelite religion originally was no other than the Canaanite one or barely differs from it in its essence and manifestation. The here presented point of view, though couched in modern terms, can hardly be qualified as "novel". New – or at any rate newer – are the arguments that can be adduced in support of this view. In-depth research like that of LEMCHE in his book can, among other things, point to the identification of the YHWH in the Psalms with gods traditionally considered as Canaanite[11]. Attention may furthermore be drawn to the fairly recently discovered inscriptions of Khirbet el-Qom (some ten kilometers west of Hebron) and Kuntillet 'Ajrud (some fifty kilometers south of Kades-Barnea in the Negeb). One of the latter inscriptions, written by an Israelite in the eighth century B.C., reads: "I bless you through YHWH of Samaria (or: 'who keeps us') and through his (i.e. perhaps: Samaria's) Asherah"[12]. On a tomb inscription in Khirbet el-Qom it can

---

[9] One trend in the field of Old Testament research even suspects the very doubts about the historicity of the literary texts, the Old Testament in its "Endgestalt" being the preaching of R, i.e. "Rabbenu", after a word of F. ROSENZWEIG, *Die Schrift und ihre Verdeutschung*, Berlin 1936, p. 47; cf. for a broader survey of the treatment of these subjects in the Dutch language also: R. OOST, *Omstreden Bijbeluitleg. Aspecten en achtergronden van de hermeneutische discussie rondom de exegese van het Oude Testament in Nederland. Een bijdrage tot gesprek*, Kampen 1986.

[10] N.P. LEMCHE, *Ancient Israel. A New History of Israelite Society*, Sheffield 1988; cf. also his *Early Israel* (VTS 37), Leiden 1985.

[11] LEMCHE, *op. cit.*, p. 226.

[12] See i.a. J.A. EMERTON, "New Light on Israelite Religion: The Implications of the Inscription from Kuntillet 'Ajrud", *ZAW* 94 (1982), pp. 2-20, here: 2f.; further F. STOLZ, "Monotheismus in Israel", in: O. KEEL (ed.), *Monotheismus im Alten Israel und seiner Umwelt* (Bibl. Beitr. 14), Fribourg 1980, pp. 167-174; J.H. TIGAY, *You Shall Have No Other Gods. Israelite Religion in the Light of Hebrew Inscriptions* (Harvard Semitic Studies 31), Atlanta 1986, pp. 26-30.

be read, i.a., "Urija, the rich one, wrote it. Blessed be Urija through YHWH, for he (i.e. YHWH) saved him from his enemies through his Asherah"[13]. "Asherah" obviously refers to the also in the Old Testament mentioned goddess or her symbol, whose name is given in connection with the Canaanite Baal religion[14]. From the papyrus inscriptions discovered in the last century, deriving from the post-exile Jewish colony on the island of Elephantine in the deep south of Egypt, "Anathjaho", among other names, and combinations with names of "Canaanite" gods were already known to us[15]. These and other discoveries only strengthen the impression that in "popular religion" YHWH must originally have been one deity among the many gods and goddesses of the Canaanite pantheon, except that YHWH in the course of the Israelite history developed into a national, and finally, during or after the Exile, into a universal god of a monolatric or even monotheistic signature, no matter how one interprets the terms "monolatry" and "monotheism"[16]. A further subject for debate is whether this YHWH in the Israelite pre- and protohistory had predominately the character of Baal[17] or that of El[18]. As is well-known, both of these latter deities are "principal gods" – if, for the sake of convenience, I may qualify them as such – in the Ugaritic pantheon as well as in the pantheon of the entire Syriac-Phoenician-Canaanite world in the times of ancient Israel, as is generally assumed.

YHWH as one of the deities of the Canaanite pantheon might very well fit into the picture we are trying to form of the oldest history of the period of Israel's kings, in particular that of Solomon. When we single out the historically more or less verifiable elements from the Deuteronomic historical work to which, since NOTH's pioneering work[19], the books of Kings are assumed

---

[13] See i.a. J.M. HADLEY, "The Khirbet el-Qom Inscription", *VT* 37 (1987), pp. 50-62, here: 51.

[14] See my *Kanaänitische goden in het Oude Testament*, Den Haag 1965, pp. 39-42.

[15] See A. COWLEY, *Aramaic Papyri of the Fifth Century B.C.*, Oxford 1923, no. 44³ (=147); further: A. VINCENT, *La religion des Judéo-Araméens d'Éléphantine*, Paris 1937, pp. 622-653.

[16] Cf. WELLHAUSEN, *op. cit.*, p. 212: "Der Monotheismus selber ist in gewissem Sinne Philosophie, das Ergebnis einer gewaltigen Abstraktion des Geistes von allem Sinnenfälligen. Ein Wunder ist nur, dass den Juden ihr Gott kein Abstractum geworden, sondern die lebendigste Persönlichkeit geblieben ist". See also the expositions of B. HARTMANN and F. STOLZ in: O. KEEL, *op. cit.* (see above, footnote 12), pp. 50-81 and 144-189; J.C. DE MOOR, *Uw God is mijn God. Over de oorsprong van het geloof in de ene God*, Kampen 1983, pp. 48f.; further N. LOHFINK, "Zur Geschichte der Diskussion über den Monotheismus im Alten Israel", in: E. HAAG (ed.), *Gott, der einzige. Zur Entstehung des Monotheismus in Israel* (Quaestiones Disputatae 104), Feiburg usw. 1985, pp. 9-25.

[17] See e.g. the dissertation by Mrs. C.J.L. KLOOS, *Yhwh's Combat with the Sea*, Leiden 1986.

[18] See i.a. U. OLDENBURG, *The Conflict between El and Ba'al in Canaanite Religion*, Leiden 1969; cf. also J. BLOMMENDAAL, *El als fundament en exponent van het oud-testamentische universalisme*, Utrecht 1972.

[19] NOTH, *Überlieferungsgeschichtliche Studien. Die sammelnden und bearbeitenden Geschichtswerke im Alten Testament* (Schriften der Königsberger Gelehrten Gesellschaft, Geisteswissensch. Klasse 18 (1943), pp. 43-266) = Tübingen 1957²; Darmstadt 1967³.

to belong, the picture of Solomon – and that of his father David – that emerges is decidedly different from the generally accepted one[20]. We may take it, however, for granted that David, notwithstanding much struggle and opposition, established a dynasty that Solomon continued with great tact and thorough strategic acumen.

One ingredient indispensable for realising a powerful empire, especially in antiquity, is the pursuit of the use of one language, one jurisdiction, and, if at all possible, one nationally accepted religion. I Kings iv 7-19 allows us a glimpse of the pursuit of political unity by mentioning twelve Cis- and Transjordanian districts which partly coincided with the boundaries of the tribes known to us from other contexts. In part, however, they consisted of purely Canaanite districts, the boundaries of which are barely traceable nowadays but which, in all probability, had neither in times earlier nor later consistently been firmly held by Israel, such as, e.g., the Mediterranean coast or the adjacent region of Carmel. We know that Solomon pursued the unity with a stern and iron hand in order to make his dominion strong internally as well as externally. And succeed in this endeavour he did[21]! It is not surprising that he also aimed at unity in the performance of the cult accompanying the building of the court chapel we mentioned before. Solomon wanted to be king for and over *one* people composed of diverse groups or tribes differing in race, culture, religion and probably also in language or at any rate dialect. With a view to this end, he assumably designed the other buildings in his palace compound. To give but one example: I Kings vii 7 emphatically mentions the building of the "Hall of the Throne", i.e. a "Hall of Judgement", "where he was to give judgement".

Unity of jurisdiction, unity of religion. Like King Ahab later in the "golden age" of the Northern-Israelite State, so also Solomon in his time evidently aimed at a "policy of parity" in which he tried to be a stern, to be sure, but also a just *pater patriae*. But once again the question crops up: What did this Jerusalem cult in Solomon's temple look like? Did Solomon really have an exclusively YHWH worship in mind, intended also for his mainly Canaanite subjects? For indeed our investigation into the detailed description of the

---

[20] The question is, in how far was Solomon's father David Israelite or Judaean? See e.g. G.W. AHLSTRÖM, "Was David a Jebusite Subject?", *ZAW* 92 (1980), pp. 285ff.; cf. also E. SELLIN, *Das Zwölfprophetenbuch* I (KAT XII/1), p. 335: "Ob zwischen beiden Ephrats noch ein besonderer Zusammenhang vorliegt, so dass etwa ein ephraimitischer Clan einmal in die Landschaft von Bethlehem ausgewandert, David mithin *dem Blute nach* [italics mine, MJM] kein Judäer gewesen wäre, ist noch nicht aufgeklärt". It remains an intriguing question why David was so "easy" in his association with the Philistines, and recruited his bodyguard from "Kerethites and Pelethites". Were childhood and youth legends applied as literary forms to legitimate the genuineness of the lineage and to justify the later lawful kingship of the dynasty?

[21] See also our article "Koning Salomo als politiek realist", in: M.B. TER BORG and L. LEERTOUWER (eds.), *Het realisme in de politiek theologisch beschouwd*, Baarn 1987, pp. 50-58.

building of the temple itself as well as the entire composition of the temple and palace structure give the impression that Solomon's YHWH worship must have been a mixture of Canaanite and early-Israelite religious components[22]. It has been pointed out repeatedly that along with the temple design, the pre-Jerusalemite cult of El, or at any rate a variant form of the local cult of a Jebusite deity had been preserved by the Solomonic cult officiants, and was subsequently integrated into the later Jahwistic theology[23]. Undoubtedly one is right in surmising that there must have been continuity between the pre-Jebusite and the later Solomonic temple cult, but it is far from easy to deduce the *nature* of this cult from the sparse pointers offered by the Old Testament itself[24].

This attempt at a reconstruction of what was *possibly* the course of Israel's religious history may serve to show how up until today attempts are made – justly so – to find reasonable explanations for what later was to be called the "uniqueness" of YHWH. The more or less peaceful coexistence of Canaanite gods, rites and cults on the one hand and the worship of YHWH on the other rightly keep engaging the scholarly debates. At the end of the last and the beginning of this century, the foremost question was: "Was this process a matter of apostasy or of development?"[25]. Continuing studies in the fields of archaeology, literature, comparative religion, sociology and cultural anthropology have meanwhile made it abundantly clear that the dilemma can no longer simply be reduced to a common denominator. And rather than thinking in terms of revolution and/or deformation, we now start from the notions revolution and/or reformation. In this connection, it will be useful to point to two recent lines of development.

In the *first* place, there is the theory of the rising and flourishing of the so-

---

[22] Cf. also G.W. AHLSTRÖM, *Aspects of Syncretism in Israelite Religion* (Horae Soederblomianae 5), Lund 1963, pp. 43-46.

[23] A well-known example is the deity El 'Eljōn, see G. WANKE, *Die Zionstheologie der Korachiten in ihrem traditionsgeschichtlichen Zusammenhang* (BZAW 97), Berlin 1966, p. 47.

[24] LEMCHE, *op. cit.*, p. 228, rightly points out that a wide-ranging study of the west-Semitic religion in the first millennium B.C. might make clear that it is impossible to find out which of the two west-Semitic gods, Baal or El, has most influenced the understanding of YHWH's essence. The identification of the two was furthered by the idea of both being "kings". This contributed to a better understanding of the "royal" character of YHWH in the time of the kings.

[25] See A. KUENEN, *De Godsdienst van Israël tot den ondergang van den joodschen staat* I, Haarlem 1869, p. 218. We may also be reminded here of J. RIDDERBOS, *Israel en de Baäls. Afval of ontwikkeling*, Nijverdal 1915, in which he opposes "that which Scripture testifies to about these things" to "the evolutionistic concept, whose insufficiency is evident in all sorts of ways". Unfortunately, this otherwise still very worthwhile lecture overlooks the fact that in particular the Old Testament itself presents a lot of support for the "evolutionistic" standpoint of the critical science repudiated by RIDDERBOS. A more acceptable position was taken by e.g. G. WILDEBOER in his lecture "Jahwedienst en Volksreligie in Israël", incorporated in *Nieuw Licht over het Oude Testament. Verspreide Opstellen*, Haarlem 1911, pp. 28-61.

called "Yahweh-alone movement" in the period of Israel's kings[26]. According to the followers of this theory, the first vestiges of this movement trace back to the ninth century B.C., when for political reasons the cult of the "Tyrian Baal" in the northern kingdom threatened to become a formidable rival to the cult of YHWH. The book of Hosea may be seen as a kind of basic document of the movement. The movement becomes manifest in Judah in the cult reformation in king Hezekiah's time, while an important stage of the movement is reached with the reformation by king Josiah, whose aim was to achieve *Kulturreinheit* and *Kultureinheit*[27]. The crisis caused by the Exile, finally, brings about the breakthrough of the movement to all those deported to Babylon, establishing the triumph of YHWH-monotheism. In the process, polytheistic remnants in the popular religion were assimilated. The goal of the movement was the pursuit of the exclusive worship of YHWH, to which end neither power politics nor an almost blatant show of opportunism were shunned.

The procedure as sketched above implies that Israel before and during the monarchy was polytheistic. True, YHWH had been worshipped from the beginning, but only as one god – at best a tribal or family god – among many others. In fact he was rather the "family" or "national" god of the Israelites and their territory, whose *specialité de la maison* was foremostly to be found in kingdom, war and peace. In addition to YHWH there were gods of other families and nations, city gods, spirits of the dead and numerous other *numina*, each having an established specific place and function in the religion. If necessary, each of them could in turn function exclusively. Likewise YHWH, too, would for centuries have been a "national" god, not necessarily excluding or standing in the way of other family, local or fertility deities. That is was specifically YHWH in whose honour such a "Yahweh-alone movement" could come into being was, among other things, due to the fact that in the pantheon only YHWH stood alone and unrelated, that only he was worshipped without the use of images, and that he was the deity of the Israelites in particular. Whenever Israel was endangered, it was YHWH on whom all attention was focused[28]. Therefore, a continued state of emergency continued

---

[26] M. SMITH, "Religious Parties among the Israelites before 587", in: *Palestinian Parties and Politics that Shaped the Old Testament*, London 1971 ($1987^2$), pp. 11-42; B. LANG, "Die Jahwe-allein-Bewegung", in: B. LANG (ed.), *Der einzige Gott. Die Geburt des biblischen Monotheismus*, München 1981, pp. 47-83; English version: "The Yahweh-Alone Movement and the Making of Jewish Monotheism", in: B. LANG (ed.), *Monotheism and the Prophetic Minority: An Essay in Biblical History and Sociology*, Bradford-on-Avon 1983, pp. 13-59.

[27] See G. BRAULIK, "Das Deuteronomium und die Geburt des Monotheismus", in: E. HAAG (ed.), *Gott, der Einzige. Zur Entstehung des Monotheismus in Israel* (Quaestiones disputatae 104), Freiburg etc. 1985, p. 115.

[28] See for the above LOHFINK, *op. cit.*, pp. 20f. B. LANG formulates i.a. the hypothesis that in the ancient Near East it must have been customary to observe strict forms of monolatry in times of hardship until the moment the emergence had come to an end.

monolatry. Thus it was that the YHWH monolatry in Israel and Judah originated in a protracted state of emergency which lay at the root of the "Yahweh-alone movement".

In the *second* place, there is the research into the proper names of people living during the period of the Israelite monarchy. M. Rose, in a study published in 1978, has pointed out that many names contained the theophoric element YHWH in a reduced form, namely YHW[29]. In the Elephantine papyri from the fifth century B.C., mentioned above, this triliteral form is also attested to as an independent name of God, as is the case in inscriptions from the eighth or seventh century B.C. found in Palestine. And everyone more or less familiar with the Old Testament will undoubtedly know personal names compounded with the form YHW, such as Yeho-natan or Yeho-shuah[30]. Rose points out that it is not very likely that there would have been a division between the cult in which the Tetragrammaton was used on the one hand, and the profane practice of naming in which only the first three consonants were used on the other[31]. Underlying this distinction, there is, in his opinion, an authoritarian idea that must have brought about this drastic alteration. What, then, could be more obvious than to call to mind the period of the reign of king Josiah, whose name is permanently linked with the finding of an ancient code on the one hand, and the radical reformation of the Judaean cult on the other (II Kings xxii f.)? For within the frame of reference of that time and of Josiah's work, the "monojahwism" of the Deuteronomistic school and the growing number of discovered inscriptions and other material containing personal names with YHWH as theophoric element can easily be explained[32].

The portent of Rose's exposition will by now have become clear: the triliteral YHW is the original form of the name of God, and only had to yield pride of place to the Tetragrammaton YHWH a little before or during the reformation of Josiah, in other words in the period of the decline of the Judaean kings, with all the concomitant far-reaching theological consequences. Rose's rather radical view can be queried on several points, on the basis of material

[29] M. Rose, *Jahwe. Zum Streit um den alttestamentlichen Gottesnamen* (Theol. Studien 122), Zürich 1978; *idem*, "Jahwe", *TRE* 16 (1987), pp. 438-441.

[30] Already M. Noth, *Die israelitischen Personennamen im Rahmen der gemeinsemitischen Namengebung* (BWANT III/10), Stuttgart 1928 (= Hildesheim 1966²), pp. 101-114, had payed attention to the difference between the longer independent form YHWH and the shorter form YHW in proper names. Rose thinks, i.a., that Noth omitted to substantiate his theory of the "Kürzungstendenz" in proper names. According to him, one does not find reduced forms of names of gods in proper names with other Semitic peoples either.

[31] Rose, *op. cit.*, pp. 22-27.

[32] In this connection, we may also remind of Deut. vi 4: "YHWH, our God, is YHWH the One". The attributive cardinal "one" specifically defines the YHWH-quality of the deity of Israel, see M. Rose, *Der Ausschliesslichkeitsanspruch Jahwes. Deuteronomische Schultheologie und die Volksfrömmigkeit in der späten Königszeit* (BWANT 106), Stuttgart etc. 1975, pp. 134-143.

found in inscriptions and otherwise epigraphical data[33]. Even assuming that the Tetragrammaton had indeed been introduced in Josiah's time as a name of God carrying authority and power, how did it relate to the YHW of the popular devotion prior to that time? Can we assume a continuity of essence, manifestation and cult of this deity? Do we, for that matter, actually refer to one and the same god when we speak about YHW before Josiah's reformation and YHWH after that period, and should we not rather think in terms of "an infinitely qualitative distinction" between the tetragrammatic God and the triconsonantic god who would have been merely one among the many Canaanite gods? If so, the solution to the problem we formulated at the beginning of this article would be obvious: not only did Solomon rebuild an existing *Jebusitic* temple, but he also restored the prevailing *Canaanite* cult, at best completed with a family or tribal god YHW, irrespective of the origin of the latter.

Recent statistical studies by J.H. TIGAY of the University of Pennsylvania point out that the problem of personal names compounded with the theophoric element YHWH or YHW also draws attention to another aspect[34]. He reports that not only the Old Testament itself but also epigraphical, inscriptional and other Israelite and Judaean data from, in particular, the later monarchy, contain an exceptionally high percentage of proper names with YHWH as a theophoric element; evidently, it was but seldom that a name with a deity other than YHWH was chosen for a newborn. The ratio of Yahwistic to non-Yahwistic names in the inscriptions is well over 94% to 6%, while in the Old Testament itself it was 89% to 11% for all pre-exilic periods. According to TIGAY, the onomastic evidence contradicts the accusations found in the Old Testament saying that the people were "pagan" and polytheistic, in particular during the later monarchy. In other words, the Old Testament is far too emphatic about the Canaanite impact on Israel and especially on Judah at the time, which means that the prophets and the authors would have grossly exaggerated the "apostasy" from YHWH. The doctrine of the collective responsibility induced prophets and historiographers to generalise the guilt of individuals or small groups. It was, e.g., Achan who violated the ban of plunder at Jericho, but all the same God said to Joshua: "Israel in its entirety has sinned" (Josh. vii 11)[35]. Impressive though this statistical material collected

[33] We may think here of the mention of the Tetragrammaton in the well-known Moabitic Mesha-inscription from the 9th century B.C.: *KAI* 181, 18; cf. J.C.L. GIBSON, *Textbook of Syrian Semitic Inscriptions* I, Oxford 1971, pp. 71-83. Do we have here the usual form of God's name, or, as ROSE has it, is it a matter of suffix /h/ appended to the three-consonantal YHW?

[34] See his work mentioned above, note 12, and further his "Israelite Religion: The Onomastic and Epigraphic Evidence", in: P.D. MILLER, Jr., P.D. HANSON and S.D. MCBRIDE (eds.), *Ancient Israelite Religion* (Festschrift Frank Moore Cross), Philadelphia 1987, pp. 157-194.

[35] See TIGAY, *op. cit.*, p. 40. On the same lines was already before TIGAY argued by the Jewish scholar Y. KAUFMANN, *The Religion of Israel. From its Beginnings to the Babylonian Exile* (transl. M. GREENSBERG), London 1961, pp. 122-149, to whom TIGAY repeatedly refers.

by TIGAY may be, the corpus is in itself too limited to justify such far-reaching conclusions; moreover, it is silent concerning the quality of the worship of YHWH in the later years of the monarchy. At best it gives some information about the range of the YHWH cult at the time.

We shall dwell on the subject of Solomon's temple still a little while longer. On the strength of the research mentioned in the beginning of this paper[36], it can hardly be called a temple only for YHWH, at least not in the sense later tradition attached to it. Indeed, also the tradition transmitted to us occasionally makes it perfectly clear that during the Judaean monarchy the temple was the stage of a Syriac-Canaanite cult rather than a Jahwistic one (see, e.g., II Kings xvi 10-18; cf. also Ezek. viii). Similarly the temple of Baal in Jerusalem at the time of queen Athaliah (II Kings xi 18) seems to have been (part of) the famous temple compound belonging to the royal palace rather than a separate sanctuary elsewhere in the city. When we go on leafing through the Old Testament, we shall find that it implicitly as well as explicitly censures the notion that the temple would be an ideal abode for YHWH. We may, again by way of example, remind ourselves of II Sam. vii 5f., where it says that it should be passed on to David as the word of God: "Do you want to build me a temple to dwell in? I have not dwelt in a temple at all since the day I brought up the people of Israel out of Egypt, but I have been moving about in a tent as if it were a permanent abode".

Also elsewhere in the Old Testament, accommodating YHWH in a built temple is obviously subject to criticsm. Immediately at the inauguration of the temple, described in the Deuteronomistically coloured chapter viii (12f.) of I Kings[37], Solomon utters his so-called "dedication of the temple", which freely translated runs roughly as follows: "YHWH has said that he prefers to live in darkness; verily I have built Thee an exalted dwelling place, a fixed abode for Thee to dwell in for ever". As may be known, the Septuagint not only incorporated these verses at another place in chapter viii, but also gives an intriguing addition to this dedication[38]. The Septuagint affirms that the proverb under discussion derives from a source other than the Deuteronomistic one. Nonetheless, we shall with regard to the form adhere to the version transmitted in the Hebrew Bible. This states explicitly that YHWH conceals himself in "darkness" (*'rpl*), an expression found also elsewhere in the Old Testament

---

[36] See above, note 3.

[37] See for this chapter now also the dissertation by E. TALSTRA, *Het gebed van Salomo. Synchronie en Diachronie in de kompositie van I Kon. 8, 14-61*, Amsterdam 1987.

[38] Cf. the translation by J. WELLHAUSEN, *Die Composition des Hexateuchs und der historischen Bücher des Alten Testaments*, 1963[4], p. 269. The Septuagint has a first line: "YHWH has set the sun in the heavens ...", and it adds to this that the dedication occurs in the "Book of the Ode", perhaps better interpreted as the "Book of Jashar" or the "Book of the Upright", from which also elsewhere in the Old Testament (Josh. x 13; II Sam. i 18) songs are quoted.

(Ex. xx 21; Deut. v 22)[39]. This "darkness" is, as it were, a manifestation and representation of the *deus absconditus*. The paradoxically concealed manifestation of YHWH thus attested to by our verse was *nota bene* cited at the consecration of the Solomonic temple. This indicates that YHWH may not actually be "incarcerated" in an earthly dwelling, as is also emphatically stated in the sequel (verse 27). So in the introductory words of the dedication formula something of the tension surrounding the approval of the temple as a fixed abode for YHWH, that must have made itself felt up until the time of the Deuteronomistic author, becomes almost palpable.

The aversion to a temple as a permanent dwelling for YHWH is also present in the criticism expressed by the prophets. In this connection Jeremiah, in his temple sermon denouncing his compatriots who shout "the temple of the Lord, the temple of the Lord, the temple of the Lord is this" (Jer. vii 4), is not even the first to come in our mind. For this is not a valid criticism within the scope of our argument, even if one would be inclined to assume that these shouters were uttering a self-fulfilling prophecy. The criticism is even more outspoken in Amos v 25f., when he ridicules the obstinate sacrificial ceremonies of, to be true, Israel, adding the much discussed words: "When, forty years long, you brought me sacrifices and gifts in the wilderness, did you then carry Sakkuth, your king, and Kewan, your principal god, those images that you made for yourselves?"[40]. Here we touch a sensitive chord revealing both immanent criticism of Israel's current temple cult and the memory of YHWH's exclusivity "in the desert".

In the later time of the kings and in the Exile, Israel was fully aware of the fact that the start of its existence as a nation, or at any rate of certain tribes of the nation, must have taken place outside of the region of the Canaanite culture, to wit in the southern steppes. This awareness was based on the concept of YHWH being the "God of the desert", specifically of Mount Sinai (Deut. xxxiii 2; Judg. v 5; Ps. lxviii 18; I Kings xix 8), in any case the God of the Israelite tribes from before the time of the kings. Obviously this deity could not live in a permanent sanctuary but must have "resided" in a "tent of meeting" – not to be identified with the so-called "Tabernacle" – where now and then he deigned to manifest himself[41]. It is clear that this God was considered and known as the "God of Israel". Several passages in the Old Testament testify to this notion, sometimes in veiled terms, sometimes unambiguously. The question as to where we should look for the source of this notion can as yet only be answered hypothetically, and requires further investi-

[39] See for further information about this word our article in *TWAT* 6 (1989), pp. 397-402.
[40] Here we (roughly) follow the translation of C. VAN LEEUWEN, *Amos* (POT), Nijkerk 1985, p. 228.
[41] See for the problems concerning i.a. the "Ark": R. SCHMITT, *op. cit.* (above, note 7), pp. 36ff.

gation. It may suffice here to remind ourselves only of the so-called "Kenites hypothesis", also supported by earlier professors of the University of Leiden, such as G. WILDEBOER, A.J. WENSINCK and B.D. EERDMANS[42]. In brief, this hypothesis holds that Israelite tribes after their flight from Egypt encountered Kenites, roaming desert smiths, in the wilderness. Jethro, Moses' father-in-law, was one of the Kenite priests of the related tribe Midian (cf. Judg. iv 11). It was among these Kenites that the Israelites would have come to know their God as YHWH.

However much criticism may be levelled at the "Kenites hypothesis", it can not be denied that in the history of Israel during the time of the kings there are elements pointing to the years spent in the desert. We mention Jeremiah xxxv, a remarkable chapter wherein the Rechabites are put on the stage. These Rechabites, descendants from a certain Jonadab – who in his turn was also called "son of Rechab" –, were given commandments from time immemorial, which they observed up until the days of Jehoiakim son of the reformer king Josiah: they refrained from wine, did not plant vineyards, did not build houses nor sow seed, but remained dwellers in tents all of their lives; in short, they lived nomadic lives. Though insignificant in number, they scrupulously and even somewhat fanatically observed the rules. The prophet Jeremiah held them up as an example to the people of Jerusalem and Judah equally, which in itself does not necessarily mean that he actually agreed with their principles, though the reverse can also not be proven. As has already been said, these Rechabites descended from Jonadab, an ardent follower of king Jehu who ruthlessly and bloodily fought the Baal worship in the northern state of Israel (II Kings x 15-27). Jonadab turns out to have been as ruthless a "zealot" on behalf of YHWH as was Jehu himself. A concealed genealogical statement in I Chron. ii 55 (cf. also iv 12) closely links these harsh Rechabites to the Kenites, who may well have laid the foundation of the worship of YHWH in Israel, considering that they themselves had been worshippers of YHWH originally[43].

All doubts about the origin and customs of the Rechabites notwithstanding, there is, in our opinion, at least a core of truth in the statements about them, to wit that the triumph of YHWH in Israel was to a large extent – if not for the greater part – brought about by prophets of YHWH inspired by "Rechabistic" ideals[44]. Indeed, many an Old Testament prophet was unmistakably

[42] See G. WILDEBOER, *op. cit.* (above, note 25), pp. 40f.; A.J. WENSINCK, *Semietische Studiën uit de nalatenschap van Prof.Dr. A.J. Wensinck*, Leiden 1941, pp. 37f.; B.D. EERDMANS, *De godsdienst van Israël* I, Huis ter Heide 1930, pp. 35-39, and now also LEMCHE, *Early Israel* (above, note 10), pp. 148-152; and I. KALIMI, "Three Assumptions About the Kenites", *ZAW* 100 (1988), pp. 386-393.

[43] For the Rechabites, cf. e.g. the articles by M.H. POPE or otherwise F.S. FRICK, in: *IDB* 4 (1962), pp. 15f., or *Suppl. Vol.*, pp. 726ff.

[44] A. KUENEN, *De Profeten en de profetie onder Israël* II, Leiden 1875, p. 365, talked about the "ethical monotheism" of the prophets.

possessed, often reluctantly, with an ideal that was unique and self-explanatory both in their eyes at the time and now in ours: to shape Israel into a nation belonging to YHWH only, cultically as well as ethically. Thus, their message was often diametrically opposed to the "parity policy" of Judaean and Israelite kings, and equally against the practices of the religious and economic leaders. As individuals with a calling they knew themselves to be servants of YHWH, just as centuries later Muhammad knew himself to be Allah's servant[45]. All this, of course, is known well enough. What is new, however – at least as we see it – is that a gradual development of the syncretistic YHWH worship from the previous periods cannot be the only explanation of the breakthrough of the YHWH exclusiveness in the seventh century, but that it was brought about mainly by a revolutionary infringement on the Canaanite and Israelite society in which the "parity policy" had pride of place among its kins and leaders. To be sure, any revolutionary breakthrough, sudden and radical though it may seem in our eyes, is bound to have had a more or less long "incubation period" of an economic, social and/or political nature. But that does not alter the fact that such revolutions contain elements that can not entirely be explained in a purely rational way, even if – in this case – we did possess many more documents from Israel and Judah than we now have at our disposal. The revolutionary spark of, e.g., the prophets of the eighth and seventh centuries was at the roots of king Josiah's reformation, short-lived as it may seem at first sight and actually a failure in the eyes of many. And yet it was in this very period that the so-called Deuteronomistic theology blossomed. The result was that during and long after the Exile, the exclusivity of YHWH had come into being, enriching us with the ethically and religiously most fascinating "epos" of the Old Testament and the creation of Deutero-Isaiah.

Again, and perhaps monotonously – all in MULTATULI's tradition – we pose the question we asked before: Was Solomon's temple a YHWH temple? In the light of our arguments the answer to this direct question has to be: No; and then again, be it with qualifications: Yes! Indeed even the Deuteronomistic theologians have not been able to get away from the fact that Solomon – and not only towards the end of his life – had not been a very faithful worshipper of YHWH, at least not in our eyes. Not only did he acquire a considerable number of wives – which at the time was not such a very objectionable royal status symbol –, but into the bargain he built for them altars and other devotional constructions, the tangible and repugnant remnants of which were, according to II Kings xxiii 13, centuries later still considered as abominations. If YHWH did have any significance to Solomon at all, it was certainly only

[45] Cf. also WENSINCK, *op. cit.*, pp. 39ff., who points out analogies between the actions of Moses and Muhammad respectively.

marginally so in his personal life. As regards the exclusivity of the YHWH cult, he was in no way different from the kings reigning over Judah and Israel after him. The court temple was constructed by *Phoenicians* in conformity with their customary measurements and materials on the very spot where previously the Jebusites had performed their Canaanite rites. As was the case under many kings succeeding him – openly attested to by prophets and other authors –, so the pre-Josian temple was in the eyes of many YHWH-worshippers blatantly incompatible with the essence and kingship of YHWH. The reformations of king Josiah, known as one of the most "devout" kings of the entire Davidic dynasty, could barely stem the tide of aversion for the temple many pre-exilic YHWH followers still harboured. Even the Deuteronomistic colouring of the history of the earliest period of the kings with Solomon's building of the temple as its culmination point could not totally obscure the traces of antipathy to the temple, even in the Old Testament. Only Ezekiel in his temple vision, and, later on, the author of Chronicles, succeeded in making the temple figure in the Jewish and Christian history as an unalloyed YHWH temple even as cleary as the time of David in his capacity as cult reformer, and as a monument for later generations. By then we have arrived at the temple called the "Second Temple" in the Jewish tradition, the exclusive abode of and for YHWH; and we hear the final chords of our Hebrew bible, obfuscating the original character of Solomon's temple with their resounding beauty.

# "I WILL BREAK HIS YOKE FROM OFF YOUR NECK"

*Remarks on Jeremiah xxx 4-11*

BY

BOB BECKING

*Utrecht*

After a Deuteronomistic introduction[1] the prophecies in Jeremiah's book of consolation open with the textual unit Jer. xxx 4-11. According to the Masoretes these verses are to be regarded as a textual unit. They placed a *petûḥa* before vs. 4 and one after vs. 11[2]. A form-critical analysis of the text shows that it consists of three distinctive units. Is it, however, necessary to make a literary-critical division on the basis of form-critical observations? In the following lines I will discuss this question. Before giving an answer it will be necessary, I think, to describe the units mentioned.

## I

1. xxx 4 *Introduction*[3].

These are the words, that the LORD spoke to Israel and to Judah.

This verse formed the introduction to a pre-dtr composition of prophecies. I regard them as from another hand than the foregoing introduction. Because

[1] W. THIEL, *Die deuteronomistische Redaktion von Jeremia 26-45* (WMANT 52), Neukirchen/Vluyn 1981, pp. 20-21, 101; S. BÖHMER, *Heimkehr und neuer Bund* (GTA 5), Göttingen 1976, pp. 47-49; N. LOHFINK, "Der junge Jeremia als Propagandist und Poet", in: P.-M. BOGAERT (ed.), *Le livre de Jérémie* (BEThL LIV), Leuven 1981, p. 352, n. 6; *idem*, "Die Gotteswortverschlachtelung in Jer. 30-31", in: L. RUPPERT, P. WEIMAR and E. ZENGER (ed.), *Künder des Wortes* (Festschrift J. SCHREINER), Würzburg 1982, p. 107, and C. WESTERMANN, *Prophetische Heilsworte im Alten Testament* (FRLANT 145), Göttingen 1987, p. 106. For the view that xxx 1-3 are redactional, but not deuteronomistic: A. WEISER, *Das Buch des Propheten Jeremia* (ATD 20/21), Göttingen 1960[4], pp. 273, 276; W. RUDOLPH, *Jeremia* (HAT I, 12), Tübingen 1968[3], p. 189; G. FOHRER, "Der Israel-Prophet in Jeremia 30-31", in: A. CAQOUT and M. DELCOR (eds.), *Mélanges bibliques et orientaux* (Festschrift H. CAZELLES) (AOAT 212), Neukirchen/Vluyn 1981, p. 135, and R.P. CARROLL, *From Chaos to Covenant*, London 1981, p. 205, and *idem*, *The Book of Jeremiah* (OTL), London 1986, pp. 568, 571-573.

[2] See J.M. OESCH, *Petucha and Setuma* (OBO 27), Fribourg 1979.

[3] According to J. BRIGHT, *Jeremiah* (AB 21), Garden City NY 1965, p. 278, vs. 4 is the heading of the complex poem 5-24; see also G. FOHRER, "Israel-Prophet", p. 135, and C. WESTERMANN, *Heilsworte*, p. 106.

of the occurrence of the words "and Judah" in the ancient versions there is no necessity to delete them in the text[4].

2. xxx 5-7 *Description of the awful terror on the day of oppression.*

5 So thus speaks the LORD[5]: a
"We[6] hear a cry of anguish b
of terror. And there is no peace[7]. c
6 Ask now and see a
if a man bears a child. b
Why then do I see every young man c
with his hands on his loins like a woman who bears? d
Why[8] then have all faces changed e
and did they become[9] pale? f
7 Because that day is great a
there is none like it. b
It will be a time of oppression for Jacob. c
And shall he be saved out of it?"[10] d

---

[4] Contra W. Rudolph, *Jeremia*, pp. 188-189; A. van Selms, *Jeremia* II (POT), Nijkerk 1974, p. 63; N. Lohfink, "Junge Jeremia", p. 353; cf. R.P. Carroll, *Jeremiah*, p. 571, although from a redaction-critical point of view the words are subject to doubt, cf. W. Thiel, *Redaktion*, p. 20; "and Judah" may be an insertion from a redactor who applied the oracles in Jer. xxx-xxxi to the whole of Israel.

[5] The first line is a necessary introduction to a new sub-unit, contra A. Weiser, *Jeremia*, p. 268; J. Bright, *Jeremiah*, p. 269.

[6] *šm‘nw*, "we hear"; LXX read a 2 plur. form taking Israel and Judah as subject. In parallel with *r’yty*, "I see", in 6c the suggestion of i.a. BHS should be taken over that "the LORD" is also subject in 5b and that the form originally was *šm‘ty*. The plural form of the MT should be compared with *šm‘nw* in the parallel context of Jer. vi 24.

[7] *w’yn šlwm* is not a negated nomen regendum related to *qwl* but an independent nominal clause; cf. A. van Selms, *Jeremia* II, p. 64.

[8] I agree with the suggestion of G. Fohrer, "Israel-Prophet", pp. 136-137; L.T. Brodie, "Jacob's Travail (Jer. 30:1-13) and Jacob's Struggle (Gen. 32:22-32)", *JSOT* 19 (1981), p. 37, and R.P. Carroll, *Jeremiah*, p. 573, that the interrogative "why" governs the whole of 6c-f.

[9] *hôy* is not the introduction of a "woe-oracle" (see below) but an incorrect reading of *hayû* which ought to be incorporated in verse 6, cf. LXX; A. Weiser, *Jeremia*, p. 268; A. van Selms, *Jeremia* II, p. 168; W. Rudolph, *Jeremia*, p. 190; G. Fohrer, "Israel-Prophet", p. 137; L.T. Brodie, *JSOT* 19 (1981), p. 37, and N. Lohfink, "Junge Jeremia", p. 354 n. 17; contra J. Bright, *Jeremiah*, p. 269; C. Hardmeier, *Texttheorie und biblische Exegese* (BETh 79), München 1978, pp. 192, 342, 384, and R.P. Carroll, *Jeremiah*, p. 574. See also W. Janzen, *Mourning Cry and Woe Oracle* (BZAW 125), Berlin – New York 1972, p. 73.

[10] The sequence adverb-verb with a *qāṭal*-form in 7d indicates that the clause is an interrogative sentence, cf. W.L. Holladay, "Style, Irony and Authenticity in Jeremiah", *JBL* 81 (1962), pp. 53-54 (and in other publications of Holladay on Jeremiah), and J.R. Lundblom, *Jeremiah: A Study in Ancient Hebrew Rhetoric* (SBL DS 18), Missoula 1975, p. 33; contra J. Bright, *Jeremiah*, p. 297; S. Böhmer, *Heimkehr*, p. 57; G. Fohrer, "Israel-Prophet", p. 137; L.T. Brodie, *JSOT* 19 (1981), p. 37; R.P. Carroll, *Jeremiah*, p. 574; J. Unterman, *From Repentance to Redemption* (JSOTS 54), Sheffield 1987, p. 135, and C. Westermann, *Heilsworte*, pp. 106-107. N. Lohfink, "Junge Jeremia", p. 354, leaves the question open.

The text consists of the following elements:

| | | |
|---|---|---|
| A | 5a | Introductory formula |
| B | 5b-6b | Descriptive statements |
| C | 6c-f | Questions about the changed situation |
| D | 7a-c | Answer |
| E | 7d | Question about the future |

This unit gives the description of a transformation which has taken place. I will indicate this transformation as Trans I.

Element B describes the awful situation after the ruin of a city or a state. *ḥ$^{a}$rādā*, "anguish", is used in I Sam. xiv 15; in Isa. xxi 4 and Ez. xxvi 16 for human reactions after the destruction of a city or to describe the cruel end of the lives of 20 Philistines. In Deut. xxviii 67 *paḥad*, "terror", summarises the human reaction to the executions of the curses of the covenant. Isaiah uses the noun in two texts related to Jer. xxx 5-7. Isa. ii 10 summons the Israelites to hide themselves from the terror on the day of the LORD. Isa. ii 19, 21 shows that the people answered the prophetic summons. In the context of a prophecy of doom Isa. xxiv 17-20 pictures the judgement in terms of creation becoming chaos anew. This judgement leads to terror (Isa. xxiv 17, 18). The author of a prophecy against Moab took over the phraseology of Isa. xxiv 17-18 in Jer. xlviii 43-44.

The sentence "We hear the voice of anguish and terror" refers to a reversal as has become clear from the analysis of the nouns *ḥ$^{a}$rādā* and *paḥad*. This reversal has already been stated by Jeremiah:

> I will make to cease from the cities of Judah and the streets of Jerusalem the sound of joy and the sound of gladness, the voice of the bridegroom and the voice of the bride[11].

In Jer. vii 29-34 the reversal is God's reaction to the sins of the people. The "removal of joyful sounds" is an element in the curses of the treaty made between Matiel of Arpad and Barga'yah of Ktk:

> [29]Nor may the sound of the lyre be heard in Arpad; but among its people (let there rather be) the din of *affliction* and *the noi[se of cry]ing* [30]and lamentation[12].

[11] Jer. vii 34; cf. xvi 9 and xxv 10.

[12] Sefîre I = KAI 222 A:29-30; cf. on this text C.H.W. Brekelmans, "Sfire I A 29-30", *VT* 13 (1963), pp. 225-228; J.A. Fitzmyer, *The Aramaic Inscriptions of Sefîre* (BeO 19), Roma 1967, pp. 14-15, 47-48; A. Lemaire and J.-M. Durand, *Les inscriptions araméennes de Sfiré et l'Assyrie de Shamshi-Ilu*, Genève – Paris 1984, p. 133. This motif is also extant in Neo-Assyrian inscriptions, cf. D.R. Hillers, *Treaty Curses and the Old Testament Prophets* (BibOr 16), Roma 1964, pp. 57-58.

The word *šālôm* in the nominal clause "and there is no peace" (5c) has a broad meaning. In the context it refers to the absence of both material and spiritual prosperity. Since the presence of *šālôm* was understood in ancient Israel as a gift of the LORD, its absence was suffered as desolation[13].

In vs. 6 the author describes the situation of terror by posing a question about a world turned topsy-turvy. This theme is well known from the Neo-Assyrian inscriptions.

For instance in the "proto-apocalyptic" Akkadian prophecies the time of a "bad prince" is described i.a. by the following words:

I ii 14 The nobility will lose prestige.
Another man who is unknown will arise
15 and seize the throne.

II ii 16 *The rich man* will extend his hand to the poor man.
(i.e. in order to beg)[14].

Another Akkadian prophecy qualifies a bad reign like this:

10 Paupers will become rich,
the rich will become paupers[15].

In his apologetic "Babylonian Inscription"[16] Esarhaddon writes that the sins of his predecessor caused the anger of the lord of the gods, Marduk. The then unchained "bad powers" thereupon started to disrupt the symmetry of the universe[17]. One of the consequences of this disruption was that

---

[13] See recently J.P. Sisson, "Jeremiah and the Jerusalem Conception of Peace", *JBL* 105 (1986), pp. 429-442.

[14] KAR 421; ed. A.K. Grayson and W.G. Lambert, "Akkadian Prophecies", *JCS* 18 (1964), pp. 7-30. On the "proto apocalyptic" nature of the Akkadian prophecies see J.-G. Heintz, "Note sur les origines de l'apocalyptique judaïque à la lumière des 'propheties akkadiennes' ", in: F. Raphael *et al.*, *L'apocalyptique* (EHR 3), Paris 1977, pp. 71-87; P. Höffken, "Heilszeitherrschererwartung im babylonischen Raum", *WdO* 9 (1977-78), pp. 57-71; R.R. Wilson, *Prophecy and Society in Ancien Israel*, Philadelphia 1980, pp. 119-123; H. Ringgren, "Akkadian Apocalypses", in: D. Hellholm (ed.), *Apocalypticism in the Mediterranean World and the Near East*, Tübingen 1983, pp. 379-386; R.D. Biggs, "The Babylonian Prophecies and the Astrological Traditions of Mesopotamia", *JCS* 37 (1985), pp. 86-90, and K. van der Toorn, "L'oracle de victoire comme expression prophétique au Proche Orient ancien", *RB* 94 (1987), p. 65.

[15] K. 7127 + //; text A.K. Grayson and W.G. Lambert, *JCS* 18 (1964), pp. 7-30; revisions on the basis of the parallel texts K. 1849 and Nippur document 2NT21 in R.D. Biggs, "More Babylonian Prophecies", *Iraq* 29 (1987), pp. 117-132.

[16] Ed. R. Borger, *Die Inschriften Asarhaddons Königs von Assyrien* (AfO Beiheft 9), Osnabrück 1967², pp. 10-29 = § 11, on this text see now M. Cogan, "Omens and Ideology in the Babylonian Inscription of Esarhaddon", in: H. Tadmor and M. Weinfeld (eds.), *History, Historiography and Interpretation*, Jerusalem 1983, pp. 76-87.

[17] Esarh. Bab. A-G, Episode 6, R. Borger, *Asarhaddon*, p. 14. I do not agree with M. Cogan, *op. cit.*, pp. 78-80, who here translates À. MEŠ ḪUL-*tim* with "bad omens".

> 9 Esagila and Ba[by]lon 10 became wasteland and 11 were like the open country[18].

In the oracles of Balaam found in Tell Deir 'Allā the reversal is also present. Although the context is broken, I think that Comb. I 11-12, 13 describes in imaginative language the possible future:

> 11 [ a fool(?)] laughs at the wise.
> A poor woman prepares myrrh.
> The priestess 12 ...
> 13 ... [ ] and the deaf hear from afar[19].

The reversal phrased by "if a man bears", however, has to my knowledge no closer parallel than the epitheton for Ishtar in a bilingual Old Babylonian song to Inanna:

> It is within your (power), Ishtar, to change men into women and women into men[20].

It should be noted, however, that the transformation in Jer. xxx 6 is phrased in the form of a question. Elsewhere in the Old Testament the theme of the "reversed universe" is formulated in the form of a question as well: Am. vi 12, Jer. ii 32, viii 4, xiii 23, xviii 14[21].

The questions put in element C underscore the theme of transformation. The first elaborates on the last theme of element B. The verbs in the second question *hpk* ni. and *hyh l* stress the change in the situation. The last phrase "they became pale" has parallels in the Old Testament, although Isa. xiii 8; Joel ii 6 and Nah ii 11 are using other words than *yerāqôn*, which is etymologically related to words for "green", to describe sudden fright.

Element D is the answer to the questions put in C. This verse has not the *form* of a woe-oracle. As pointed out in note 9 the Old Greek supports the view that Masoretic *hôy* is a misreading of *hayû*. Moreover, the typical elements of a woe-oracle are absent in Jer. xxx 7[22]. *Hôy* is not followed by a descriptive

---

18 Esarh. Bab. A-G, Episode 7 Fassung b: 9-11; R. Borger, *Asarhaddon*, p. 14.

19 Text J. Hoftijzer and G. van der Kooij, *Aramaic Texts from Deir 'Allah* (DMOA 19), Leiden 1976, pp. 174, 180; cf. H. Weippert, "Der Beitrag ausserbiblischer Prophetentexte zum Verständnis der Prosareden des Jeremiabuches", in: P.-M. Bogaert (ed.), *Le livre de Jérémie* (BEThL LIV), Leuven 1981, pp. 89-90. For a full bibliography on the Deir 'Allā plaster texts see now: A. Lemaire, "L'inscription de Balaam trouvée à Deir 'Alla: épigraphie", in: J. Amital (ed.), *Biblical Archeology Today*, Jerusalem 1985, pp. 322-323, n. 4.

20 Text: P. Haupt, *Akkadische und Sumerische Keilschrifttexte* (AB 1), Leipzig (1881-)1882, p. 130: 47-48; cf. D.R. Hillers, *Treaty Curses*, pp. 66-68.

21 See H. Weippert, "Beitrag", p. 89, n. 34.

22 See C. Westermann, *Grundformen profetischer Rede* (BETh 31), München 1960, pp. 136-140; W. Janzen, *Mourning Cry*, pp. 81-83, and C. Hardmeier, *Texttheorie*, pp. 154-173.

nominal clause. The accusation (*Anklage*) is missing. Merely the element of announcement (*Ankündigung*) could be seen in vs. 7.

The answer given in vs. 7 to the questions of the foregoing verses is that the day of transformation is incomparable in history. The expression *'ēt ṣārā* "a time of oppression" is sometimes combined with the concept of the "day of the LORD"[23]. This concept, however, is not used by Jeremiah when speaking to Judah or Israel. In Nah i 7 Nahum uses the term *yôm ṣārā* for the day when the LORD enters the history of mankind to be a shelter for some but a revenger for others. In my opinion the "day" of Jer. xxx 7 is comparable to Nah. i 7. But note that in the whole of Jer. xxx 5-7 the LORD is not to be held responsible for the transformations which have occurred or will take place.

Finally, element E consists of a question of despair. The transformations are that great that no hope for salvation remains. In interpreting this verse as a question and not as an affirmation[24] a presumed tension within the unit is solved. The verse is not an "unerwartete Heilszusage", but stresses the gloomy future for Jacob[25].

With WEISER I think that the "Form" of Jer. xxx 5-7 is the description of a "Notzeit für Jakob"[26]. Even in the questions, the language has a descriptive character. Therefore, I do not think that these verses can be looked upon as a complaint[27].

3. xxx 8-9 *Prophecy of liberation.*

8 "But it will happen on that day" a
says the LORD of hosts, b
"that I will break his[28] yoke from off your neck c
and I will burst your bonds"[29], d
so that they shall no longer serve[30] strangers for it[31]. e
9 But they shall serve the LORD their God a

[23] S. BÖHMER, *Heimkehr*, p. 57, and R.P. CARROLL, *Jeremiah*, p. 575; but see N. Lohfink, "Junge Jeremia", pp. 359-360.

[24] See note 10.

[25] Contra S. BÖHMER, *Heimkehr*, pp. 57-58. C. WESTERMANN, *Heilsworte*, pp. 106-107, removes the tension by interpreting 7d as introduction to 8-9.

[26] A. WEISER, *Jeremia*, pp. 276-278.

[27] Against R.P. CARROLL, *Jeremiah*, p. 579.

[28] LXX have changed the pron. pers. in this verse in order to give a better understanding; but see below II.

[29] The direct speech is limited to 9a-d, see below.

[30] Cf. LXXJer. xxxvii 8; *y'bdw* is vocalised in MT as a Qal, not as a Hiph'il, contra R.P. CARROLL, *Jeremiah*, p. 575.

[31] The preposition in *bô* is interpreted as a $b^e$-pretii as in Gen. xxix 18, 20, 25 and Hos. xii 13.

and David their king, b
whom I will raise up for them. c

This prose-unit speaks of the future in terms of liberation for Israel. The hope uttered is twofold: the LORD will break the yoke of foreigners and He will restore the Davidic kingship.

4. xxx 10-11 *Oracle of salvation*[32].

10 "And you, my servant Jacob, fear not" a
says the LORD, b
"and be not prostrated, Israel. c
Because here I am, who will save you from afar d
and your offspring from the land of their captivity. e
Jacob will return and rest. f
He will be safe and nobody shall startle him. g
11 I am with you" a
says the LORD, b
"to save you. c
For I will make an end to all the nations, d
amongst whom I scattered you. e
But of you I will not make an end. f
But I will chasten you with justice. g
By no means I will leave you unpunished". h

Jer. xxx 10-11 has the structure of an "oracle of salvation". I will not discuss this *Gattung* nor will I treat the question whether or not we should speak about a "*priestly* oracle of salvation"[33]. The oracle of salvation in Jer. xxx 10-11 has the elements shown in Fig. 1 (p. 70).

Jer. xxx 10-11 shows that the sequence of the elements within an oracle of salvation is not always the same.

The text of Jer. xxx 10-11 has some parallels with DtIsa.:

| | |
|---|---|
| Do not fear | Isa. xl 9; xli 10, 13, 14; xlii 1, 5; xliv 2; li 7; liv 4. |

[32] The words have a parallel in MTJer. xlvi 27-28 = LXXJer. xxvi 27-28. LXX lacks them here = LXXJer. xxxvii 10-11. Most scholars take the words in Jer. xxx for original, cf. R.P. Carroll, *Jeremiah*, p. 577, but see N. Lohfink, "Gotteswortverschachtelung", p. 106.

[33] Literature (among others, see especially the commentaries on DtIsa.): J. Begrich, "Die Priesterliche Heilsorakel", *ZAW* 52 (1934), pp. 81-92 = *Gesammelte Studien zum Alten Testament* (ThB 21), München 1964, pp. 217-231; C. Westermann, "Das Heilswort bei Deuterojesaja", *EvTh* 24 (1964), pp. 355-373; A.M. Schoors, *I am God your Saviour* (SVT 24), Leiden 1973, pp. 32-46; S. Böhmer, *Heimkehr*, pp. 55-56, 60-61; M. Weippert, "De herkomst van het heilsorakel voor Israël bij Deuterojesaja", *NTT* 36 (1982), pp. 1-11; E.W. Conrad, "The "Fear Not" Oracles in Second Isaiah", *VT* 34 (1984), pp. 129-152, and *idem*, *Fear Not Warrior: A Study of 'al tira' Pericopes in the Hebrew Scriptures* (BJS 75), Chico 1985.

| Elements | Jer. xxx 10-11 |
|---|---|
| 1. Introduction | |
| Botenformel | (10b, 11a) |
| address | 10a, c |
| 2. Assurance of salvation | |
| including summons "do not fear ..." | 10a, c |
| 3. Divine self-introduction | 10d, 11a |
| 4. Announcement of salvation | |
| a. in nominal clauses | 10d-g |
| b. in verbal clauses | |
| 5. Outcome | |
| on behalf of the supplicatn | 11f-h |
| as regards the enemy | 11d-e |
| 6. Final goal | 11c |

*Fig. 1.* Elements in the oracle of salvation.

| | |
|---|---|
| My servant Jacob | Isa. xliv 1, 2; xlv 4[34] |
| Be not prostrated | Isa. li 7 |
| Jacob will return | cf. Isa. li 11: "The redeemed by the LORD will return" |

On the bais of these parallels the authenticity of this text has been questioned. Many scholars[35] think that DtIsa. is prior to Jer. xxx 10-11. The affinities with DtIsa. occur, however, for the greater part in the framework of the oracle.

On the other hand, Jer. xxx 10-11 has some affinities with pre-exilic and early exilic texts. For instance, the expression "to make an end to" (*kālā ʿśh*), occurs in Jer. iv 27; v 10, 18; Nah. i 8, 9 and Ez. xi 13 and is not attested in DtIsa.

Moreover, Jer. xxx 10-11 shares some formal elements with the Neo-Assyrian prophecies for Esarhaddon and Assurbanipal dating from the midst of the eighth century B.C. The assurance of salvation (2. in Fig. 1) has a parallel in the words *la tapallaḥ* which occurs frequently in these oracles[35]. The words also have a parallel in the Aramaic inscription of Zakkur king of Hamath: *'l tzḥl* "Do not fear!"[36].

---

[34] See also Isa. xlvii 20 "the LORD has released his servant Jacob".

[35] See among others: J. Lust, "'Gathering and Return' in Jeremiah and Ezekiel", in P.-M. Bogaert (ed.), *Le livre de Jérémie* (BEThL LIV), Leuven 1981, pp. 131-132; S. Böhmer, *Heimkehr*, pp. 60-61, and C. Westermann, *Heilsworte*, p. 107.

[36] M. Weippert, "Assyrische Prophetien der Zeit Asarhaddons und Assurbanipals", in: F.M. Fales (ed.), *Assyrian Royal Inscriptions* (OAC XVII), pp. 71-115, esp. Tabelle 3 and 4 "Beschwichtigungsformel". I wonder if the view of E.W. Conrad, *Fear Not*, pp. 52-62, 79-107, 120-123, that the *'al tira'*-Formel is used in Isaiah to encourage a warrior before battle, is also valid for Jer. xxx 10.

The "outcome for the enemy" (5. in Fig. 1) occurs in the Neo-Assyrian prophecies as well, although a literal parallel to Jer. xxx 11d cannot be found. The closest parallel is:

> With my hands I will make an end to your enemies[37].

These parallels show that the *Gattung* of the oracle of salvation already existed in pre-exilic times.

It should be noted that two expressions in Jer. xxx 10-11 have affinities with Israel's legal traditions and especially with the covenant terminology. Both in Lev. xxvi 6 and Deut. xxviii 26 the words *w*$^{e}$*'ên maḥ*$^{a}$*rîd*, "and nobody will startle him", occur in the prosperity formula of the covenant between the LORD and his people. In the prophetic traditions of Israel the words stress the promises for the future of the people[38]. The same holds true for the phrase "I will by no means leave you unpunished"[39]. The paranomastic construction is only attested in two additions to the old confession "Merciful and gracious is the LORD ..." in Exod. xxxiv 7 and Num. xiv 18 and in the theological introduction to the book of Nahum (Nah. i 3). The function of the expression in the verses quoted combined with the fact that the verbum finitum construction of *nqh* pi occurs in both versions of the Decalogue (Exod. xx 7; Deut. v 11), suggests that the expression in Jer. xxx 11 might have a covenantal connotation. In another article, I hope to prove that the author of Jer. xxx-xxxi understood his world and history in the framework of a covenantal paradigma.

When taken together, these observations render it possible that the author of Jer. xxx-xxxi used an already existing literary form in order to frame his own words[40]. Although I do not know whether Jer. xxx 10-11 is an authentic Jeremian prophecy or stems from a pseudepigraphic "Israel-Prophet", I do agree with FOHRER when he considers the author of Jer. xxx-xxxi* a predecessor of DtIsa[41].

## II

In recent scholarly publications the unity of Jer. xxx 4-11 is disputed. Briefly summarised, Jer. xxx 5-7 is considered to be authentic, i.e. stemming from the author of the "Grundstock" of Jer. xxx-xxxi. The prose of Jer. xxx 8-9 is

---

37 K. 4310 III 7′-IV 35:xviii, see M. WEIPPERT, "Assyrische Prophetien", pp. 84-87 (literature).

38 Isa. xvii 2; Jer. vii 33; Mic. iv 4; Nah. ii 12.

39 According to C. WESTERMANN, *Heilsworte*, p. 107, the words have a secondary character to Jer. xxx 11.

40 See also J. UNTERMAN, *Repentance*, pp. 136-137.

41 G. FOHRER, "Israel-Prophet", p. 136.

mostly looked upon as an insertion, while 10-11 is regarded as post-DtIsaianic[42]. WESTERMANN[43] separates vv. 5-9 from vv. 10-11 (Post Dt-Isa.). CARROLL states that the oracle of salvation is often uttered after a lament, stating the individual or communal complaint about present circumstances. In that case, the oracle of salvation (10-11) would be a fitting response to vv. 5-7. The description of the terrible day may be regarded as equivalent to a formal lament. Vv. 8-9 interrupt the coherence of the pericope and must be regarded as secondary additions to the cycle[44].

The arguments for such a literary-critical division are different. BÖHMER's view is very explicit. He uses a form-critical argument: 5-7 and 10-11 are poetry, 8-9 is prose. Then he makes philological remarks: the phrase "breaking the yoke" is used in a different way in Jer. ii 20 and v 5, while *zārîm* in Jer. ii 25 and iii 13 refer to "other gods" and in xxx 8 to "other nations". On a theological level he finally states that the expectation of a new Davidic king is not Jeremaic[45].

Above I have argued that Jer. xxx 10-11 need not be regarded as a later addition. I agree with the remarks of CARROLL regarding the relationship between 5-7 and 10-11. I will go one step further in arguing that 8-9 is not necessarily an insertion.

First I would like to make a remark about the method of form-criticism. On the basis of extra-Biblical material – the Neo-Assyrian oracles and the Balaam inscription –, H. WEIPPERT has shown that the variation of prose and poetry should not lead us by necessity to a literary-critical division of prophetic texts. Her research provides us with a falsification of the statement that form-critical distinctions must lead to literary-critical divisions[46]. I do not contend that form-critical distinctions never give us cause to such a division. I think, however, that when other arguments or observations regarding a particular text point in the same direction, one ought not make a stand against assuming different traditions, sources or redactions. My problem is whether or not there are enough additional arguments that lead to a division in Jer. xxx 4-11.

---

[42] S. BÖHMER, *Heimkehr*, pp. 59-61; J. LUST, "Gathering", p. 136; N. LOHFINK, "Junge Jeremia", pp. 351-368; N. LOHFINK, "Gotteswortverschachtelung", p. 106; W. THIEL, *Redaktion*, p. 21; I. RIESENER, *Der Stamm ʿbd im Alten Testament* (BZAW 149), Berlin – New York 1979, pp. 174, 179-181; C. LEVIN, *Die Verheissung des neuen Bundes* (FRLANT 137), Göttingen 1985, pp. 178-183; U. SCHRÖTER, "Jeremias Botschaft für das Nordreich", *VT* 35 (1985), p. 312, and J. UNTERMAN, *Repentance*, pp. 135-136.

[43] C. WESTERMANN, *Heilsworte*, pp. 106-107.

[44] R.P. CARROLL, *Jeremiah*, p. 579; see G. FOHRER, "Israel-Prophet", p. 137, n. 2: 8-9 is a "verheissende Glosse".

[45] S. BÖHMER, *Heimkehr*, pp. 59-61.

[46] H. WEIPPERT, "Beitrag", pp. 83-104; see also her *Die Prosareden des Jeremiabuches* (BZAW 132), Berlin – New York 1973, and J.L. CRENSHAW, "A Living Tradition: The Book of Jeremiah in Current Research", in: J.L. MAYS and P.J. ACHTEMEIER (eds.), *Interpreting the Prophets*, Philadelphia 1987, pp. 102-103.

Therefore, I will now turn my attention to the unit 8-9. In my opinion, this unit consists of two sub-units:

A 8a-d Direct speech
B 8e-9 Indirect speech

Both sentences are focalised by the prophetic author of the text. A distinction between direct speech and indirect speech clarifies the change in number and person of the intended persons. Besides the LORD, there are two "actants" in this unit: the oppressed and the oppressor. I label them (A) and (B). They are indicated in the unit 8-9 as follows:

| | | | | |
|---|---|---|---|---|
| (A) | A | 8c | suff. 2.m.s. | *ṣw'rk* |
| | | 8d | suff. 2.m.s. | *mwsrwtyk* |
| | B | 8e | verb 3.m.p. | *y'bdw* |
| | | 9a | verb 3.m.p. | *w'bdw* |
| | | 9a | suff. 3.m.p. | *'lhyhm* |
| | | 9b | suff. 3.m.p. | *mlkm* |
| | | 9c | suff. 3.m.p. | *lhm* |
| (B) | A | 8c | suff. 3.m.s. | *'lw* |
| | B | 8e | nomen subject 3.m.p. | *zrym* |

*Fig. 2.* The actants (A) and (B) in the unit 8-9.

After the direct speech of the LORD the prophetic author describes its effect. In the direct speech (A) is addressed in the 2.m.s. and (B) is referred to with 3.m.s. forms. In the prophetic speech (A) is indicated with 3.m.p. forms.

Both the divine speech and the prophetic sermon describe a transformation, which I will designate as Trans II. This Trans II indicates a threefold change in the relationship between (A) and (B).

1. The yoke of oppression will be broken.
2. The bonds of oppression will be burst.
3. The object of (A)'s serving will change from *zārîm* (8e) to the LORD (9a) and his representative: an earthly king from the house of David[47]. By this transformation the character of serving is changed. The relationship between (A) and (B) in 8e is that of a vassal and an overlord[48]. In the new situation *'bd* indicates the renewed cultic and moral serving of the LORD[49]. The adver-

[47] As in Hos. iii 5; Ps. lxxxix 20ff.; Ez. xxxiv 23 and xxxvii 24 "David" in Jer. xxx 9 means the "second David"; cf. H. Kruse, "David's covenant", *VT* 35 (1985), pp. 153, 156.

[48] See L.T. Brodie, *JSOT* 19 (1981), p. 39, and I. Riesener, *Stamm 'bd*, pp. 143, 149, 174.

[49] Cf. Isa. xiv 1-23 and Ez. xxxiv 27.

bial construction *lo' ... 'ôd* underscores that this Trans II will never recur again[50].

The protagonist in this Trans II is the LORD. By breaking the yoke and bursting the bonds HE causes the change in the relationship between (A) and (B). This unit is related to Jer. xxx 5-7 and 10-11.

The unit 5-7 gives an answer to two questions. These verses characterise the oppression which is presumed in 8-9. Furthermore, the unit 5-7 describes how the oppression came into existence, i.e. through a transformation to anguish and terror (Trans I). In the unit 5-7 the question of the protagonist of Trans I is left open. In my opinion, the unit 8-9 answers this question. The actant (B) can be held responsible for it, leaving open the question whether or not this (B) was only an instrument in the hands of the LORD.

The unit 10-11 answers the question why the LORD is willing to act for His people in this way. The three motifs in Trans II are elaborated on in 10-11:

1. and 2. in 10d-e and 11d-e and

3. in the final note of xxx 11: "By no means I will leave you unpunished", which implies an ongoing or renewed servant relationship between Israel and the LORD. Finally, one should note that after the change in servitude Israel is called "my servant Jacob" (10a) and not merely "Jacob" (7c).

One last point. On the manifestation level of the text a shift is visible towards the position of the people Jacob/Israel. In the first unit (5-7) the situation is one of anguish and despair. In the third unit (10-11) there is an outlook that the terror will change into salvation. CARROLL already noted this connection between both units. This shift is paralleled by the Trans II described in the second unit (8-9). The coherence of Jer. xxx 4-11 lies in the fact that the LORD will bring his oppressed and anguished people (5-7) to a new situation of salvation (10-11) by breaking the yoke and the bonds of the oppressor (8-9). Therefore, there is no need for a literary-critical division of Jer. xxx 4-11. There are no repetitions in the text and it is possible to interpret the supposed contradictions within the scope of the total unit.

There are, however, some arguments against the unity, which are not countered. I refer to the philological remarks[51]. They are, however, not arguments against the unity of Jer. xxx 4-11, but against the authenticity of the text. If they are valid, they are pointing to the non-Jeremaic provenance of the oracles in the book of consolation[52].

This thematic unity of Jer. xxx 4-11 makes it impossible to defend the thesis

---

[50] Cf. M. FISHBANE, *Biblical Interpretation in Ancient Israel*, Oxford 1985, p. 374 and n. 141.

[51] See for instance BÖHMER, *Heimkehr*, pp. 59-61; and above, pp. 71-72.

[52] There is no room here for a discussion on the authenticity of Jer. xxx-xxxi. The main points of view are those of S. MOWINCKEL, *Zur Komposition des Buches Jeremia*, Kristiana 1914 (from the hand of "D", an anonymous prophet of salvation); H. WEIPPERT, *Prosareden*, pp. 2, 201 (for the greatest part authentic); S. BÖHMER, *Heimkehr*, pp. 47-88 (Jer. kernel in a dtr-redaction

of BRODIE that the story of Jacob's struggle in Pniel (Gen. xxxii 22-32) is to be regarded as a text "rewriting" the story of Jacob's travail. Apart from the fact that the textual affinities between Jer. xxx 1-13 and Gen. xxxii 22-32 are much smaller than BRODIE suggests, the fabric of Jer. xxx 4-11, existing in Trans I and Trans II, has no parallel in Gen. xxxii 22-32[53].

## III

I will conclude with an exegetical note on the phrases "I will break his yoke off your neck" and "I will burst his bonds". The imagery is adopted from the agricultural sphere. *'ôl*, "yoke", and *môsēr*, "bond", refer to the harshness which cows suffered when they were ploughing. In ancient Near Eastern texts this imagery is used to indicate a vassal-relationship (both in religious and in political concepts). It denotes the oppressing charactere of human responsibility in relation to God or a human overlord.

The phrases "to break the yoke" and "to burst the bonds" with man as subject express rebellion against God or a king. For *šbr 'ôl* see Jer. ii 20[54] and v 5. The expression has a parallel in a Neo-Assyrian fragment from the epic of Atrachasis:

> ²...]. X *i ni-iš-bi-ir ni-ra*
> ...]. let us break the yoke![55]

Although the fragment is broken and its relationship to the Old-Babylonian Atr. I is not clear, it is evident that the phrase *šebēru nira* refers to the rebellion of the Igigi against the Anunnaki. SCHMOLDT[56] points to an Assyrian expression for "breaking the yoke". The inscriptions he quotes, however, do not contain this expression. ARAB II, 27 gives the translation of the Display-inscription of Sargon II. In the account of the campaign against Kiakki of Sinuhtu, however, the expression *salû nira*, "to throw off the yoke", is used, which occurs in many places in inscriptions of Sargon II, Esarhaddon and Assurbanipal[57]. ARAB II, 218 contains a fragment describing a campaign of Esarhaddon against the city of Arzani. I do not agree with LUCKENBILL's

---

added with later material); G. FOHRER, "Israel-Prophet", p. 148 (from an anonymous proto-eschatological prophet), and L. LOHFINK, "Junge Jerermia", pp. 351-368 (the "Grundstock" is authentic and from the earliest time of Jeremiah's prophetic career).

[53] L.T. BRODIE, *JSOT* 19 (1981), pp. 31-60, see also H.A. MCKAY, "Jacob Makes it Across the Jabbok", *JSOT* 38 (1987), pp. 3-13.

[54] Read *šbrt* 2.f.s. cf. LXX.

[55] K. 10082 = CT 46.7:2 see W.G. LAMBERT and A.R. MILLARD, *Atra-Hasis*, p. 44. This fragment J has no parallel in the Old Babylonian version of the epic.

[56] H. SCHMOLDT, "Art. *'ôl*", *ThWAT* VI, K. 79.

[57] Cf. *CAD*, N, II, p. 263, and *AHw*, pp. 1076-1077.

translation. From parallel accounts referring to this campaign it becomes clear that one ought to read here: "[I laid upon him] my yoke"[58].

"To burst the bonds" (*ntq môs$^{e}$rôt*) indicates rebellion in Jer. ii 20[59], v 5 and Ps. ii 3.

Both expressions also occur with God as subject indicating the liberation of His people. The greater part of these occurrences are found in the pseudo-prophetic speech of Hananjah, Jer. xxviii 2, 4, 11, 14. Further, the expressions are found in the prophecies of salvation in Nahum i 13, directed towards the Israelites in their Assyrian exile:

> I will break his yoke (*môtā*), which is upon you,
> I will break your bonds.

The same motif is found in Ps. cvii 14.

Since there are striking parallels between the prophecy of Nahum and Jeremiah's book of consolation, I will not exclude the possibility that the author of Jer. xxx 8 adopted the expression and the theological concept lying behind it from Nahum[60]. In Jer. xxx 8 both expressions underscore that Trans II is a deed of liberation of the LORD on behalf of his people.

It is not necessary to look upon the phrases as an addition occasioned by an optimistic theology. There is one fact which distinguishes them from the pseudo-prophetic speech of Hananjah. The author of Jer. xxx 4-11 has inserted them in his composition after Trans I. The difference between Hananjah and Jer. xxx 8 is that the former sees the "breaking of the yoke" as an escape from the threat. For Jer. xxx 8 the "breaking of the yoke" is a metaphor indicating the LORD's final answer after the ruination of His people. Hananjah is only speaking about a hopeful future. Hananjah leaves open the theological question concerning the cause of the threat. The author of Jer. xxx 4-11, however, states that even after Trans II "Jacob" will not be left unpunished by the LORD.

---

[58] Esarh. Frt. A:16; cf. R. BORGER, *Asarhaddon*, p. 110.
[59] Read *ntqt* 2.f.s.; see note 54.
[60] Cf. R.P. CARROLL, *Jeremiah*, p. 576.

# HEZEKIAH AND ISAIAH

## *A Study on Ben Sira xlviii 15-25*

BY

P.C. BEENTJES

*Utrecht*

In the course of the last twenty years, Old Testament scholars have published several studies dealing with Hezekiah and Isaiah[1]. To the best of my knowledge, however, no special study has been written about the presentation and function of this king and this prophet in the Book of Ben Sira. This alone raises the question of how they are dealt with in Ben Sira xlviii 15-25.

## I. Text

The Hebrew text[2] of Sir. xlviii 15e-25 forms part of the so-called Ms. B., a portion of nine leaves which, together with other fragments, were acquired for the Bodleian Library in Oxford by Professor Archibald Sayce (1846-1933)[3]

[1] E.g. B.S. Childs, *Isaiah and the Assyrian Crisis*, London 1967; R. Clements, *Isaiah and the Deliverance of Jerusalem* (JSOT Suppl. Ser. 13), Sheffield 1980; P.R. Ackroyd, "Isaiah 36-39: Structure and Function", in: W.C. Delsman *et al.* (Hrsg.), *Von Kanaan bis Kerala* (Festschrift J.P.M. van der Ploeg) (AOAT 211), Neukirchen/Vluyn 1982, pp. 3-21; A.K. Jenkins, "Hezekiah's Fourteenth Year; A New Interpretation of 2 Kings xviii, 13 – xix, 37", *VT* 26 (1976), pp. 284-298; O. Kaiser, "Die Verkündigung des Propheten Jesaja im Jahre 701", *ZAW* 81 (1969), pp. 304-315; W. Zimmerli, "Jesaja und Hiskia", in: H. Gese und H.P. Rüger (Hrsg.), *Wort und Geschichte* (Festschrift K. Elliger) (AOAT 18), Neukirchen/Vluyn 1973, pp. 199-208, reprinted in *Studien zur alttestamentlichen Theologie und Prophetie* (ThB 51), München 1974, pp. 88-103; K.A.D. Smelik, "Distortion of Old Testament Prophecy. The Purpose of Isaiah xxxvi and xxxvii", *OTS* 24 (1986), pp. 70-93; M. Hutter, *Hiskija, König von Juda. Ein Beitrag zur judäischen Geschichte in assyrischer Zeit*, Graz 1982; E. Vogt, *Der Aufstand Hiskias und die Belagerung Jerusalems 701 v. Chr.* (AnBib 106), Rome 1986. I had no access to A.H. Konkel, *Hezekiah in Biblical Tradition* (PhD at Westminster Theological Seminary), 1987 (UMI, NEJ 87-20640).

[2] For the Hebrew text of the Book of Ben Sira we consulted: *Facsimiles of the Fragments hitherto recovered of the Book of Ecclesiasticus in Hebrew*, London 1901; F. Vattioni, *Ecclesiastico. Testo ebraico con apparato critico e versioni greca, latina e siriaca* (Testo I), Napoli 1968; Z. Ben-Ḥayyim, *The Book of Ben Sira. Text, Concordance and an Analysis of the Vocabulary* (The Historical Dictionary of the Hebrew Language), Jerusalem 1973.

[3] A detailed report by S. Minocchi, "La découverte du texte hébreu original de l'Ecclésiastique", *Compte rendu du quatrième congrès scientifique international des catholiques*, Deuxième section, Fribourg 1897, pp. 283-296, esp. 287-289.

and published by A.E. COWLEY and A. NEUBAUER[4]. The text of the passage under discussion is found on both sides of the folio which COWLEY and NEUBAUER labelled "fol. 9 recto/fol. 9 verso"[5]. Due to new discoveries in later text editions this is now indicated by other sigla[6]. One side of the folio contains the Hebrew text of Sir. xlviii 12c-22b, while the other side of this leaf shows the text of Sir. xlviii 24-xlix 10. As the bottom of the folio is severely damaged, however, the Hebrew text of Sir. xlviii 22c-23 and Sir. xlix 11-12 is lacking. Yet it is absolutely certain that these lines originally formed part of this folio. This is indicated, first of all, by the fact that all the leaves of Ms. B. always have eighteen lines on each side[7], whereas on this badly damaged folio there are only sixteen verse lines. Secondly, the original text of the lost Hebrew lines of this folio is certainly corroborated by the fact that they have been preserved in translation by all the important versions (Greek, Syriac, Latin).

## II. THE CONTEXT AND THE SCOPE OF THIS SECTION

The passage under discussion is one section of the celebrated *Laus Patrum*. Scholars not only disagree on the precise limits of the "Praise of the Fathers"[8], but also hold different views with regard to the main purpose intended by Ben Sira when he included this special section in his book. Ben Sira seems

---

[4] A.E. COWLEY and A. NEUBAUER, *The Original Hebrew of a Portion of Ecclesiasticus (xxxix, 15 to xlix, 11)*, Oxford 1897.

[5] COWLEY and NEUBAUER, *op. cit.*, pp. 38-40.

[6] E.g. "B 16 r./B 16v." by R. SMEND, *Die Weisheit des Jesus Sirach, Hebräisch und Deutsch*, Berlin 1906, pp. 56-57 (to be quoted: SMEND, *HuD*). The notation "16a/16b" has been used by H.L. STRACK, *Die Sprüche Jesus', des Sohnes Sirachs* (Schriften des Institutum Judaicum in Berlin, Nr. 31), Leipzig 1903, pp. 50-52.

[7] "The Ms. is written on oriental paper, and is arranged in lines, eighteen to the page ...": COWLEY and NEUBAUER, *op. cit.*, p. XIII. "Da B auf jedem Blatt 36 Zeilen hat ...": SMEND, *HuD*, p. VII.

[8] The following authors regard Ben Sira xliv-xlix as a unit; the chapter on Simon, the High Priest is regarded by them as an appendix at best. Th. MAERTENS, *L'Eloge des pères*, Bruges 1956; E. JACOB, "L'histoire d'Israel vue par Ben Sira", *Mélanges bibliques A. Robert*, Paris 1957, pp. 288-294; R.T. SIEBENECK, "May Their Bones Return to Life! – Sirach's Praise of the Fathers", *CBQ* 21 (1959), pp. 411-428; R.A.F. MACKENZIE, "Ben Sira as Historian", in: Th.A. DUNNE and J.M. LAPORTE (eds.), *Trinification of the World* (A Festschrift in Honor of Fr.E. CROWE), Toronto 1978, pp. 312-327 (to be quoted: MACKENZIE, *Historian*); W. FUSS, *Tradition und Komposition im Buche Jesus Sirach*, Tübingen 1963; R. SMEND, *Die Weisheit des Jesus Sirach erklärt*, Berlin 1906, p. 412 (to be quoted as: SMEND); V. HAMP, *Sirach* (Die Heilige Schrift in deutscher Uebersetzung, Echter-Bibel Lfg. 13), Würzburg 1951, p. 136.

Another group of scholars lays stress on the unity of Ben Sira xliv-1: G.A. TE STROETE, "Van Henoch tot Simon", in: A.R. HULST (ed.), *Vruchten van de Uithof* (Festschrift H.A. BRONGERS), Utrecht 1974, pp. 120-133; J.D. MARTIN, "Ben Sira – A Child of His Time", in: J.D. MARTIN and P.R. DAVIES (eds.), *A Word in Season*. Essays in Honor of W. MCKANE (JSOT Suppl. Series 42), Sheffield 1986, pp. 141-161; *idem*, "Ben Sira's Hymn to the Fathers. A Messianic Perspective", *OTS* 24 (1986), pp. 107-123; B.L. MACK, *Wisdom and the Hebrew Epic. Ben Sira's Hymn*

to stress the continuity of God's *b<sup>e</sup>rît* in the history of Israel. Starting with Noah (Sir. xliv 17)[9], a series of promises is brought into effect which will eventually culminate in God's promise to Phinehas (Sir. xlv 24-25): i.e. in the days of Ben Sira himself he would be personified in the High Priest Simon, to whom the author dedicates the whole of the last chapter of his *Laus Patrum*[10]. Whereas the establishment of the covenants is especially accentuated in the first part of Ben Sira's Hymn (ch. xliv-xlv)[11], it is – as B.L. MACK has argued in his fascinating study of the "Praise of the Fathers"[12] – the history of prophets and kings which gives structure to the second major block (ch. xlvi 13-xlix 11)[13].

Scholars disagree, however, on the question of which verse – following the passage on Elijah and Elisha – might be the opening line of the new pericope dealing with Hezekiah and Isaiah. Quite different positions have been adopted. Whereas SEGAL[14] regards Sir. xlviii 15-25 as a single literary unit, VAN DEN BORN[15] prefers xlviii 16-25. Whereas PETERS, HAMP and, more recently, SKEHAN and DI LELLA[16] are convinced that we have to limit this passage to xlviii 15e-25, commentators like KNABENBAUER, EBERHARTER and MACKENZIE[17] have opted for xlviii 17-25. Both the inner logic of the text itself and its literary structure, however, suggest that Sir. xlviii 15ef (*wyš'r lyhwdh*

---

*in Praise of the Fathers*, Chicago 1985; P.C. BEENTJES, *Jesus Sirach en Tenach*, Nieuwegein 1981, pp. 175-199; *idem*, "The 'Praise of the Famous' and its Prologue", *Bijdragen* 45 (1984), pp. 374-383 (to be quoted as: BEENTJES, "Praise"); E. JANSSEN, *Das Gottesvolk und seine Geschichte*, Neukirchen 1971, pp. 16-33; Th.R. LEE, *Studies in the Form of Sirach (Ecclesiasticus) 44-50*, Berkeley 1979.

9 See BEENTJES, "Praise", pp. 380-382.

10 It was H. STADELMANN, *Ben Sira als Schriftgelehrter* (WUNT 2. Reihe, Band 6), Tübingen 1980, who arrived about simultaneously as I and yet completely independent of one another, at more or less the same conclusion (*op. cit.*, pp. 146-176, esp. 146-159). There came further strong support by J.D. MARTIN, "Ben Sira's Hymn", pp. 113-116.

11 In my opinion, it is not by chance that *bryt* occurs *seven* times between Sir. xliv 1 and xlv 26 (xliv 12a *Mas.*; xliv 17d, 20b, 22c; xlv 15c, 24, 25a). Between Sir. xlvi 1 and l 24 we find the word only *once* (lxv 24-25), when Ben Sira reverts to the *bryt* with Phinehas.

12 MACK, *op. cit.*, pp. 37-65, esp. 37-47 (cf. my critical review of this book in *JSJ* 17 (1986), pp. 259-261).

13 According to MACK the Hymn "consists of three major units (Establishment of the Covenants, History of Prophets and Kings, Climactic Hymn in Praise of Simon) and two transitional units (Conquest of the Land, Restoration) in chiastic or concentric correlations" (*op. cit.*, p. 41).

14 M.H. SEGAL, *Sēpēr ben Sîra' haššalēm*, Jerusalem 1958$^2$, pp. 333-336.

15 A. VAN DEN BORN, *Wijsheid van Jesus Sirach (Ecclesiasticus)* (BOT VIII), Roermond 1968, pp. 232-233.

16 N. PETERS, *Das Buch Jesus Sirach oder Ecclesiasticus* (EHAT, 25. Band), Münster 1913, pp. 413-417; HAMP, *op. cit.*, pp. 133-134; P.W. SKEHAN and A.A. DI LELLA, *The Wisdom of Ben Sira* (A.B. 39), New York 1987, pp. 536-539.

17 I. KNABENBAUER, *Commentarius in Ecclesiasticum* (CSS 2/VI), Paris 1902, pp. 456-457; A. EBERHARTER, *Das Buch Jesus Sirach oder Ecclesiasticus* (Die Heilige Schrift des Alten Testaments. VI. Band), Bonn 1925, pp. 154-155. R.A.F. MACKENZIE, *Sirach* (Old Testament Message, Vol. 19), Wilmington 1983, pp. 184-185; MACKENZIE, *Historian*, p. 322.

*mz'r*[18] / *w'wd lbyt dwd qṣyn*) should be treated as the starting point of a new paragraph in the "Praise of the Fathers". There is strong evidence that the section, which deals with the Northern kingdom and begins in xlvii 23-25, ends in xlviii 15a-d. In the first place, it should be noticed that the author uses an important *inclusion* with *ḥṭ't* (xlviii 23f., 24b/xlviii 15b), a noun which occurs nowhere else in the "Praise of the Fathers". The description of the deportation of the Northern kingdom (xlviii 15c-d) functions as a second *inclusio*; the theme of xlvii 24a is recalled explicitly. A minor correspondence between the beginning and the end of the section dealing with the Northern kingdom is the use of *'m* ("people") in xlvii 23d and xlviii 15a. As soon as the treatment of the Northern kingdom – note the literary technique of at least three inclusions – has come to an end, Ben Sira starts his evaluation of the Kingdom of Judah in xlviii 15e-f, picking up the remark from xlvii 22 about the mercy of the Lord towards the house of David. This "feedback" is an additional indication for considering xlvii, 23-xlviii 15d as an "independent" literary unit. Whereas xlviii 15e-f shows a change of subject, it is the *yš . . . wyš*-sentence[19] in Sir. xlviii 16 which, to a considerable degree, determines the structure of the following section(s)[20].

The first colon *yš mhm 'św ywšr* (xlviii 16a) is elaborated by the author in xlviii 17-25; xlix 1-3, whereas the second colon of xlviii 16b (*wyš mhm hply'w m'l*)[21] is briefly expanded in xlix 4-6. At first sight, the author seems to be using stereotyped Deuteronomistic language in this passage. On closer inspection, however, it can be ascertained that Ben Sira was creating some formula of his own. Even though the so-called Deuteronomistic History uses the phrase *'āśâ hayyāšār* in order to approve a king's reign[22], we find *'św ywšr*[23], a construction with a noun[24] in Sir. xlviii 16a. As is the case with the very remarkable word combination *hply'w m'l* in the next colon, expressions which occur nowhere else in the entire Old Testament can be found here. The most plausible inference is that they reflect the author's own creative style. It is pre-

[18] It is absolutely unclear to me how D. BARTHÉLEMY and O. RICKENBACHER, *Konkordanz zum hebräischen Sirach*, Göttingen 1973, p. 215 did come by ὀλιγόπιστος as the Greek rendering of *mz'r* in the Hebrew text of Sir. xlviii 15e.

[19] Cf. Sir. iv 21; x 30; xx 4; xx 5; xliv 8-9.

[20] In my opinion, MACKENIE, *Historian*, p. 322 is not consistent in his argumentation. On the one hand he argues that Sir. xlviii 15-16 marks the *end* of a section. On the other hand, however, he states that verse 16b "prepares for the destruction to be recalled in 49:6".

[21] I do not agree with G. SAUER, *Jesus Sirach* (JSHRZ III/5), Gütersloh 1981, p. 627, who applies this judgement to the kings of Israel too. His view is contradicted by Sir. xlix 4d (*mlky yhwdh*).

[22] E.g. I Kings xv 11; xxii 43; II Kings xii 3; xv 3; xviii 3; xxii 2.

[23] I do not understand SMEND's translation of this colon: "Einige aus *ihm* taten was *dem Herrn* gefiel" (italics by me, P.C.B.); SMEND, *HuD*, p. 87.

[24] The adjective *yāšār* is to be found in the Book of Ben Sira in the plural only (xi 15; xxxix 24 marg.).

cisely the interaction between the biblical narratives relating to Hezekiah and Isaiah and the way in which Ben Sira incorporated them into his "Praise of the Fathers" which now needs to be examined more closely.

## III. Ben sira's portrait of hezekiah

King Hezekiah is introduced by Ben Sira in a very special way. His first appearance in the text is described with the help of a pun: *yḥzqyhw ḥzq 'yrw* (vs. 17a). According to some scholars[25], Ben Sira is using or even imitating here II Chron. xxxii 5. This, however, does not seem to be the case. The Ben Sira text itself provides us with a number of arguments in favour of the view that the Jerusalem sage is here working out his own understanding of Hezekiah. It appears that *the pun* is one of his favourite devices in this particular section. It is not by chance that the author concludes his description of Hezekiah with another pun, using the *same* verb: [*w*]*yḥzq bdrky dwd* (vs. 22b). It should also be noticed that, in a small number of verse lines, a very interesting change occurs with respect to the verb *ḥzq*. In the opening line (vs. 17a) Ben Sira uses it to describe Hezekiah's activities[26] with respect to the water supply for the city. At the end of the passage (vs. 22b), the same verb *ḥzq* acquires a very important theological sense, which is similar to such standard Deuteronomistic phrases as *wayyelæk b<sup></sup>ekål dæræk dāwid* (I Kings xxii 43; II Kings xxii 2)[27]. In addition, Isaiah is introduced by Ben Sira with the help of a pun too: *wywšy'm byd yš'yhw* (vs. 20d)[28]. So it is plausible to assume that it was Ben Sira himself who invented and elaborated upon the special framework in which he portrays king Hezekiah[29].

How is this good king (cf. Sir. xlix 4) portrayed in Ben Sira's text? Is it just a question of re-telling the biblical narratives of II Kings xviii-xx; Isa. xxxvi-xxxix; II Chron. xxix-xxxii, or can we see at work a creative sage?

Ben Sira's view (vs. 17ab) of Hezekiah's fortification of "his city"[30] both in wording and in content differs from the biblical data. First of all, it is striking to read that, whilst Old Testament texts speak about *two* separate activi-

[25] Smend, p. 464; I. Lévi, *L'Ecclésiastique* I, p. 140; Segal, *op. cit.*, p. 334; van den Born, *op. cit.*, p. 232; Skehan and di Lella, *op. cit.*, p. 538.

[26] Cfr. Sir. l 1d, 4.

[27] For expressions of the same kind see the texts mentioned in note 22.

[28] Wordplay relating to names: Sir. xlvi 1 (Joshua); xlvi 13bc (Samuel); xlvii 23cd (Rohoboam). With respect to the last text Skehan and di Lella, *op. cit.*, p. 530 believe that the name *rḥb'm* in Ms. B. is disturbing the line. In my opinion, we absolutely need this name here, as has been indicated by T. Penar, *Northwest Semitic Philology and the Hebrew Fragments of Ben Sira* (Biblica et Orientalia, n. 28), Rome 1975, p. 82.

[29] B.L. Mack also points to the fact that Ben Sira "constructed his hymn without recourse to a Deuteronomistic view of Israel's history", *op. cit.*, p. 120.

[30] The function of this rather vague term will be discussed later on in connection with *ṣywn* (vs. 18c).

ties of Hezekia – viz. improving the walls (II Chron. xxxii 5; Isa. xxii 10b) and making provisions for a good supply of water (II Kings xxii 20; II Chron. xxxii 3, 30; Isa. xxii 9, 11) – in Sir. xlviii 17ab[31] the "fortification" by Hezekiah consists only in bringing water within the city[32]. In the next bicolon (vs. 17cd), it is specified in what way king Hezekiah carried out that project[33]. No doubt a very remarkable aspect of this particular line is that Ben Sira does not use here either the phraseology or the vocabulary which could be derived from the Old Testamental passages which are relevant[34]. On the contrary, Ben Sira uses for example the verb *ḥṣb*[35] in combination with *ṣwr*, a combination of words which is found twice in the so-called Siloam-inscription[36]; whilst for his presentation of king Hezekiah in xlviii 17, he is virtually composing his own text. With respect to the introduction of the Assyrians in xlviii 18ab (*bymyw ʿlh snḥryb / wyšlḥ ʾt rb šqh*), however, he adopts the precise wording of the biblical passages reporting this Assyrian raid[37]. But, as soon as the adjutant's first activity is reported (vs. 18c), Ben Sira frames a colon of his own: *wyṭ ydw ʿl ṣywn*. Here I disagree completely with all those commentators[38] who consider this phrase to have been adopted by Ben Sira from Isa. x 32b (*ynpp ydw hr byt ṣywn*). It should be stressed here that Ben Sira did know the combination of *nwp* (hif.) with *yd*, as is proved by Sir. xii 18; xxxvi 3; xlvi 2 and xlvii 4. If he had intended to rely on the text of Isa. x 32b, he would certainly have used the verb *nwp* (hif.). Instead, the combination of *nṭh* plus *yd* which belongs to Ben Sira's vocabulary (xiv 25; xliii 12; xlvi 2), can be found. This biblical formula is found *nowhere* in the Assyrian context of II Kings xviii-xx and Isa. xxxvi-xxxix[39].

---

[31] Cf. J.H.A. Hart, "Sir. xlviii, 17ab", *JTS* 4 (1903), pp. 591-592; Ch.E. Hauer, "Water in the Mountain?", *PEQ* 101 (1969), pp. 44-45; R. Wenning und E. Zenger, "Die verschiedenen Systeme der Wassernützung im südlichen Jerusalem und die Bezugnahme darauf in biblischen Texten", *UF* 14 (1982), pp. 279-294.

[32] The translation as given by Skehan and di Lella, *op. cit.*, p. 536 ("Hezekiah fortified his city *and* had brought water within it") is the only one, which suggests *two* different activities.

[33] I do not discuss here the very complicated archaeological problems with respect to the above-mentioned texts. See N. Avigad, *Discovering Jerusalem*, Nashville 1983, pp. 45-60; Y. Shiloh, *Excavations at the City of David* I (Qedem 19), Jerusalem 1984, pp. 21-29 and stratum 12 (3-12 *passim*); M. Broski, "The Expansion of Jerusalem in the Reigns of Hezekiah and Menasseh", *IEJ* 24 (1974), pp. 21-26; K. Kenyon, *Digging Up Jerusalem*, London 1974, pp. 129-165.

[34] One could point to *mqwh* only. I like to stress, however, that this word is a hapax legomenon in the entire Old Testament (Isa. xxii 11), whereas Ben Sira is using it rather frequently (Sir. x 13; xliii 20d; xlviii 17d; l 3).

[35] Not *ḥṣr*, as indicated by Skehan and di Lella, *op. cit.*, p. 538.

[36] For the text see *KAI*, no. 189.

[37] Sir. xlviii 18a corresponds with II Kings xviii 13/Isa. xxxvi 1; Sir. xlviii 18b refers to II Kings xviii 17/Isa. xxxvi 2.

[38] Smend, p. 465; Strack, *op. cit.*, p. 51; Segal, *op. cit.*, p. 335; van den Born, *op. cit.*, p. 232; Skehan and di Lella, *op. cit.*, p. 538.

[39] The expression *nṭh yd* is found about forty times in the Old Testament, but nowhere in II Kings; in the Book of Isaiah it occurs in v 25; ix 11, 16, 20; x 4; xiv 26-27; xxiii 11; xlv 12.

The use of the name *ṣywn* is another reason it can be convincingly argued that the text of Sir. xlviii 18c is a creation of Ben Sira himself. In the biblical accounts of II Kings xviii-xx/Isa. xxxvi-xxxix and II Chron. xxxii, one cannot find a single text in which "Jerusalem"[40] is called "Sion"[41]. Although Ben Sira uses the names "Jerusalem" and "Sion" in parallelism (xxiv 10-11; xxxvi 13-14 [Gr. 18-19])[42] in other passages of his book, he seems to have omitted this deliberately in xlviii 15-25. This is especially the case in vs. 17a, where he has given a rather vague description: i.e. "his city". It is virtually certain, however, that Ben Sira in vs. 18c used the name "Sion" on purpose. In this way he explicitly anticipates the expression *'bly ṣywn* in vs. 24b, which is a literal quotation from Isa. lxi 3[43].

In Sir. xlviii 18d (*wygdp 'l bg'wnw*)[44] there is the expression *gdp 'l* ("to blaspheme God"). In biblical Hebrew it occurs seven times[45]: mainly in the Assyrian passage under discussion. It could be argued that Ben Sira borrowed this wording from the biblical report of the Assyrian raid. There is, however, at least one major difference. Both in II Kings xix 6/Isa. xxxvii 6 and in II Kings xix 22/Isa. xxxvii 23 the verb *gdp* forms part of an oracle to Hezekiah by the prophet Isaiah which is preceded both times by a reference to a prayer.

In Ben Sira's text, all these data have been conflated anew. Although in II Kings xix 14-19/Isa xxxvii 15-20 it is explicitly stated that it was king Hezekiah who prayed to God, and in II Chron. xxxii 20 it is said that it was king Hezekiah and the prophet Isaiah, it is the *community* to whom the author attributes the role of intercession before the Most High in Sir. xlviii 20. With respect to this action Ben Sira uses the expression [*wyqr*] *'w 'l 'l 'lywn*[46], which in the "Praise of the Fathers" can be found several times: xlvi 5 (Joshua); xlvi 16 (Samuel); xlvii 5 (David). This is even more striking because the "references to actions of religious ... piety in general are so few"[47].

---

[40] II Kings xviii 2, 7, 22, 35; xix 10, 31; Isa. xxxvi 2, 7, 20; xxxvii 10, 32; II Chron. xxxii 2, 9, 10, 12.

[41] Cf. *bat ṣiyyōn* (II Kings xix 21/Isa. xxxvii 22); *har ṣiyyōn* (II Kings xix 31/Isa. xxxvii 32).

[42] The name "Jerusalem" also occurs in Sir. xlvii 11, where it is text-critically disputed, as all versions speak here of "Israel".

[43] Further details are discussed in P.C. Beentjes, "Relations between Ben Sira and the Book of Isaiah. Some Methodical Observations" (forthcoming).

[44] *gdp* is also found in Sir. iii 16 (Ms. C.). According to H.-P. Rüger, *Text und Textform im hebräischen Sirach* (BZAW 112), Berlin 1970, Ms. C. represents "die ältere Textform" (*op. cit.*, p. 29). As to the translation of the "crux interpretum" *bg'wn lbm* (Sir. xlviii 19a) see: T. Penar, *op. cit.*, p. 83.

[45] Num. xv 30; II Kings xix 6, 22/Isa. xxxvii 6, 23; Ez. xx 27; Ps. xliv 17.

[46] The formula *qr' 'l + 'l* as such does not occur in the Old Testament. With *'lhym* it is found in II Sam. xxii 7; Jona i 6; iii 8; Ps. l 17. With *YHWH* in Judg. xv 18; xvi 28; I Sam. xii 17, 18; I Kings xvii 20-21; Jona i 14; ii 3; I Chron. xxi 26; II Chron. xiv 10.

[47] Mack, *op. cit.*, p. 210. In my opinion all these texts dealing with the theme "call upon God" should be connected with Sir. ii 10.

Here, the next colon (*wyprśw 'lyw kpym*) should also be taken into account, because it is the only verse in the entire Book of Ben Sira where in a context of prayer the concomitant gesture is also mentioned explicitly[48].

## IV. Ben sira's view of isaiah

Quite different from the biblical accounts, Ben Sira by making use of a pun (*wywšy'm byd yš'yhw*) emphasises the role of the prophet Isaiah (vs. 20d) as God's answer to the distress of the praying community. In the next part, however, we are confronted by an intriguing problem. Doubtlessly the colon [*wyk bm*] *ḥnh 'šwr* (Sir. xlviii 21a) refers to II Kings xix 35/Isa. xxxvii 36 or is even a quotation of it[49]. But, even if Ben Sira here quotes literally, he at the same time is creating a whole new context. For, in Ben Sira's presentation, the one who "struck the Assyrian camp" (vs. 21a) is certainly not the Angel of the Lord[50] as is the case in the biblical and deutero-canonical accounts[51]. Theoretically, this verse could refer to the prophet Isaiah.

At first sight this supposition is strengthened by the expression *byd yš'yhw* in vs. 20d: "God saved them by the hand of Isaiah". Then it could be the prophet who "struck the Assyrian camp" (vs. 21a). But some serious problems arise with respect to the interpretation of vs. 22. In Ben Sira's view, it is Hezekiah's positive way of life – not his prayer! –, which caused the defeat of the Assyrian army. It is very significant that the author stresses the fact that in vs. 22c[52] Hezekiah's adherence to David's "paths" was ordered by the prophet Isaiah. Because of this *indirect* function of the prophet, and because of the syntactical structure of vv. 20c-21, the most plausible inference is to consider God himself as the subject of vs. 21ab[53]. For this reason and because of a similar expression in Sir. xlix 6c we should translate *byd* as: "because of"[54].

---

[48] A detailed investigation into the function of prayer within the Book of Ben Sira is urgently needed.

[49] For a detailed analysis of II Kings xix 35: A. van der Kooij, "Das assyrische Heer vor den Mauern Jerusalems im Jahr 701 v. Chr.", *ZDPV* 102 (1986), pp. 93-109.

[50] Contra MacKenzie, *Historian*, p. 323: "by sending his Angel into the Assyrian camp". In the Greek translation by Ben Sira's grandson this problem has been "solved" by adding ὁ ἄγγελος αὐτοῦ in vs. 21b.

[51] In texts like I Macc. vii 21 and II Macc. xv 22-24 the Angel of the Lord has been mentioned explicitly too.

[52] As the Hebrew text of vv. 22c-23 has been lost, we have to rely upon the Greek and Syrian translation.

[53] Skehan and di Lella even have *added* the word "God" to their translation of this Hebrew line to stress that aspect: "God struck the camp of the Assyrians" (*op. cit.*, p. 536).

[54] Cf. *byd yrmyhw* (Sir. xlix 6c). One should try to translate both lines – and xlvi 4a as well – in a similar way. With respect to xlix 6c it is impossible to translate: "by Jeremiah". I am convinced we should follow Penar's suggestion: "because of" (*op. cit.*, p. 84).

As the Hebrew text of Sir. xlviii 22cd-23 has been lost, it is necessary to rely completely on the Greek version. These two bicola seem to contain a number of important and interesting implications with respect to the structure of the "Praise of the Fathers". It is particularly unfortunate, therefore, that it is impossible to verify this on the basis of the original Hebrew text. SMEND[55] has stated that the phrase Ησαίας ὁ προφήτης (vs. 22c) is an impossible combination in this particular line, since Isaiah is already mentioned in vs. 20d. There are at least two reasons to challenge this view.

First of all, there is a direct link between Ben Sira's phrase "Isaiah the prophet" and the biblical accounts about Hezekiah which are continuously mentioned in this article. It is hardly accidental that it is precisely in the context of II Kings xix-xx and Isa. xxxvii-xxxix that the combination "Isaiah the prophet"[56] can be found, since this formula is never found in other Old Testament texts where the prophet's role is emphasised[57].

Secondly, the originality of the phrase "Isaiah the prophet" is confirmed by Ben Sira's Hymn itself. In the "Praise of the Fathers" the *nby' / nbw'h*-motif is very important[58]. To which it could be added, as MACK has done recently, that, in the "Praise of the Fathers" "a figure's office is an essential component in the pattern of characterization" common to all heroes[59]. That the expression "Isaiah the prophet" cannot be overlooked in vs. 22c is strongly confirmed by an analysis of the subsequent lines as well.

The way in which Ben Sira formulates vs. 22d suggests a link with xlvi 15. This line, which lays stress on the trustworthy (*'mn*) prophetic activity of Samuel, forms part of a passage which has been framed by Ben Sira with the help of the word *nbw'h* (xlvi 13c, 20b). In xlviii 22d Ben Sira seems to recreate this prophetical "atmosphere". One wonders if it is mere coincidence that Samuel is introduced by a pun too[60]: whilst the formula *qr' 'l 'l* is also used with respect to him in xlvi 16a.

When considering Sir. xlviii 23, a similar pattern is evident. On the one hand, the whole line unmistakably recalls the biblical accounts. "In his days the sun went backward"[61] refers to the passage in II Kings xx 9-11/Isa. xxxviii

---

[55] "Da Jesaja schon v. 20 genannt ist, kann er hier nicht als "Jesaja, der Prophet" bezeichnet sein"; SMEND, p. 467.

[56] II Kings xix 2; xx 1, 11, 14; Isa. xxxvii 2; xxxviii 1; xxxix 3.

[57] An exception is II Chron. xxvi 22; xxxii 32.

[58] *nby'* in Sir. xlviii 1, 8; xlix 7, 9, 10; *nbw'h* in Sir. xliv 3; xlvi 1, 13, 20. For me it cannot be merely coincidence that elsewhere in the Book of Ben Sira the words "prophet" and "prophecy" emerge in very "theological" contexts: Sir. xxiv 33; xxxvi 16 (Gr. 21) and xxxix 1. Cf. my article "Profetie bij Jesus Sirach", to be published in the Festschrift in honor of C.A. VAN LEEUWEN, Utrecht 1989.

[59] MACK, *op. cit.*, p. 19.

[60] *hmšw'l / šmw'l* (xlvi 13b, 13d).

[61] VATTIONI, *Ecclesiastico*, p. 264 gives the reading ἐνεπόδισεν, which in fact is attested by just one minuscule (603, Paris, 13th-14th cent.). According to ZIEGLER's text edition, we should read

8[62]; whereas the phrase "and he prolonged the life for the king" echoes II Kings xx 5b-6/Isa. xxxviii 5. On the other hand, Ben Sira has nevertheless created something special of his own: another internal parallel within the "Laus Patrum". The way in which vs. 23a is formulated suggests a direct link with xlvi 4a. Looking at the context of both passages, there are also other striking resemblances. Both Joshua and Isaiah are introduced by a wordplay on *ysʿ*[63]. This is all the more striking because, elsewhere in the "Laus Patrum", the root *ysʿ* only occurs in xlix 10. Both texts contain the phrase *qrʾ ʾl ʾl ʿlywn* (xlvi 5; xlviii 20): and the characteristic *bydw / byd* (xvli 4a; xlviii 20d) as well[64].

Scholars have, therefore, failed to grasp the full significance of Sir. xlviii 24-25. Much attention and energy has been devoted in order to emphasise that, in these two lines, Ben Sira considers the prophet Isaiah as the author of the whole of the Book of Isaiah in its final, canonical shape[65]. The usual way in which this has been done by the commentators is very significant. Words (e.g. *ʾḥryt*; *hgyd*) or combinations of words (e.g. *brwḥ gbwrh*) are isolated from their context in order to prove that Ben Sira is quoting or alluding to all three parts of the Book of Isaiah in this passage. Such an approach can lead to strange and forced interpretations. Instead of taking e.g. Sir. xlviii 24b (*wynḥm ʾbly ṣywn*) as a close parallel to Isa. lxi 2c-3, a rather impressive number of exegetes tried to prove that *wynḥm* must be seen as a parallel to *nḥmw nḥmw* in Isa. xl 1[66].

If we do not consider Sir. xlviii 24b as a conflation of two different passages (Isa. xl 1; lxi 3), but, rather, as a reference to one specific text (Isa. lxi 2c-3), the question now arises of whether Ben Sira is pursuing a special aim here. Whereas vs. 24a and vs. 25 share a rather general atmosphere[67], vs. 24b not only strikes the eye because it is a biblical *quotation*, but also because of its content. To the best of my knowledge the phrase *wynḥm ʾbly ṣywn* is nothing less than the key to a remarkable problem which has generally been unnoticed by Ben Sira scholars. Whereas much attention is paid to the absence of Ezra in

---

ἀνεπόδισεν; J. ZIEGLER, *Sapientia Iesu Filii Sirach* (Septuaginta ... Gottingensis, vol. XII/2), Göttingen 1965, p. 354. A similar problem can be found in the Greek texts of Sir. xlvi 4a.

[62] I do not agree with the translation "In his lifetime he turned back the sun", as given by SKEHAN and DI LELLA, *op. cit.*, p. 536.

[63] *yhwšʿ / tšwʿh* (xlvi 1a, 1d); *ywwšyʿm / yšʿyhw* (xlviii 20d).

[64] See note 54.

[65] See all commentators and J. SCHILDENBERGER, "Die Bedeutung von Sir 48, 24f. für die Verfasserfrage von Is 40-66", in: H. JUNKER (Hrsg.), *Alttestamentliche Studien*, Festschrift Fr. NÖTSCHER (BBB 1), Bonn 1950, pp. 188-204.

[66] Further details in: BEENTJES, "Relations" (cf. note 43; forthcoming).

[67] As to the specific function of prophetic texts in Ben Sira's time I like to point to a very illuminating article of F. GARCÍA MARTÍNEZ, "Profeet en profetie in de geschriften van Qumran", in: F. GARCÍA MARTÍNEZ *et al.* (eds.), *Profeten en profetische geschriften* (Festschrift A.S. VAN DER WOUDE), Kampen – Nijkerk n.d. (= 1987), pp. 119-132. The transliteration of Sir. xlviii 24 as given on p. 127 unfortunately is not correct; instead of *gbw ḥzh* one should read *gbwrh ḥzh*.

the "Laus Patrum"[68], with the exception of MacKenzie nobody seems to have noticed that in Ben Sira's presentation of the history of Judah an allusion to the *Babylonian exile* is completely absent. MacKenzie has raised this question in connection with his analysis of Sir. xlix 4-6[69]. He certainly made an original observation. This statement, however, gives rise to a new problem. There is absolutely nothing in the text of Sir. xlix 4-6 which indicates that Ben Sira actually bridges the "gap" constituted by the exile. Nevertheless, *Sir. xlviii 24b* could perform this particular function. It is not by accident, therefore, that Ben Sira uses a *biblical quotation* in precisely this passage. By quoting Isa. lxi 2-3, the Sage created a pattern which, further on, enabled him to eliminate all references to the period of the Babylonian exile in his "Laus Patrum"[70].

It is not only the quotation from Isa. lxi 2-3 to which Ben Sira has given a remarkable depth; its immediate context also reveals some very fascinating aspects. Until now, scholars have commented on Sir. xlviii 24a and 25 in a rather single-minded way. The verse lines, and especially some words (*'ḥryt*[71], *hgyd*[72], *bw'n*) have elicited elsewhere a stereotyped enumeration of Deutero-Isaian texts (Isa. xli 22f.; xlii 9; xliii 9; xliv 7; xlv 21; xlvi 10; xlvii 13; xlviii 3). The point which has certainly been overlooked here, however, concerns the question of whether Ben Sira simply quotes here some words or phrases from the Book of Isaiah, or whether he (with the help of this prophetical vocabulary) elaborated a new interpretation. Since, in the past, hardly any attention has been devoted to the latter alternative, it is necessary to discuss briefly a number of peculiarities in the last verse lines of the Ben Sira passage in question.

First of all, it must be stressed that, in most of the listed references to Deutero-Isaiah, it is *God* (or "the gods") to whom the words under discussion relate, whereas Ben Sira uses the same vocabulary to describe the activities of

---

68 P. Hoeffken, "Warum schwieg Jesus Sirach über Esra?", *ZAW* 87 (1975), pp. 184-201; C. Begg, "Ben Sirach's Non-Mention of Ezra", *BN* 42 (1988), pp. 14-18.

69 "At this point we come to the most personal and distinctive feature of Ben Sira's Bible history: he says nothing of any 'Babylonian exile'; moreover, he implicitly denies it": MacKenzie, *Historian*, p. 323.

70 As a working hypothesis MacKenzie advances "that Ben Sira was descended from a family whose members had not been exiled by the neo-Babylonian officials, but had remained in Palestine" (*op. cit.*, p. 324). This very interesting question needs further research.

71 The use of *'hryt / ta eschata* within the Book of Ben Sira has been investigated by M. Fang Che-Yong, "Sir 7,36 (Vulg 7,40) iuxta hebraicam veritatem", *VD* 40 (1962), pp. 18-26; *idem*, "Ben Sira de novissimis hominis", *VD* 41 (1963), pp. 21-38. Because *'hryt* in Sir. xlviii 24 in his opinion has a "sensus messianicus vel eschatologicus" the verse line has been put aside by him. V. Hamp, "Zukunft und Jenseits im Buche Sirach", in: H. Junker (Hrsg.), *op. cit.*, pp. 86-97 does not discuss Sir. xlviii 24 too.

72 As to the special meaning of *ngd* hi. in Deutero-Isaiah cf. *THAT* II, 31-37, esp. 35-36; W.A.M. Beuken, *Jesaja* IIA (POT), Nijkerk 1979, p. 96.

*the prophet Isaiah*. In view of this observation, it seems that Sir. xlviii 25 – with its remarkable chiastic structure – contains some important data. The verse line exhibits a highly typical pair of words (*nhywt / nstrwt*), a combination which does not occur in the Hebrew Old Testament[73]. Yet exactly the same combination of words is used elsewhere in Ben Sira: *mḥwh ḥlypwt nhywt / wmglh ḥqr nstrwt* (Sir. xlii 19). This bicolon forms part of the introduction (vv. 15-25)[74] to the "Hymn of Creation" (Sir. xlii 15-xliii 33)[75], which can be regarded as the first half of a diptych of which the "Laus Patrum" is the counterpart[76]. Whereas in Sir. xlii 19 the author stresses the fact that it is the *Most High* who reveals the past, the future and the deepest secrets[77], it cannot be accidental that in Sir. xlviii 25 he typifies the activity of *the prophet Isaiah* by using exactly the same vocabulary. Here, a similar pattern is encountered to the one which has already been observed with respect to Ben Sira's reception of the texts from Deutero-Isaiah. With the help of *identical* vocabulary, Ben Sira at the same time emphasises significant *theological* differences or accents. In this way, he has effectuated his purpose to underline the special place of Isaiah as the prophet of God "par excellence".

## V. Conclusion

It has already become evident that the Ben Sira passage on Hezekiah and Isaiah cannot be explained fully by simply cataloguing Old Testament quotations which the author probably used in his text.

Several times it appeared to be important to investigate which *new* context has been created by the Jerusalem Sage with the help of *traditional* material.

On the other hand, it has been proved that the verse lines dealing with Hezekiah and Isaiah must be construed primarily in the context of the Book of Ben Sira. Especially in his "Laus Patrum" the author has done much more than just re-tell Old Testament narratives[78].

---

[73] Only *nstr(w)t* is to be found twice: Deut. xxix 28; Ps. xix 13.

[74] The word *nstrwt* has been used again in the *conclusion* of the Hymn (Sir. xliii 32).

[75] A lengthy analysis of the Hymn has been published by G.L. Prato, *Il problema della teodicea in Ben Sira* (AnBib 65), Rome 1975, pp. 116-208; not a single word, however, with respect to Sir. xlii 19.

[76] P.C. Beentjes, "Praise", pp. 374-375.

[77] Cf. Sir. xxxix 19-20.

[78] I should like to thank Dr. P. Staples, who was so kind to correct my English.

# JOSHUA V 10-12: ANOTHER APPROACH

BY

C. BREKELMANS

*Leuven*

There was a period in which it was quite normal to speak about the "Hexateuch". In this situation the passage of Jos. v 10-12 could be ascribed to the priestly tradition without any problem. Scholars referred to the exact dating of the 14th day of the month in vs. 10 and to the combination of *pèsaḥ* and *maṣṣōt* which was supposed to occur in the priestly tradition only. This same position is held nowadays by e.g. E. KUTSCH and G. FOHRER[1]. As a consequence of this approach no special attention was given to our passage: it was one text among others of the priestly tradition in which *pèsaḥ* and *maṣṣōt* are seen as one and the same liturgical feast.

The situation has changed since M. NOTH introduced a clear separation between the Pentateuch/Tetrateuch and the Book of Joshua. But even before this time some scholars tried to distinguish in our text older and later elements. For M. NOTH himself the exact date in vs. 10 and *b$^{e}$ʿèṣèm hayyōm hazzèh* are due to later priestly redaction, whereas the rest of the passage may be ascribed to the "Sammler"[2]. The feast of *pèsaḥ* and the manna are presupposed to be well known from the desert period. The main concern of the passage is the new situation in the cultivated land and the *maṣṣōt* are mentioned as characteristic of this new situation.

A much greater importance has been given to our text by H.J. KRAUS[3]. Leaving aside the exact dating of vs. 10, our verses preserve an old tradition of the *pèsaḥ-maṣṣōt* feast in the central sanctuary of Gilgal in commemoration of the Exodus and the Entrance in the land, as described in Jos. iii-iv. So our passage is "für die Erforschung des alttestamentlichen Passah-Massot-Kultes ... von großer Bedeutung". It shows that such a feast already existed before the monarchy. It was then forgotten during the monarchy and reintroduced by king Josia.

A very important place has our passage again in the study of E. OTTO: "Da

---

[1] E. KUTSCH, "Erwägungen zur Geschichte der Passafeier und des Massotfestes", *ZThK* 55 (1958), pp. 1-35; G. FOHRER, *Geschichte der israelitischen Religion*, Berlin 1969, p. 90.

[2] M. NOTH, *Das Buch Josua* (HAT), Tübingen 1953$^{2}$, p. 39.

[3] H.J. KRAUS, *Gottesdienst in Israel*, München 1962$^{2}$, p. 190f.

diese Überlieferung sowohl für die Rekonstruktion der in Gilgal gefeierten kultischen Begehung als auch für die Geschichte von Passa und Mazzotfest überhaupt eine zentrale Bedeutung hat, müssen wir uns diesen Text ausführlich zuwenden''[4]. According to OTTO the reference to *pèsaḥ* in our text must be a secondary element, because in the older tradition *pèsaḥ* was a family feast, whereas the *maṣṣōt* feast includes a pilgrimage to a sanctuary. Therefore, the combination of both feasts, as proposed by KRAUS, cannot be old. But the *maṣṣōt* feast at Gilgal may be ascribed to the Yahwistic tradition. In a more recent study G. KUHNERT[5] tries to show that our text preserves the old tradition that ''the feast of the desert'' which the Israelites in Egypt asked permission for to celebrate and which may be identified with the nomadic *pèsaḥ*, was continued after the arrival in Canaan in the plain of Jericho. The eating of unleavened bread and roasted corn as the first fruits of the land shows that this custom was taken over from the Canaanites. No altar, no priest and no sanctuary are mentioned in the text, in accordance with the nomadic past of the Israelites[6]. All this belongs to the Yahwistic tradition.

M. ROSE also published a long study on Jos. v 10-12 in order to establish the relationship of this text with Ex. xvi 35[7]. For this last text as for our passage he states that manna and desert belong together and that the manna disappears with the entrance in the land. And in accordance with the general tendency of his study (i.e. the Yahwist depends on the Deuteronomist), he concludes that Ex. xvi 35 is dependent on Jos. v 10-12. The whole *pèsaḥ*-item in this last text is ''deuteronomistisch, geschichtstheologisch motivierter Eintrag der mit II Kön. xxiii 21-23 zusammenzusehen ist und der später priesterschriftlich noch mit exacter Datierung versehen wurde''[8]. The Passover of Jos. v 10 is a literary and theological counterpoint to the Passover of king Josia. But besides this Passover feast, the central theme of the passage is the transition from the desert period (manna) to the cultivated land. This transition is presented as the offering of the first fruits (cf. Deut. xxvi 1ff. and Lev. xxiii 10). This cultic background has disappeared almost completely under the influence of the Pèsaḥ(-Maṣṣōt) tradition which now dominates the scene[9].

To all these rather divergent interpretations of our text we could add that of E. ZENGER who holds that the taking up of Ex. xvi 35a in Jos. v 12 and the celebration of the Passover just before the desert period (in Ex. xii) and

---

[4] E. OTTO, *Das Mazzotfest in Gilgal* (BWANT 107), Stuttgart 1975, p. 175.
[5] G. KUHNERT, *Das Gilgalpassah*, Mainz 1982, pp. 69ff., 159ff.
[6] *Ibid.*, p. 168.
[7] M. ROSE, *Deuteronomist und Jahwist* (AThANT 67), Zürich 1981.
[8] *Ibid.*, p. 42.
[9] *Ibid.*, p. 43.

immediately afterwards (in Jos. v 10) are both elements of the Yahwistic tradition[10].

Is it possible to say something new about a passage on which there are so many different opinions? The only thing on which scholars nowadays seem to agree is that the exact dating (on the 14th day of the month) and the clauses *mimmoḥ°rat happèsaḥ* (which is missing in the LXX) and *b'èṣèm hayyōm hazzèh* are later explanations[11]. I see no reason not to subscribe to this judgement.

Let us try another approach to our text. If we leave out for a moment the Passover of vs. 10, there can, it seems, be no doubt at all that the transition from the desert to the cultivated land is the main and only theme of vv. 11-12. Twice it is said that the period of the manna has come to an end (12aα and 12aβ) and even three times that the Israelites were eating the products of the land. I return to this shortly. The produce of the land is specified as *maṣṣōt* and *qālūy*, unleavened bread and toasted or roasted corn. The roasted corn especially has created many problems for those who interpret *maṣṣōt* as referring to a cultic feast. What is the roasted corn doing in such a context? There is no other place in which it is mentioned in connection with the feast of unleavened bread. This proves, as some scholars say, that this text cannot be of priestly origin, but preserves a much older tradition (so E. Otto). But that there existed once such a tradition seems very improbable to me. It is my impression that whatever cultic interpretation, be it young or old, does not know what to do with the roasted grain. But must we look for a cultic interpretation? The text of Lev. xxiii 14 could give us a new lead for the interpretation of our text. There we read that before the offering of the first fruits of the harvest the Israelites are not allowed to eat anything of that harvest: no *lèḥèm*, no *qālī*, no *karmèl*. This seems a kind of list of all possible food prepared from grain. Could it be that our text gives us such a list too? It is perhaps not so astonishing that *karmèl* is missing here. If *karmèl* means new corn[12], it seems included in the other two items of the list. But we must explain at least why *lèḥèm* is missing and *maṣṣōt* appears instead. This is not as difficult as it seems to be. The produce of the land, immediately after the entrance of the Israelites, is the very first harvest in the land after the desert period. Before that the Israelites were eating the manna and so there was no dough at all to leaven the bread. So our text takes it for granted that the first bread was unleavened. And this explains why *lèḥèm* is not mentioned in our text and is replaced by *maṣṣōt*. If this could be the right interpretation of the combination

[10] E. Zenger, *Die Sinaitheophanie* (FzB 3), Würzburg 1971, p. 137.

[11] For the LXX see S. Holmes, *Joshua, the Hebrew and Greek Texts*, Cambridge 1914; A.G. Auld, "Joshua, the Hebrew and Greek Texts", *VTS* 30 (1979), pp. 1-14.

[12] For the meaning of *karmèl* see now M. Mulder in *ThWAT* IV, c. 343.

of unleavened bread and roasted corn in our text, it is quite superfluous and even impossible to bring this text in connection with a cultic ceremony, be it the *maṣṣōt* feast or the offering of the first fruits.

After having found this approach to the text, I thought I had found something new. But as occurs more often, when looking at commentaries of older scholars, I found that C. STEUERNAGEL already had proposed the very same interpretation when he wrote: "Zunächst muss es (sc. Israel) sich mit ungesäuertem Brot und gerösteten Ähren begnügen, da es noch kein Sauerteig besitzt"[13]. It is a great pity that this explanation of STEUERNAGEL has been overlooked completely by exegetes. Many later interpretations could have been avoided, I think.

We already mentioned that vv. 11-12 say three times that the Israelites did eat the produce of the land and twice that the manna ceased. This fact has brought with it the distinction of two sources (11-12aα and 12aβb)[14]. As for 12a this seems not very probable. The second time the manna is mentioned indicates that it did not only cease at that very moment, but that it never came back in the future. This underlines the definitive character of the closing of the desert period. This "Doppelung", therefore, has a clear function in the text and so any literary-critical distinction is uncalled for. Moreover, there are other texts in which certain statements are followed by *w*$^{e}$*lō hāyāh ('ōd)*, such as Ex. ix 14; Jos. v 1; I Kings xx 13, 15; Jer. xiv 4. In all these cases this clause introduces further precisions of the preceding statements.

In vs. 12b the situation is much more complicated, because it shows several new elements. Instead of the hapax *'*$^{a}$*būr* in 11 and 12a here the produce of the land is called *t*$^{e}$*bū'āh*; instead of *'èrèṣ* we find *'èrèṣ k*$^{e}$*na'an*; finally, the time indication *baššānāh hahī'* also is new. It has been said that *t*$^{e}$*bū'āh* mainly occurs in later writings[15], although it is found already in Ex. xxiii 10; Prov. x 16; xiv 4; xvi 8; xviii 20 and Gen. xlvii 24. Also *'èrèṣ k*$^{e}$*na'an* is almost absent from older texts (those of the Pentateuch are said to be of priestly origin). M. ROSE says that this specific element of vs. 12b introduces, besides the opposititition desert – cultivated land, the claim on that land[16]. And according to KUHNERT the time indication betrays the same interest for exact dating as the later priestly elements of vv. 10-11. The interpretation of M. ROSE, on the other hand, is quite different. He considers the time indication as an allusion to the end of the "fourty years" of Ex. xvi 35.

There can be no doubt that there is a connection between our verse and Ex.

---

[13] C. STEUERNAGEL, *Das Buch Josua* (HKAT), Göttingen 1899, p. 169.

[14] See e.g. G. VON RAD, *Die Priesterschrift im Hexateuch* (BWANT 65), Stuttgart 1934, p. 146: 12aβb = $P^{A}$ und 11-12aα = $P^{B}$. See also M. ROSE, *op. cit.*, pp. 35ff. and 41ff.

[15] P. LAAF, *Die Pascha-Feier Israels* (BBB 36), Bonn 1970, p. 88; M. ROSE, *op. cit.*, p. 36 and note 169.

[16] M. ROSE, *op. cit.*: "symbolhafte Inanspruchnahme des ganzen geographischen Bereiches".

xvi 35. Both texts mention the period of the desert as the period of the manna; both texts express the idea that this ends with the entrance in the land; both texts give great attention to the eating (Ex. xvi 35 two times, our text three times); both texts also speak of *'èrèṣ k^ena'an*. Is this not a clear indication that both texts are from the same hand? Since WELLHAUSEN, the prevailing opinion has been that Ex. xvi 35 can best be divided into two parts, 35a being from the Yahwist, 35b from the priestly tradition, although M. NOTH accepts just the reverse. The two more recent studies on Ex. xvi, however, by RUPPRECHT and MAIBERGER, reckon in Ex. xvi with a basic priestly narrative and various later expansions[17]. According to both scholars 35a belongs to the older priestly narrative, whereas 35b is a later specification of *'èrèṣ nōšèbèt* (not Transjordan, but *'èrèṣ k^ena'an*)[17]. If this is accepted, Jos. v 12b (or 12aβb) could belong to such a later redaction too.

The whole of the manna tradition thus seems to be of priestly origin and is therefore rather late[18]. This must be the case then also for Jos. v 11-12. A reflection which sees the whole of the desert period as characterised by the eating of the manna indeed presupposes concrete stories about this manna and so must be younger than these stories themselves.

However this may be, the reflection of Jos. v 11-12 is in a certain way the continuation and the fulfilment of Ex. xvi 35. Whereas in this last text all attention is given to the desert period and the eating of the manna during all these fourty years until they reached the frontier of Kanaan, Jos. v 11-12 directs our attention to the moment on which this period comes to an end and a new period begins in which there is no manna any longer and the Israelites are eating the produce of the land they have entered.

For a long time scholars have discovered in both texts an older tradition alongside a later priestly redaction[19]. While for Ex. xvi this approach now seems to be abandoned, for Jos. v 10-12 this opinion still stands. This makes M. ROSE say that Jos. v 10-12 contains a tradition which is older than that of Ex. xvi, although he admits not to be able to offer a reconstruction of this older tradition. I must acknowledge that I am not very much impressed by such statements. As I said before, it is much more probable that the same hand is at work in Ex. xvi and Jos. v, this last text being the continuation and the fulfilment of Ex. xvi 35. I cannot find any priority of one text over against the other. Both are on the same level.

---

17 E. RUPPRECHT, "Stellung und Bedeutung der Erzählung vom Manna-Wunder", *ZAW* 86 (1974), pp. 269-307; P. MAIBERGER, *Das Manna. Eine literarische, etymologische und naturkündliche Untersuchung* (ÄguAT 6), Wiesbaden 1983; *idem*, art. man, *ThWAT* IV, c. 968-975.

18 RUPPRECHT accepts two holder texts in Num. xi 6 and xxi 5.

19 See P. MAIBERGER, art. man, c. 973: "Die Mannaerzählung Ex 16 gehört zu den literarkritisch umstrittensten und schwierigsten des ATs. Einig ist man sich nur über ihre Uneinheitlichkeit".

This means that there is here a redactional element which shows a relationship between the Pentateuch and the book of Joshua. If the book of Joshua is part of the Deuteronomistic history, there is at some level a common redaction with the Pentateuch (Tetrateuch) too. It seems that this conclusion cannot be avoided.

We now must return to vs. 10 and the passover. When the foregoing interpretation of the vv. 11-12 is right, there seems to be no direct connection with the passover feast of vs. 10. That the end of the desert period with the manna and the eating of the produce of the land after that was commemorated at the passover feast in any way, is fully unknown in the biblical tradition, notwithstanding the thesis of KRAUS that the Exodus and Entrance in the land were celebrated together in the central sanctuary of Gilgal.

Other scholars say that the passover was introduced at this very place with the purpose of making Joshua the prototype of king Josia. Our passage is then "a retrojection of the figure of Josia in the classical past"[20]. Others again prefer to see Joshua as a new Moses[21]. It is, however, not so easy to point out elements in our text for such an interpretation, because Joshua is not mentioned at all in our text. And in this respect, our text differs very much from the rest of ch. v. At best we could say, with M. ROSE, that the Deuteronomist "als literarischen Kontrapunkt eine Passah-Feier in der vor-Königszeit benötigt". But even so, II Kings xxiii 22 says that a Passover like that of king Josia had not been celebrated since *the Judges*. Why then do we find no direct reference here to Joshua or to the conquest period? This is what one would expect, if our verse is meant to be a counterpoint to II Kings xxiii 22.

It has been said that the terminology of the passover in vs. 10 cannot be attributed to the priestly tradition, because a) our text refers to a national feast and not to a family feast, b) the feast takes place *b*$^{e}$*'èrèb* (as in Deut. xvi 4) and not *ben ha'arbayim* as in P, c) the formula *'āśāh happèsaḥ*, although common in P, already occurs in Deut. xvi 1, Ex. xxxiv 23 (here in connection with the feasts of weeks) and in II Kings xxiii 21-23[22]. But this approach only stands when the exact datings of our verse are considered as secondary elements. When, however, the whole of vs. 10 is secondary, such an interpretation is rather difficult. It seems more probable that the presence of *maṣṣōt* in vs. 11 created the occasion for the introduction of the passover in vs. 10. At the same time this brought with it some of the expansions in vs.

---

[20] R.D. NELSON, *The Double Redaction of the Deuteronomist History* (JSOT Suppl. 18), Sheffield 1981, p. 125; *idem*, "Josiah in the Book of Joshua", *JBL* 100 (1981), p. 531-540.

[21] See now G.W. COATS, "The Book of Joshua: Heroic Saga or Conquest Theme", *JSOT* 38 (1987), pp. 15-32.

[22] P. LAAF, *op. cit.*, p. 89.

11. This means that the combination of *pèsaḥ-maṣṣōt* is a very late element in our text. And when vv. 11-12 already are of priestly origin, vs. 10 is an even later addition, originating from the same priestly circles.

# TIME AND THE STRUCTURE OF THE ABRAHAM CYCLE

BY

J.P. FOKKELMAN

*Leiden*

Time is omnipresent in every story and its importance can scarcely be overestimated. Time is functioning in two ways in every sentence of the story, as *narration* time and *narrated* time. The narration time corresponds to the speaking, reading and hearing of the text, for the simple reason that any use of language takes place sequentially in time. The narrated time, however, is all-pervasive, too, whether the plot carries on, or whether the narrator decides to halt momentarily to provide information or explanation. The first carrier of the narrated time – and I limit myself now to the Hebrew narrative art – is the verb, which as a rule represents the predicate and practically always has its temporal aspect. We are all very familiar with the backbone of Hebrew narration: the stream or concatenation of *wayyiqtol* forms. The sparing and well-considered disruptions of the stream, brought about by the inversion of the type x + *qatal* for example, and by nominal and circumstantial clauses, achieve an analepsis (flash-back) or pause in the temporal progress. It is often worthwhile for the interpreter to compare the narration time and the narrated; this will usually provide him with a satisfactory entrance into the text.

The story of the patriarch Abraham in the book of Genesis is so rich in meanings that it is not possible to determine the right arrangement or structure on the grounds of content. The themes are too much intertwined for that. For instance, the criterion cannot be revelation of God himself to Abraham or how the promises of land and progeny are dispersed throughout the text. As thematically or theologically important as the elements are, and as often as we come upon them, they are of such differing weight in the various units – and sometimes so ingeniously interwoven – that they can not serve as the basis for the structure.

In this article the position is taken that the organisation of time offers us the key to the proper articulation of the Abraham cycle. This should come as no surprise to anyone who considers that this cycle uses and thematises time in an unusual way. Indeed, the life of Abraham (as rendered in Gen. xii-xx) is dominated by a faithful, trusting and despairing wait, for how and when God shall keep his promise that Abraham shall have progeny, counter to the obstacle of Sarah's infertility. Thus the influence of time is raised to a higher power.

If I understand it correctly, the use of explicit references to time in this section of Genesis stands out in one respect against the rest of Hebrew narrative art. What is unique in the biography of Abraham is that the coordination system of time and space is carried in the first place by *a specific series of references to age*. They follow here, with the lines from or about the patriarch himself in italics:

| | verse in Gen.: |
|---|---|
| *a*) Terach was 205 years old, when he died in Haran. | xi 32 |
| *b*) *Abraham was 75 years old when he departed from Haran.* | xii 4 |
| *c*) Sarai (. . .) took (. . .), *after Abram had lived ten years in the land of Canaan.* | xvi 3 |
| *d*) *Abram was 86 when Hagar bore him Ishmael* | xvi 16 |
| *e*) *When Abram was 99, the Lord appeared unto him.* | xvii 1 |
| *f*) *He* (Abraham) *laughed and said to himself: "Can a child be born to a man a hundred years old, or can Sarah bear a child at ninety?"* | xvii 17 |
| *g*) *Abraham was 99 years old when he circumcised himself* | xvii 24 |
| *h*) Ishmael was 13 years old when he was circumcised. | xvii 25 |
| *i*) *Abraham was 100 years old, when his son Isaac was born.* | xxi 5 |
| *j*) Sarah lived 127 years (. . .) and she died. | xxiii 1-2 |
| *k*) *This is the number of years that Abraham lived: 175 years* | xxv 7 |
| *l*) This is the lifetime of Ishmael: 137 years | xxv 17 |

Going over this series of data just once is already sufficient to see that they have their own order and invite systematic attention. If we turn to three great German commentators on Genesis from this century – GUNKEL, VON RAD, WESTERMANN, each in his own way very representative of historical-critical Bible studies – we notice that they have done nothing with the series of age references. A pointed example of historical-critical scholarship thinking itself able to analyse literary texts without first schooling itself in a genuinely literary method or respecting the literary conventions that order a text. Benno JACOB does not help us much here either, even though he has made many calculations using numbers from the genealogies. Let us then examine the series of ages ourselves, determine their internal cohesion and accompanying functions, and finally draw conclusions about the structure of the text by relating the organisation of the narrated time to the cycle as a whole.

We have before us a series of twelve passages from Genesis with thirteen numbers referring to age. Initially I shall remain on *the syntagmatic axis* of the text by proceeding linearly with the references to age, and I make the following observations. The elements *a* and *b* are a pair, Haran being mentioned in both. It is the country where the father stays behind in his grave, and which is for Abram the departure point for his journey towards the unknown. The narrator has in the meantime skipped 75 years. The long journey Haran-Canaan is apparently the first event in Abram's life that is important enough to be reported. The line that follows in our list, element *c*, is the only one that once more places space by time and chooses for that purpose the polar entity Canaan – the land of destination that is the subject of the divine promise to the patriarchs. The lines *c* and *d* are likewise a pair, occurring in the same literary unit; they form the temporal framework for the first story about Hagar and Ishmael, Genesis xvi. Both related to the decision of Sarai to counteract the affliction of her infertility by an adoption via a slave, they refer to a first year of fertility in the patriarchal family. This solution is only temporary and fifteen years later it will be overshadowed – pass into oblivion I would almost say.

The elements *d* and *e* are also coupled. This pair attracts attention by the sharp contrast between the narration time and the narrated time. Indeed these verses xvi 16 and xvii 1 border each other and yet are separated by a gap of thirteen years of narrated time. The narration time between xvi 16 and xvii 1 is zero and they seem to collide; so abrupt is the leap by the narrator who does not wish to relate anything about more than a dozen years of Abram's life. This hiatus between the two stories would be a good choice for a boundary mark, if we wish to divide the whole cycle.

Element *f* is Gen. xvii 17. It is prominent as being the only element which is not a report (a narrator's text), but a dialogue (character's text), and consisting of *two* lines having numbers. This verse deserves more extensive attention shortly, with its *parallelismus membrorum* that despairs of the parenthood of the spouses Abraham and Sarah. The elements *g* and *h*, about the circumcision of the father and son on the same day, are likewise a parallelism and again form a pair. Moreover, they mark together the end of the unit Genesis xvii. The totals of Abraham's and Sarah's lives make xxiii 1-2 and xv 7 the pair *j* + *k*, and the identical nominal formulation in xxv 7 and 17 (*w'lh* [*ymy*] *šny ḥyy* + PN + number) places the life of Ishmael next to that of his father in the particulars with which Gen. xxv 1-18 closes the cycle.

Does this all mean that the elements *e* and *i* are alone? By no means, as we shall see if we proceed to the *paradigmatic axis*, in search of the thematic or compositional connections in the series of references to age.

I shall begin at the edges of the cycle. The outermost elements, *a*, *k* and *l* form a framework by reporting the totals of three generations: the statistics of the patriarch himself, his father and his son at the time of their deaths. By means of these totals and the genealogical particulars that form their surroundings, the cycle acquires its precise position in the whole of the book of Genesis, that is itself articulated by a system of *toledot**. The observation of the inclusion is already an indication of what precisely the limits are of Abraham's history. The short piece xi 27-32, which contains the germ of the plot of the whole cycle in the announcement of Sarai's infertility[1], is the prologue, as is generally recognised. That Gen. xxv 1-18 is the closing of "Abraham" and belongs thus to the preceding rather than to the following, is less widely known[2], but is ascertained by thematic connections[3].

Precisely three lines from the beginning and end of our list of ages, under *c* and *j*, we find Sarah in the position of subject. She is that once again, namely in the centre, in element *f*. Moving again closer to the centre, we find the elements *d* and *i*, in other words, the dating of the births of Ishmael and Isaac. In xvi 16 Abram gets a son: his first-born? No, this son of Hagar is substituted by Isaac, who is born fourteen years later, and is even called by God himself in the presence of Abraham "your only son" (three times even, *yḥydk*, xxii 2, 12, 16)[4]. Nevertheless the first that is not to remain the first shall remain a participant in God's covenant with Abraham, according to chapter xvii, and not fall outside the blessing of God. In short, Ishmael belongs and yet does not belong, and that ambiguity is also carefully heeded as far as chapter xxv[5].

The age of Abraham is precisely 100 when Sarah finally presents him with "his only" son, a large, round and undoubtedly also symbolic number. We come across this number in yet another manner, by subtracting *b* from *k*. We discover that the narration time, in other words, the text Gen. xii-xxv, covers the years 75 to 175 in Abraham's life, or at least deals with the most important events in this period. Put another way: the lines from xii 4 and xxv 7 (= *b* and

---

* I have written about the accurate distribution, in two series, of the "procreations" over the genealogical and the narrative material in Genesis, in my contribution (the chapter on Genesis) to: Robert ALTER and Frank KERMODE, *The Harvard Literary Guide to the Bible*, 1987.

1 Note that the short nominal clause *'yn lh wld* goes directly against the title (and idea of) *twldt*.

2 Chapter xxv is thus wrongly placed with the succeeding section by Dixon SUTHERLAND, in his dissertation titled *Genesis 15:16: A Study in Ancient Jewish and Christian Interpretation*, Louisville, University Microfilms 1982, and in his article "The Organization of the Abraham Promise Narratives", *ZAW* 95 (1983), pp. 337-344.

3 It concerns among other things the relationship of xxv 9-10 to chapter xxiii, of xxv 11 (end) to the well Lahai Ro'i in Gen. xvi and the end of chapter xxiv, of xxv 16c to xvii 20 (4th clause) and finally of xxv 18 to xvi 12.

4 Notice in this connection the subtle difference between the phrases with the infinitive in xvi 16 (active *yld* with the mother mentioned) and xxi 5 (passive *hwld*, without Sarah, and the word choice which emphatically calls Isaac "his son".

5 In xxv 9 Ishmaël belongs to the family: together with Isaac he buries his father. The paragraph vv. 12-17 gives him and his descendants again a place in the text that cannot be overlooked. Yet the closing lines, vs. 18, indicate much isolation for him, and when we find that "the Well of the Living One who sees me" (that the narrator had dug specifically for Hagar) is assigned to Isaac in xxiv 62 and xxv 11, then we think again: no, he is losing out.

*k*) are a pair; they form a ring between their neighbours, the rings $a+l$ and $c+j$.

Where is the attention of the narrator primarily directed in that period of precisely a hundred years that begins in Gen. xii? We make a new subtraction, *b* from *i*, and discover that the actual story of Abraham mainly occupies itself with the first quarter of the narrated century. Everything that is related to Gen. xii-xxi occurs in those 25 years. After Gen. xxi (i.e. after Abraham's hundredth year), there follows just one occurrence of dramatic importance, the sacrifice of Isaac – a test that for that matter jeopardises the focus of the macro-plot, the long-awaited son. It is striking that this fearsome event is the only "undatable"; there are no age particulars mentioned with it. What are reported in xxiii and xxiv are natural completions: the death of Sarah is in xxiii just occasion to present the sale of the property with the cavern near Hebron, and xxiv arches harmoniously back to the beginning[6].

The hiatus in the narrated time between xvi 16 and xvii 1 separates the elements *a-d* from the particulars *sub e-i*. We shall examine these lines from Gen. xvii-xxi further. The elements *e* and *g* have an identical numeral, ninety-nine, the age of Abraham, and so they are the umpteenth pair. They frame the principled chapter about the circumcision covenant, and in this manner surround the pair of numbers in xvii 17. The two lines from this last verse have an exceptional position in the series of age references. They are a speech by the hero, they are a twosome, they show *parallelismus membrorum*, they can be scanned as a very iambic bicolon with 4+6 stresses, they are rhetorical questions full of despair and above all disbelief, and their meaning refers to the miracle that is about to take place, and has just been announced. In many ways stylistically marked, Gen. xvii 17 lays claim to being the significant centre point of the series of thirteen numbers. We can expand this conclusion to the whole of chapter xvii. This unit must be of central importance, based on the fact that it contains no less than five of the thirteen age numbers and has a sixth as a boundary mark next to it (xvi 16). We group the elements *d-h* now as two pairs of lines or numbers around the central pair of lines; the double number of xvii 17 is thus flanked (beforehand) by xvi 16+xvii 1 and (afterwards) by xvii 24+25.

I shall point to one more pair, the elements *g* and *i*. The beginning of this is in xvii 1 because Abraham's age in xvii 1 is identical to that in xvii 24. We

---

[6] Gen. xxiv does that in two ways. The long and almost idyllic story sketches a long journey to and from Haran, which achieves its object, furnishing Isaac with an endogamous marriage. In the meantime the narrator – and following in his footsteps soon after, the servant of Abraham who wants to persuade the family of Rebecca that her destiny is in Canaan, at the side of Isaac – makes it quite clear at several points in his text that Abraham is definitely blessed by God and repeats how the patriarch is chosen by God. See xxiv 1b, 2, 7a, the answering of the prayer of the servant at the well, vv. 27, 35-36, 50.

can thus also refer to the pair as $(e=)\ g+l$. This twosome is the successor or the pendant of the pair $c+d$. The decisive pregnancy of Sarah herself, the second year of fertility in Abraham's life, replaces the first year of fertility, that of Hagar and the unit Gen. xvi, and surpasses it in importance and narration time.

We may now conclude that the series of thirteen explicit references to time is a refined subsystem and has its own well worked-out structure to which every element makes multiple contributions. The series has its own sense; that sense becomes visible if we represent the series and the most prominent correlations in it in *a concentric pattern* of ten members around a pivot X:

A Terach dies (age x)<br>
A′ Abram is 75 at his departure<br>
B Sarai attempts adoption (Abram is 85)<br>
C birth of the first son, Ishmael (Abram is 86)<br>
D the circumcision covenant, "Abram" (99)>"Abraham"

X *"Shall a son be born unto a hundred year old?"*<br>
*"Shall Sarah bear at the age of ninety?"*

D′ Abraham is 99, all men are circumcised<br>
C′/D′′ circumcision of his son Ishmael (13 years old)<br>
C′′ birth of "your only son", Isaac (Abraham is 100)<br>
B′ Sarah dies (age y)<br>
A′′ Abraham dies (age z)

This outline follows in the footsteps of the series *a-k*; if so desired, element *l* can be subsumed under A′′. I have represented the ages in the toledot passages with *x*, *y* and *z*. The information from line *k* (xxv 7, the life span for Abraham) is not just the counterpart of *a* (Terach's total) but of element *b* as well (xii 4, the "dating" of the great journey), because there at the start of Gen. xii is the beginning of the actual story. Therefore I have given the capital letter A to three members; together they form the framework of the whole cycle. The two components of C (the birth of a son, Ishmael the person) both return, but in keeping with the ambiguity of Ishmael's position, simultaneously split. Thus the one birth (C′′) reciprocates the other (C), while Ishmael must make room for the "real" son Isaac. Yet Ishmael gets one more mention, in C′, and that concurs with one of the emphatic instructions that Abraham receives in Gen. xvii: he may not neglect or forget the son of Hagar, Ishmael remains part of God's covenant with the patriarch.

This subsystem of the text cannot produce on its own the theme or the arrangement of the whole cycle. Hermeneutically expressed: the time dimension serves the story; we may fit the whole of the text in, but not subject it to, the coordinates of the time. Nevertheless the time scheme that has come to light can be a considerable help to us and point out which events are to be conveyed as especially important by the composition. Crucial in the life of the hero is the great journey away from Haran with which everything begins, and the births of two sons. However, the pivotal one-hundredth year of the patriarch is apparently the most important. It is covered by the elements DXD′C′D″C″ and by the elements *e*, *f*, *g*, *h* and *i*. But the special significance of Abraham's hundredth year is most clearly seen if we make a comparison between the narration time and the narrated time. The first year of fertility (with Hagar's pregnancy) is allotted just one narrative unit, chapter xvi, that barely fills one complete page of Hebrew in our standard edition. The second year of fertility, and the aforementioned hundredth year of Abraham's life, has the attention of seven or eight units, to wit in Gen. xvii-xxi, more than eight pages in the BHS. This enormous difference in size proves that *the hundredth year of Abraham's life* is the decisive period. The section of the text in which it is handled is the centre piece of the composition.

The beginning of the middle section Gen. xvii-xxi, the first boundary, is most clearly marked by the pair xvi 16 + xvii 1, and the gap of thirteen years skipped narrated time. But what about the second boundary? It has received a double temporal marking as well. The central part ends with the note that "Abraham resided in the land of the Philistines a long time". The narrator thus skips over a period of *yamim rabbim*; this one cannot be measured precisely, but it is too considerable to be ignored. In this way, the central panel appears to be framed and set apart by two big hiatuses of narrated time. In xxii 1a a new phase begins with its own time designation: "After these things it came to pass ...".

The words with which the unique chapter Gen. xxii begins cannot be interpreted without familiarity with the beginning of Gen. xv, as these introductory lines display a chiasmus and are obviously attuned to each other:

| | | | | |
|---|---|---|---|---|
| xxii 1a | *wayhi* | *'aḥar hadd$^{e}$barim ha'elle* | | title: ordeal, God speaks |
| xv 1a | *'aḥar hadd$^{e}$barim ha'elle* | | *haya* | word of God in a vision |

In Gen. xv God emphatically reassures a despondent Abraham, who has been waiting for a long time, that he shall receive a physical son, whereas Gen. xxii seems to rob him of this son; the command to sacrifice Isaac makes this chapter another focal point of despair (even if obedience eventually triumphs, and the reader knows that it is "only" a test thanks to the early disclosure in vs. 1, before the story unfolds – knowledge which the hero does not acquire until afterwards). The two chapters form a structural pair, in my opinion. Thus they distinguish themselves from the rest by concentrating themselves wholly upon the son as the object of divine promise[7], and God recognises in both the excellence of Abraham with so many words – compare xv 6 with xxii 12 and 16.

The explicit temporal introduction of Gen. xv and xxii presents us with *two time thresholds.* What does the phrase "And it came to pass after these things" actually do, separate or connect? Both simultaneously, I would say. It brings a certain consecution and in indicating a new event or phase it presupposes the coherence of the greater whole. It is also an element of articulation and brings about a temporal and material separation. This formula does not occur elsewhere with "Abraham", with one exception: directly after the sacrifice of Isaac in fact, xxii 20a. It functions there as introduction to a small genealogical paragraph, vv. 20-24. On account of the special import that the explicit references to time have in the Abraham cycle, we must consequently regard the placing of this reference as significant rather than arbitrary, and thus likewise perceive the formula in xxii 20a as a time threshold. As a result, the piece xxii 20-24 becomes the opening of the last section of the composition, and in turn that means ... but let me now first provide *the arrangement of the cycle as a whole.* This division is indeed inspired by the time demarcations, but shall derive its authority from a thematic analysis. A good division should do justice to the contents and provide the correct frames for a reliable assignment of meanings.

framework: genealogical information = prologue xi 27-32

phase I Gen. xii-xiv (journey, promised land, Abram holds his own)
phase II Gen. xv-xvi (crisis, issue: son? Night vision, adoption)
phase III Gen. xvii-xxi (covenant = circumcision, announcements of births and destruction; destruction, crisis in Gerar, birth, Hagar banished, covenant)
phase IV Gen. xxii 1-19 (crisis, sacrificing of son?, ordeal, blessing)
phase V Gen. xxii 20-xxiv 67 (acquisition of ground, journey, Rebecca succeeds Sarah)

framework: genealogical information = epilogue, xxv 1-18

Space and time are not only just in life *a priori* categories of our knowledge but also a fundamental system of coordination for practically all narration; in the first book of the Bible they are of supreme importance because they are

[7] This is valid for xv 1-6 as the first short version of the night vision (I take vv. 7ff. to be a second, longer, and mainly synchronous version of the same revelation) and xxii 1-14. The second speech of God in xxii 16-18 is again primarily about countless descendants, but traces of space as a dimension appear also in vs. 17b-18a. In the other passages with a God-Abraham dialogue, the double promise of God (land *and* progeny) gets attention; see xii 1-3, xiii 14-17, xvii 4-8, compare xxiv 6-8.

thematised in the promises of land and progeny that God makes to the patriarchs. The double promise results in a whole narrative programme, which at the end of the entire Torah still awaits eventual fulfilment; Moses may lead a thinned-out tribe of sinful Israelites only to the border of the promised land. The double promise (and the postponement of its fulfilment) creates, in other words, the macro-plot that forms the basis of the entire Torah.

Concerning Abraham, the above division allows us to see that the coordinates of *space and time* (thematised, "coloured" too, by God's promise) *alternate with each other* in importance. In Gen. xii-xiv the dimension of space dominates (while the "seed" theme is in no way absent or unimportant). Abraham makes a long journey (xii 1-9), has to detour to Egypt (xii 10-20) and upon returning, must divide the land with his nephew Lot (xiii 1-18). The text is teeming with spatial categories; thus the altar and the geographical position of xii 18 and the journey of vs. 9 are accurately reflected in xiii 1-4. The construction of altars in xii 8 (xiii 4) and xiii 18 and their consecration is a sacral deed of more than just local importance. It is a metonymical acquisition of the promised land; in so far as this contains an anticipation of history there is also a temporal aspect. In xiv Abram is caught between a coalition of four Mesopotamian and another one of five Palestinian city-states, but is able to maintain himself and even rescue his nephew. After the narrator's text xiv 1-18 (without a single spoken word!) there is a dialogue in vv. 19-24, in which Abraham shows he is unaffected by international politics, despite his intervention on behalf of Lot; he does not want to be involved because his destiny is of a completely different nature. He remains aloof and does not accept anything as a gift. Large-scale war, nine cities, campaigns, kings in tar pits, pursuit, "the highest God, who has created heaven and earth" – here too the text is teeming with spatial elements. In the character's texts xii 2 and xiii 16 God speaks of seed, but for the principal figure of the four literary units in chapters xii-xiv progeny is of no concern yet, and neither is it an issue for the plot.

In chapters xv and xvi it is much different. Suddenly the despair of the aging pair rises to the surface. Abram's lament from xv 2-3 is virtually provoked by God who repeats his promise of progeny in a revelation. In chapter xvi Sarai is so aggravated by her infertility that she consents to an emergency solution, a child fathered by Abram on a servant woman. The expectant Hagar, however, confronts her again with her frustration at being infertile. She sends the pregnant servant woman into the desert, an assault on the continuation of Abram's genealogical line. Phase IV is entirely taken up by one story and that also contains an assault on the continued existence of the family. God himself demands the "only" son as a sacrifice. The key word for Hagar in the desert (and in xvi 7ff.) had become "see" (*r'h*), she recognised God as "the Living One that is looking (*r'h*) after me". The corresponding phase IV is masterfully and richly variegated with this same key word. God "shall point out (*r'h*)" where the sacrifice must be brought, Abraham "sees the place from afar", he lies – and believes – in the presence of his questioning son that "God will provide (himself)" and because he endures the ordeal, he consecrates the mountain Moriah with a name that eternalises how God's providence turned out for the better. What was ambiguous to the point of being macabre in xxii 8, becomes an unequivocal expression of faith and thankfulness in vs. 14. Life still prevails, the Living One has once again looked after the mortal. The fact that the Aqedah by itself occupies phase IV underlines how special and unique this ordeal text is[8].

In phase V space dominates once again. The focus of chapter xxiii is the purchase of a parcel of land, over which tenacious and elegant negotiations are made in three carefully delimitated rounds of dialogue between the patriarch and the Hittites of Hebron. Sarah's decease is little more than ancillary. In xxiv her place is taken by Rebecca, just as Abraham's place is destined for Isaac. This very lengthy and harmonious story displays a well-prepared (vv. 1-9) and beautifully completed (vv. 62-67) journey of Abraham's servant to Haran and back. The rump of the story takes place at the well from which living water is drawn (vv. 11-31), and the house of Laban and Rebecca (vv. 32-61). In many details the notion of space is also to be found. The two stories in xxiii-xxiv have the air of "all's well that ends well".

The position of xxii 20-24 is intriguing. Placement is timing – as it so often is. Only now does Abraham hear that the blessing that God has given him (in xii 1-14) and that was the commencement of the reported part of his life, has been working thoroughly for a long time in the branch of the family that has remained behind in Haran. The narrator did not allow him to learn that sooner, on thematic grounds. The life of the patriarch had until then been under one, huge, arch of tension – the long wait for the fulfilling of the promise. The arch reaches from Gen. xii to xxi, and is once more gruesomely activated by the command to perform the Aqedah. During that whole time the narrator has no use for the happy tiding of the blessing of childbirth in Haran; that would harm the purity of his theme. The level of knowledge of the hero (and of ours, the readers!) is also an issue. In Gen. xii-xxii 19 Abraham must continually labour under the assumption that (the realisation) of the promise and the blessing are wholly dependent on his family, in the sense that they manifest themselves in the yet finally occurring fertility. The news that is saved until xxii 20-24 would, if revealed earlier, have destroyed the assumption of Abraham and the point of the narrator. The postponement is also positive in another way: when the Aqedah comes to a positive conclusion, and Isaac is

[8] For further study on the Aqedah, see the long article by Francis LANDY, and my response to it, in an issue of *Semeia Studies* that has just appeared: J. Cheryl EXUM (ed.), *Signs and Wonders. Biblical Texts in Literary Focus*, Missoula 1989.

spared, that joyous fact is celebrated and embellished by the happy tidings to Abraham in xxii 20-24, which must have been for the patriarch an extra confirmation, even an eye-opener, of God's dedication.

The details of xxii 20-24 form a framework, with the epilogue in chapter xxv, around the narrative material proper from phase V, the two stories from Gen. xxiii and xxiv. This short paragraph also contains genealogical information with which it anticipates the closing of xxv 1-18. This piece belongs not with the preceding but with the following, not just because of the presence of the time threshold found in vs. 20a, but also on account of the following observations on the contents. The most familiar names of vv. 20-24 refer to the genealogical framework and to Gen. xxiv, because they are prominent in the prologue and in chapter xxiv, while in the bulk of Gen. xii-xxiii they are not at all mentioned. Milka (twice in xxii 20-24) and Nahor (idem) were already introduced to us in Gen. xi. As short as the prologue is, Nahor is mentioned three times, and by means of an artificial repetition in xi 29, Milka twice. We also come upon the names of Bethuel and Rebecca in xxii 23, but we recognise these two from our reading in chapter xxiv. The man is the head of the house where Abraham's servant is a guest[9], and the woman is designated by Providence as the partner for Isaac. She is the actantial object of the plot in xxiv and the journey of the servant. Not for no reason at all is the girl emphatically presented in xxiv 15: "Rebecca came outside, begotten of Bethuel, son of Milka, the daughter of Nahor, the brother of Abraham". In appearance so much information is redundant, in reality the connections with xxii 20-24 and the names of kindred in the prologue are warranted[10].

*The central panel*, phase III (Gen. xvii-xxi), deserves our attention now. I shall close this sketching of the structure by calling attention to the placing of Gen. xvii and xx on the time scale. The question arises whether the establishment of the circumcision (Gen. xvii) and the revelation in Gen. xviii (three men visiting, two announcements) are actually at different points on the axis of the narrated time. I do not think so. The references to ages in xvii 1 (=xvii 24) and xxi 5 in theory allow for a time lapse of several months between the conclusion of the covenant in xvii and the peculiar visit in Gen. xviii. However, the gap is in any case not great, as the angels ("the men") that Abraham entertains say to him in xviii 10a that "this time next year" (*ka'et ḥayyah*) Sarah

[9] As agent (i.e. he who functions as representative of the family in Haran), Bethuel is substituted by Laban, who is not mentioned at the end of xxii; nevertheless Bethuel speaks in xxiv 50a as well.

[10] Bethuel is mentioned often enough in xxiv; see not just vs. 15/24/47, but also vs. 50a. Rebecca may repeat the genealogical chain in vs. 15 once more in vs. 24, and for those who have still not yet comprehended its importance, the narrator redoubles the identification from vv. 23-24 in vs. 47!

shall have a son. I feel that we are splitting hairs if we insist on a lapse in time between the occurrences in xvii and xviii. The age designations incline us to the contrary, and I propose therefore that the covenant in Gen. xvii and the visit with the two announcements in Gen. xviii, are part of one and the same revelation in Abraham's hundredth year. I perceive the two chapters as synchronous.

Are there arguments for this reading? As I see it, the two boundaries of the two chapters and the particular time indication in the announcement of the miraculous birth cover each other completely:

| | | | |
|---|---|---|---|
| xvii 1 | When Abram was 99 years old, the Lord appeared unto him<br>*wyr' yhwh 'l 'brm* | xviii 1 | The Lord appeared unto him,<br>*wyr' 'lyw yhwh* |
| xvii 21 | "My covenant I will establish with Isaac which Sarah shall bear unto you at this set time next year" | xviii 10 | "I will certainly return unto you at the same season, and your wife Sarah shall have a son". |
| xvii 22 | *wykl ldbr 'tw,*<br>And when He had finished speaking with him, God was gone from Abraham. | xviii 33 | *wylk yhwh k'šr klh ldbr 'l 'brhm*<br>The Lord went his way when He had finished speaking to Abraham. |

We note that the still rough reference to time in xvii 1 is succeeded and narrowed down by two precise indications in xviii 1, one of time and one of place ("by the terebinths of Mamre ... as the day grew hot"). After the general (the establishment of circumcision for all subsequent generations) comes the individual: this hero is presented this unique son-of-old-age from this specific (read: old) woman[11]. I read xviii 1 thus as a defining or refining of xvii 1 and interpret the verse as a flash-back: the Lord *had* appeared to him[12]. The working of *klh ldbr* in xvii 22//xviii 33 is a more compelling parallel if it is known that this formula occurs nowhere else in "Abraham", except in xxiv 15//45 where Providence is again working for our hero.

Let us imagine the position of the narrator. He had decided to bring to the fore the hundredth year of the patriarch as a turning point, and to do that

[11] Note that *'elaw* in xviii 1 relates to the preceding; the text does not say *'el 'abraham*!

[12] It is allowed to do that with a *wyqtl* form. See for example *wyṣ'* in Jonah iv 5 and the great importance of this as a hinge in the composition; see N. Lohfink, "Jona ging zur Stadt hinaus (Jona 4,5)", *Biblische Zeitschrift* NF 5 (1961), pp. 185-203, and the handling of it by H.W. Wolff, *Studien zum Jonabuch*, Cologne 1965, pp. 40-48.

by telling of an exceptionally significant revelation of God. This single revelation is a *pleroma* of pronouncements:
*a*) the enactment of the circumcision covenant,
*b*) the announcement of the birth of Isaac,
*c*) the announcement of the destruction of Sodom and Gomorrah.

The two announcements represent the polarity individual:collective = life: death, and that polarity brings a formidable dynamic in the central panel. Element *a* stands out against *b* and *c* as general, transpersonal, a continually repeating ceremonial vs. an individual, unique, unrepeatable occurrence. Technically it was probably too complicated for the narrator to work statements of such varying content into one plot; that single story would have been over-crowded. He decided then to place the fundamental materials in a separate chapter in front[13]. The advantage of this is that the Abraham who now may prepare himself for a no longer expected parenthood is already circumcised himself. His personal circumcision *is* the preparation, physically and spiritually. The general and institutional in Gen. xvii is however founded or anchored upon the individual. Abraham must make a concrete beginning by circumcising himself and his son. Moreover, the enactment of the circumcision can only be credible in the eyes of the addressed mortal if he does not become extinct, and so there is also an announcement already in chapter xvii of the birth of Isaac, vv. 16, 18-21 (prepared in vs. 2b and 6). We can regard circumcision, birth, fertility, promise and blessing as one large, sliding, metonymic scale, and it must be said that this metonymic complex dominates all of Genesis[14].

Each of God's announcements meets with an obstacle, with Abraham and his wife (in xvii and xviii) as well as his nephew Lot (in xix). Abraham reacts with disbelief to the announcement of the birth in xvii 17-18, Sarah does the same in xviii 11, 12, 15. Abraham acts as advocate for the perhaps fifty, forty, or finally just ten righteous in Sodom upon the announcement of massive annihilation. In the unit xviii 23-33 he puts with charming candidness "the Judge of all the earth" soundly to the test. In Gen. xix, in various ways the parallel of xviii, Lot replies to the announcement of the destruction by the angels with irksome dawdling and quibbling (vv. 16-22) and the subject of birth gets a burlesque and painful minus variant in the births of Ammon and Moab. They are fathered on his own daughters by an inebriated Lot. Thus comes the

---

[13] As the fundamental covenant "certificate", Gen. xvii 1-22 is actually composed of four great speeches of God, vv. 4-8, 9-14, 15-16 and 19-21. There is a short introduction, vv. 1-2 (again words of the deity taking the initiative), two, but brief interruptions by the patriarch (vs. 17, disbelief; vs. 18, resignation), and a conclusion that is narrator's text, the cluster of reporting sentences vv. 23-27.

[14] See my chapter "Genesis" in *The Harvard Literary Guide to the Bible*, *op. cit.*; I wrote about the obsession with continuity and survival that is perceptible in so many details and motifs.

branch of Lot, from a blissful beginning in Gen. xiii (see vs. 10!), to its ignominious end.

The polarity of individual new life and collective death in the announcements is not only repeated in chiastic order, as God carries out his plans (xix 24-29, destruction of Sodom and Gomorrah; xxi 1-8, birth of Isaac, feast). It also works masterfully on in Gen. xx (Sarah in the harem of the Philistine king Abimelech) which is a structural reversal of the usual situation. "Normal" is that the woman of Gerar get children and that Sara is infertile. But when Sarah comes into jeopardy (is she pregnant or not? An intriguing question! Shall Abimelech make sexual approaches? No, almost, but not quite; God himself holds him back with a cautionary dream, xx 3, and thus the king remains guiltless), the tables are radically turned. The very last verse reveals what has happened to the women of Gerar. They have become infertile, while Sarah is surely pregnant (now or tomorrow). That is the new form of individual life versus collective death[15]. Gen. xx thus fits organically in phase III and its position between the massive annihilation in chapter xix and individual birth is strategically chosen and a clarification. The tension that arises between Abraham and the ruler of Gerar is finally settled in xxi 22-34, as the leaders of the Philistines go to the blessed Abraham with appropriate respect and make a covenant with him. Because of its polar relation to xx, this literary unit belongs to phase III.

---

[15] For that reason too Gen. xx belongs in its place. It cannot be exchanged with the variant in xii 10-20 nor that in Gen. xxvi. A synchronic literary analysis of these texts is more adequate than a diachronic; see Klaus KOCH, *Was ist Formgeschichte?*, Neukirchen 1967, § 10, and the rightful disputation of it by Robert POLZIN in *Semeia* 3 (1975), "'The Ancestress of Israel in Danger' in Danger".

# "YHWH IS MY BANNER" – "A 'HAND' ON THE 'THRONE' of YH"

## *Exodus xvii 15b, 16a and their interpretation**

BY

C. HOUTMAN

*Amsterdam*

*Exodus xvii 14-16*

14 Then YHWH said to Moses: "Record this in writing as a memorial and impress it on Joshua that I will blot out all memory of Amalek from under heaven".
15 Moses built an altar and named it: "YHWH is my Banner!"
16 "Because", he said, "it is a 'hand' (= memorial) on 'the throne' of YH. The war of YHWH against Amalek continues to the remotest generations".

### 1. Introduction

The narrative account of Amalek's attack against Israel in Exod. xvii 8-16 can be subdivided into two main segments: vv. 8-13 and vv. 14-16. The vv. 8-13 describe the battle and in vv. 14-16 a word from YHWH is reported (vs. 14), along with Moses' response to it (vv. 15-16). In the second segment the interpretation of vs. 15b and vs. 16a has caused a lot of headaches. The purpose of this article is to acquaint the reader with various interpretations of these problematic verses and to offer an additional proposal for the solution of the cruces interpretum, followed by some comments about the compositional relationship of Exod. xvii 14-16 to xvii 8-13 in order to add additional support to the suggested proposal[1]. At this point I would like to present a few introductory remarks about the significance of the construction of the altar in Exod. xvii 15.

Attention is called, first of all, to the fact that Exod. xvii 15 reports Moses' construction of an altar but makes no mention of an offering of sacrifices (cf.,

---

* Besides well-known abbreviations, the following abbreviations are used in this article: FT = Fragmentary Targum(s) (edition M.L. Klein, Rome 1980); GMPT = Genizah Manuscript(s) of Palestinian Targum to the Pentateuch (edition M.L. Klein, Cincinnati 1986); TNf = Targum Neofiti 1 (edition A. Díez Macho, Matriti 1968ff.); TO = Targum Onqelos (edition A. Sperber, Leiden 1959); TPsJ = Targum Pseudo-Jonathan (edition M. Ginsburger, Berlin 1903).

[1] For a detailed exegesis of Exod. xvii 8-16 see volume II of my commentary on Exodus, *Commentaar op het Oude Testament*, Kampen 1989.

e.g., Gen. viii 20; xxii 9; Jos. viii 30ff.; Judg. vi 20ff.; II Sam. xxiv 21, 25; I Kings ix 25). This omission coincides with several passages in the book of Genesis, describing the erection of an altar by the patriarchs: Gen. xii 8; xxvi 25 (the construction of the altar is followed by a calling upon the name of YHWH) and xii 7; xiii 18; xxxv 7 (construction of the altar without calling upon the name of YHWH). Moreover, the erection of the altar in Exod. xvii 15 was occasioned by a revelation from YHWH (vs. 14), as was the case in Gen. xii 7 and xxxv 7 (cf. xxxv 1, 3). Furthermore, the altar of Exod. xvii 15 received a name. Such was also the case in Gen. xxii 9; xxxv 7 and Judg. vi 24 (cf. Gen. xxxiii 20). Through this name the altar continues to evoke the memory of the event that took place at its particular location. Finally, the place at which an altar was built frequently becomes a cultic site. However, in Exod. xvii 15 and in some other places the cult as such plays no role. In Exod. xvii 15 there is no reference to the bringing of sacrifices within the context of a victory celebration (cf. I Sam. xiv 31-35) nor of a spiritual worship (Gen. xii 8, etc.). In Exod. xvii 15 the naming of the altar stands at the centre of attention. Here the altar was not built for the offering of sacrifices (cf. Jos. xxii 23, 26, 29); rather, the altar is to function as a memorial (cf. Jos. xxii 27f.).

## 2. Exodus xvii 15b and xvii 16a in the versions

In view of the translation of Exod. xvii 15b, 16a in the older versions, it is evident that the interpretation of these verses was already problematic in ancient times. Since the translations of the versions are witnesses to earlier interpretations, I shall survey their respective translations of Exod. xvii 15b, 16a and add a few marginal notes.

2.1. *The translation of Exod. xvii 15b:* a review of the versions reveals, first of all, that the translators experienced difficulty in rendering the term *nissî* in the name which Moses gave to the altar in Exod. xvii 15b.

In the Septuagint the nominal clause *yhwh nissî* was translated as Κύριος καταφυγή μου, "The Lord is my Refuge". Apparently, *nissî* was derived from *nûs*, "to flee". In this connection attention is also called to the translations of two Greek-writing Jewish authors, namely, Philo Alexandrinus (*Vita Mosis* I, 219) and Flavius Josephus (*Antiquitates Judaicae* III, 60). According to Josephus, Moses called God "Victor" (νικαῖον ὀνομάσας τὸν θεόν) and, according to Philo, he called the altar "Refuge of/with God" (θεοῦ καταφυγήν). Both authors report that Moses worshipped at the altar. Philo reports that Moses offered sacrifices "with prayers of thanksgiving ... on the altar in celebration of victory". Josephus only mentions "sacrifices of thanksgiving offered by Moses". Prayer and/or worship is also attributed to Moses in the translation of Exod. xvii 15b in several targums.

TO: *wplḥ 'lwhy qdm ywy d'bd lyh nsyn*, "and he worshipped before YHWH, who performed miracles for him".

TNf: *wṣly tmn bšm mymry dyyy d'bd lyh nysyn*, "and he prayed there in the name of the Word of YHWH, who performed miracles for him".

GMPT MS AA: *wplḥ wṣly tmn bšm mymrh dy'y dy 'bd lh nsyn*, "and he worshipped and prayed there in the name of the Word of YHWH, who performed miracles for him" (cf. FT MS J.T.S. 605).

The translation of the targums cited above can be explained as follows: *wayyiqrā' šᵉmô yhwh* of Exod. xvii 15b was interpreted as *wayyiqrā' bᵉšem yhwh* (Gen. xii 8; xiii 4; xxi 33; xxvi 25). This formulaic phrase from Genesis is translated in TO as *wṣly bšm' dywy*, "and he prayed in the name of YHWH" (cf. TPsJ; with the exception of Gen. xxi 33). In TNf on Gen. xii 8 the same "double translation"[2] occurs as in GMPT MS AA on Exod. xvii 15b: *wplḥ wṣly tmn bšm mmryh dyyy*, "and he worshipped and prayed there in the name of the Word of YHWH" (cf. TNf on Gen. xxi 33 and xiii 4 in the margin; in Gen. xiii 4 and xxvi 25 only *wṣly* is used but in Gen. xxvi 25 the reading *wplḥ* is mentioned in the margin). In the above mentioned targums the Hebrew noun *nes* is understood to denote a "miracle". However, in biblical Hebrew this term does not have this meaning (cf. paragraph 4.1. below).

TPsJ on Exod. xvii 15b also interprets the term *nes* as "miracle". It reads as follows: *wyqr' šmyh mymr' dh' dyn nys' dyly dnys' d'bd 'tr bgyny hw'*, which can be translated as: "and he called the name of it 'The Word of YHWH was my miracle here', – 'for the miracle which He performed on this place was on my behalf'". However, this translation is somewhat problematic. R. LE DÉAUT defends a translation with "The Word of YHWH" as subject: "et la Parole de Yahvé le nomma 'Ce prodige (est) mien' – 'car le prodige qu'a opéré le Lieu a été (fait) à cause de moi'"[3].

In the Vulgate *yhwh nissî* was translated as: *Dominus exaltatio mea*, "The Lord is my elevation". In this translation *nissî* was derived from *nś'*.

2.2. *The translation of Exod. xvii 16a:* comparison shows that the versions differ in their translation of Exod. xvii 16a as to the starting point of the direct discourse and the reading and/or the meaning of the term *kes*.

The Septuagint translated Exod. xvii 16a as: ὅτι ἐν χειρὶ κρυφαίᾳ, "for with a secret hand (the Lord wages war against Amalek ...)". In this translation the introductory phrase *wayyo'mĕr* was not rendered and *ks yh* was apparently read as one word, *ksyh*, derived from *ksh*, "to cover"[4].

---

[2] Cf. B. BARRY LEVY, *Targum Neophyti 1. A Textual Study* I, New York – London 1986, pp. 52f.

[3] R. LE DÉAUT, *Targum du Pentateuque* II, Paris 1979, p. 145. In connection with this translation see the discussion on the question as to who is the subject of *wayyiqrā'*: Moses or YHWH, in *Mechilta* II, 159f. (edition J.Z. LAUTERBACH, Philadelphia 1931-35).

[4] For a contrary opinion see Z. FRANKEL, *Über den Einfluss der palästinischen Exegese auf*

In the Peshiṭta the direct discourse of Exod. xvii 16a is introduced by *h'* = Hebrew *hinneh*. Moreover, *ks yh* was read as one word and was translated as *kwrsj'*, "throne" (cf. the Samaritan Pentateuch, which reads *ks'* instead of *ks yh*). Apparently Exod. xvii 16a was interpreted as a solemn introduction to a divine oath: "Behold, as He has sworn ...", vs. 16b being the content of this oath.

This interpretation of Exod. xvii 16 can be readily explained in view of the fact that the hand plays an important role in oath-taking (cf. Exod. vi 8; Num. xiv 30; Deut. xxxii 40). In the swearing of a solemn oath the hand is lifted up to (*'ĕl*) heaven (Deut. xxxii 40; Dan. xii 7; cf. Rev. x 5). Heaven can denote the throne (*kisse'*) of YHWH (Isa. lxvi 1; Ps. xi 4; xciii 2; Job xxxvi 9; Acts vii 49)[5]. In the NT this particular nuance of heaven is also present in the context of oath-taking (Matth. v 34; xxiii 22). If, therefore, one takes into consideration the possibility that the occurrence of the term "heaven" at the end of Exod. xvii 14 could have contributed to an association of "throne" with "heaven" and the fact that in the later development of the Hebrew language *'al* was used in the sense of *'ĕl*[6], then the Peshiṭta's interpretation of *yd 'l-ks yh* in Exod. xvii 16a as a solemn gesture of God putting himself under oath is not at all surprising.

In the targums Exod. xvii 16a is also interpreted as the introduction to a solemn oath asseverating the complete annihilation of Amalek (vs. 16b)[7]. Similarly, the words *ks yh* are understood as denoting the throne of YHWH. TO (*'l kwrsy yqr'*) and TPsJ (*bkwrsy yqryh*) refer to an oath of YHWH "by the throne of His Glory". However, in other targums (TNf, FT MSS P and V, GMPT MSS AA and J) reference is made to an oath which has gone out "from beneath the throne of the Glory of the Lord of all the world" (see, for example, TNf: *mn tḥwt kwrsy 'yqry drbwn kl 'lm'*). With the exception of TPsJ, the Palestinian targums (TNf, FT MSS P and V, GMPT MSS AA and J) interpret the divine oath of Exod. xvii 16b to contain a picture of the future: the first Israelite monarch, Saul, will join battle with Amalek (I Sam. xv) and Mordecai and Esther will eliminate the rest of Amalek. In FT MS V and GMPT MS J Saul is typified as the first king who is destined to sit "on the throne of the kingdom of Israel" (see, for example, FT MS V: *'l kwrsyhwn dmlkwt' dysr'*). In this interpretation of the content of the oath, therefore, the

---

*die alexandrinische Hermeneutik*, Leipzig 1831, pp. 88f. ("with the hand on the throne = invisible JHWH wages war"); A.R. Müller, "Ex 17,15f in der Septuaginta", *Biblische Notizen* 12 (1980), pp. 20-23.

[5] Cf. C. Houtman, *De hemel in het Oude Testament*, Franeker 1974, pp. 168, 227, 240.

[6] Cf. *KBL*[3], p. 781, s.v. 6.

[7] Cf. *Mech.* II, 160f.; Rashi (with an explanation of the abbreviations *kes* and *yh*: when Amalek shall have been exterminated, then shall the name and the throne be complete); Ibn Ezra; Nachmanides.

phrase *ks yh* served as a key element in the explanation of the relationship between the throne of YHWH and the throne of an earthly monarch[8]. This intimate relationship between the throne of YHWH and the throne of an earthly monarch was already true in the OT. Note I Chron. xxviii 5. According to this verse, Solomon is destined to sit "on the throne of the kingdom of YHWH over Israel" (*'al-kisse' malkût yhwh 'al-yiśrā'el*; cf. *'al-kisse' yhwh* in I Chron. xxix 23; and see II Chron. ix 9; xiii 8).

In the Vulgate the direct discourse in Exod. xvii 16a begins with *quia manus solii Domini*, "Because the hand of the throne of the Lord (and the war of the Lord against Amalek will be ...)". This translation understood the term *kes* as *kisse'*, "throne", and *yh* as a divine personal name. The term *yād*, "hand", must probably be interpreted to denote a powerful (divine) intervention.

## 3. Exodus xvii 15b and xvii 16a in modern exegesis

In modern exegesis the word *nissî* of Exod. xvii 15b is normally translated as "my banner". However, there exists no general consensus about the correct translation of the term *kes* in Exod. xvii 16a. In fact, frequently this term is considered to be inappropriate and, consequently, preference is often given to the reading *nes*. Given this disagreement, I shall first give a summary of the interpretations based on the Masoretic text and then of the interpretations based on the proposal to emend the Masoretic text to read *nes*.

3.1. *Interpretations based on the Masoretic text:* those who defend the reading of the Masoretic text in Exod. xvii 16a interpret the noun *kes* to mean "throne" and translate the noun-clause *yād 'al-kes yh* as: "The hand on the throne of the Lord". This interpretation of *kes* is the starting point for diverse explanations of the meaning of the text under discussion:

Israel must follow the example of Moses and wage the battle against Amalek with its hand lifted up in prayer to the celestial throne of YHWH (see, e.g., C.F. Keil; W.H. Gispen[9]); Moses swears a solemn oath with his hand raised to the celestial throne of YHWH (cf. Gen. xiv 22) (A. Dillmann[10]); Israel must take an oath with the hand on the throne of YHWH = the seat of Exod. xvii 12 = the altar[11] (G. Beer[12]); a hand (= Amalek) was against

[8] Cf. *bSanh.* 20b and see Nachmanides.

[9] C.F. Keil, *Genesis und Exodus*, Leipzig 1878; W.H. Gispen, *Het boek Exodus* II, Kampen 1951².

[10] A. Dillmann, *Exodus und Leviticus*, Leipzig 1880².

[11] Cf. H. Schmid, *Mose*, Berlin 1968, p. 63.

[12] G. Beer, *Exodus*, Tübingen 1939. The problem is, however, that in the OT the altar is never called "throne". By many exegetes the ark is considered to be a "throne". In fact, F.M.Th. Böhl, *Exodus*, Groningen – Den Haag 1928, is of the opinion that *kes*, "throne", refers (secondarily) to the ark. A similar position is held by K. Möhlenbrink, "Josua im Pentateuch", *ZAW*

the throne of YHWH (= Israel)[13]. The hand is also understood as the hand of God, the power, which God extends from his heavenly throne to protect his people and to destroy his enemies (Amalek)[14].

3.2. *Interpretations based on an emended text:* against the interpretation of *kes* as "throne" it is objected that it isolates Exod. xvii 16a from xvii 15b. On the basis of similar etiological passages (see, e.g., Exod. ii 10, 22) one would expect a play on words in Moses' naming of the altar[15]. For this reason, therefore, it has been proposed that the reading *kes* in Exod. xvii 16a MT should be emended to read *nes* and translated as: "The hand on the banner of YH!" This conjectural textual emendation has also occasioned disparate interpretations:

H. GRESSMANN argues for a connection between the *nes* of Exod. xvii 15b and the staff of Exod. xvii 9. On the basis of this identification he interprets the naming of the altar in Exod. xvii 15b-16 as follows: the altar represents "Jahve unter der Form des Stabes geweiht" (p. 157); YHWH is the God who is actively present in the staff; the staff stands by the altar and bears the serpent as its symbol; oaths were sworn by this staff and such is also the case with the oath taken in the battle against Amalek (cf. Exod. xvii 16b); YHWH assures the effectuation of such oaths[16]. Although others also identify the staff of Exod. xvii 9 and the banner of Exod. xvii 15b[17], this identification is problematic[18]. Moreover, it should be noted that H. GRESSMANN makes a rather artificial connection between the staff and the altar. While they do not adopt H. GRESSMANN's proposed identification, a number of commentators consider Exod. xvii 16a to be a summons to swear an oath of allegiance ("Fahneneid") (see, e.g., B. BAENTSCH[19]).

---

59 (1943), p. 57. Since *nes* (xvii 15b) can be compared with an altar, F. STOLZ (who also reads *nes* in Exod. xvii 16a instead of *kes*), *Jahwes und Israels Kriege*, Zürich 1972, p. 99, maintains that it is natural to think of "einen Kasten in der Art der Lade".

[13] See, e.g., H.S. REIMARUS, *Apologie oder Schutzschrift* etc. (edition Frankfurt am Main 1972, I, pp. 361f.); J.H. HERTZ, *The Pentateuch and Haftorahs*, London 1938; cf., e.g. J.G. MURPHY, *The Book of Exodus*, Edinburgh 1866; F. MICHAELI, *Le livre de l'Exode*, Neuchâtel 1974. This explanation has as an advantage over those cited before that *'al* is given a recognised meaning, but for the rest it is unconvincing.

[14] See the Nestorian Father Ishōdad of Merw (edition *CSCOS* 80, 81); cf. the marginal notes of the Dutch *Statenvertaling* of 1637.

[15] E. MEYER, *Die Israeliten und ihre Nachbarstämme*, Halle a.S. 1906, p. 63, n. 4, considers *nissî* to be a play on Massah (Kadesh); cf. F.M.Th. BÖHL, *op. cit.*. F.C. FENSHAM, *Exodus*, Nijkerk 1970, opts for a play of words with *nsh*, "to test" (cf. Exod. xvii 7); see already Ephraim (edition *CSCOS* 71, 72) and Ishōdad.

[16] H. GRESSMANN, *Mose und seine Zeit*, Göttingen 1913, pp. 157f., 354f.; *idem*, *Die Anfänge Israels*, Göttingen 1922², pp. 100ff.

[17] See, e.g., M. BUBER, *Moses*, Heidelberg 1952², p. 110; E. AUERBACH, *Moses*, Amsterdam 1953, p. 85; SCHMID, *op. cit.*, pp. 63f.

[18] See R. GRADWOHL, "Zum Verständnis von Ex. xvii 15f.", *VT* 12 (1962), pp. 491-494 (492).

[19] B. BAENTSCH, *Exodus-Leviticus*, Göttingen 1903.

M. NOTH[20] presupposes that the altar with the name "YHWH is my banner" was a rallying-point for warriors in the time that Southern Israel was embattled with the Amalekites and that Exod. xvii 16a represents the battle cry whereby the warriors were summoned to muster around the banner of God in order to march out to battle (cf. also G. TE STROETE; B.S. CHILDS[21]). As in the case of the explanation of B. BAENTSCH *et al.*, M. NOTH's interpretation is open to the objection that it only establishes a superficial relationship between Exod. xvii 15b and xvii 16a because in this explanation the term *nes* does not have the same meaning in Exod. xvii 15b and xvii 16a. Moreover, it is doubtful whether *'al* can denote "upon (the banner)"[22].

R. GRADWOHL maintains that Exod. xvii 16a refers to a votive hand on the standard of YHWH by the altar. This votive hand is a symbol of God's helping hand and a guarantee for continuation of the battle against Amalek[23].

A principle objection against all the proposed interpretations based on the reading *nes* in Exod. xvii 16a is that this reading is really no more than a conjecture, which lacks direct support from the text traditions and the ancient versions.

The foregoing discussion presented a conspectus of the disparate interpretations of the passage under discussion[24]. In this survey each one of the interpretations considered proved to be inadequate. Therefore, I shall now proceed to an exposition of my own proposed interpretation.

## 4. PROPOSAL FOR A NEW INTERPRETATION OF EXODUS XVII 15B AND XVII 16A

4.1. I would like to begin my exposition with a consideration of the term *nes*. It occurs twenty-one times in the OT (always in the singular) and is usually interpreted as: "banner", "ensign" or "pole"[25]. However, this interpretation is contested by B. COUROYER[26]. On the basis of Egyptian pictorial engravings he concludes that *nes* is not a portable ensign but a visible sign, a piece of material, a cloth (Ez. xxvii 7), which is hoisted (*nś'*) on a pole or mast so that it is visible from afar. As such, *nes* functions as a signal which marks a rallying point for people, points to danger and summons mobilization. It

[20] M. NOTH, *Das zweite Buch Mose Exodus*, Göttingen 1973⁵.

[21] G. TE STROETE, *Exodus*, Roermond – Maaseik 1966; B.S. CHILDS, *Exodus*, London 1974.

[22] Cf. A.B. EHRLICH, *Randglossen zur hebräischen Bibel* I, Leipzig 1908, p. 330.

[23] R. GRADWOHL, *VT* 12 (1962), pp. 493f. For the function and meaning of the hand as a symbol in the Ancient Near East see S. SCHROER, "Zur Deutung der Hand unter der Grabinschrift von Chirbet el Qôm", *UF* 15 (1983), pp. 191-199.

[24] Cf. also B. COUROYER, "Un Egyptianisme en Exode, XVII, 15-16: YHWH-nissi", *RB* 88 (1981), pp. 333-339; R. ALTHANN, "Unrecognized Poetic Fragments in Exodus", *JNSL* 11 (1983), pp. 9-27 (19ff.); E. ZENGER, *Israel am Sinai*, Altenberge 1985², pp. 77, 95ff.

[25] Cf. H.J. FABRY, *ThWAT* V, Sp. 468ff.

[26] B. COUROYER, "Le nēs Biblique: signal ou enseigne?", *RB* 91 (1984), pp. 5-29.

can also denote the pole or mast itself (Num. xxi 8f.; Isa. xxx 17; xxxiii 23).

In my opinion, this debated issue is not really crucial for the interpretation of Exod. xvii 15. Of significance for the exegesis of this verse is that the use of *nes* in the OT clearly indicates that with the name *nissî* Moses typifies YHWH as his personal point of orientation, as the one through whom he allows himself to be mobilised and on whose signal and command he comes into action (cf. Isa. v 26; xiii 2; xviii 3; xlix 22; Jer. iv 6, 21; li 27; Ps. lx 6). In this sense the use of a term which belongs to the vocabulary of military operations is most appropriate in a passage in which a battle stands at the very centre. In the mouth of Moses the name "YHWH is my banner" is a confession[27]. From the mouth of Moses one hears that his active role in the battle against Amalek (Exod. xvii 10-12) stood under the sign of YHWH's strategy (cf. I Sam. vii 12; Ps. xx 6, 8). In the altar Moses' confession is eternalised in stone. With its name the altar bears this confession throughout the ages. In this manner this confession retains its power and continues to summon new generations to orientate on God, as did Moses (i.e. to enter the battle against Amalek with their eyes stayed on Him).

4.2. In the light of the function and meaning of *nes* in Exod. xvii 15b it is also vitally important to note that this signal could have been placed on a mountain (Isa. xiii 2; xviii 3), a hill (Isa. xxx 17) or another elevated place (Jer. li 12). However, Exod. xvii 15 itself seems to imply that Moses erected the altar on the very place where he had stood/sat during the battle with Amalek, i.e. on the top of the hill (Exod. xvii 10-12). Consequently, as Moses dominated the vicinity from the top of this hill, so the altar also dominates this same area. It is visible from afar. As a result the altar itself is also a sign (cf. Num. xxvi 10), which retains the memory of that which happened at this location and directs the observer's attention to the consequences of this event for the future (Exod. xvii 14, 16). Through its name and its location on the top of the hill, therefore, the altar functions as a signal.

4.3. This important function of the altar also contains the key to unlocking the meaning of *yād* in Exod. xvii 16a: "hand" = "memorial" (cf. I Sam. xv 12; II Sam. xviii 18; Isa. lvi 5)[28]. Perhaps the use of the term *yād* in this verse was also intended to evoke associations with the important role of the hand(s) in the battle against Amalek (Exod. xvii 9, 11, 12).

4.4. The altar fulfills its function as memorial "on the throne of YH"[29]. As was suggested in the previous paragraphs, the altar/memorial was built

---

[27] By W.H. Brownlee, "The Ineffable Name of God", *BASOR* 226 (1977), pp. 39-46, the name is interpreted as: "He creates my standard".

[28] Cf. M. Delcor, "Two Special Meanings of the Word *yād* in Biblical Hebrew", *JSSt* 12 (1967), pp. 230-240.

[29] *kes*, the abbreviated form of *kisse'/kisseh* (I Kings x 19; Job xxvi 9) was chosen with regard to the pun with *nes*.

"on the top of the hill" (*'al-ro'š haggib'â*) (Exod. xvii 9). Therefore, it can justifiably be concluded that *'al-kes yh*, "on the throne of YH", corresponds with "on the top of the hill". For a clear understanding of this placename it must be recalled that "the throne of YHWH" and similar designations are used elsewhere with reference to Jerusalem/Zion or the temple located there (Jer. iii 17; xiv 21; xvii 12; Ez. xliii 7; cf. also Ps. xciii 2 and, for example, Isa. lx 13; Lam. ii 1)[30]. Consequently, "the throne of YH" designates the place where YHWH is present.

4.5. Applying this concept to the narrative as a whole, it may be said that during the battle against Amalek Moses was standing/sitting "on the throne of YH". Viewed in this manner, his powerful action as a "magician" also becomes comprehensible (Exod. xvii 10-12; cf. II Kings i 9 ?). As a result of the peculiar nature of the place where Moses was standing/sitting he had special powers at his disposal. By building the altar – evidently it is presupposed that he used the stone on which he sat – Moses marked this location as a sacred place (cf. Gen. xxviii 18ff.)[31].

All in all, the question arises whether the narrative account of the battle against Amalek (Exod. xvii 8-16) was not also associated with the Mountain of God (Exod. xvii 6; xviii 5), just as the narratives in its immediate context (i.e. Exod. xvii 1-7; xviii).

## 5. Compositional place and function of Exodus xvii 14-16

5.1. In the above exposition it has simply been assumed that Exod. xvii 8-16 can be interpreted as a unified literary whole. Moreover, the literary-critical issues inherent in this pericope were left aside, nor will they be dealt with at length in this summary[32]. However, my proposed interpretation of Exod. xvii 15b, 16a obliges me to devote some more attention to the *compositional relationship between Exod. xvii 14-16 and xvii 8-13*. In my judgement, Exod. xvii 14-16 occupies a special compositional and thematic position in relation to Exod. xvii 8-13. To sustain this opinion attention is called to two important differences between these two narrative segments.

First of all, it is noted that Moses (5 ×) and Amalek (5 ×) stand at the centre of attention in Exod. xvii 8-13. YHWH is not mentioned in this narrative section. In fact, there is not even a reference to a divine instruction to Moses in this part of the narrative. Instead, Moses is reported to have taken the initia-

[30] Cf. E. Lipiński, *La royauté de Yahwé*, Brussel 1968², pp. 117f.

[31] Cf. C. Houtman, "What Did Jacob See in His Dream at Bethel?", *VT* 27 (1977), pp. 337-351.

[32] For a detailed literary-critical analysis see H. Valentin, *Aaron*, Freiburg – Göttingen 1978, pp. 145ff.; Zenger, *op. cit.*, pp. 76ff.; cf. W. Fuss, *Die deuteronomistische Pentateuchredaktion in Exodus 3-17*, Berlin – New York 1972, pp. 352ff.

tive in Exod. xvii 9 and in vv. 11-12 all the attention is focused on him. As a result of his personal intervention as a "magician" the military threat of Amalek was repelled. Consequently, the whole scene (Exod. xvii 8-13) is dominated by the person of Moses. Moses' dominant role in Exod. xvii 8-13 explains why this narrative section had been classified as a heroic saga or legend[33]. However, it should not be overlooked that the mention of "the staff of God" (Exod. xvii 9) in the introduction colours the episode as a whole. Indeed, it already provides this episode with a significant pointer to "above". In the light of this important allusion it is evident that Moses was able to control the threatening emergency situation at hand because he had been endowed with "supernatural" powers. Therefore, Moses did not act as a hero but as a man of God[34].

Secondly, it should be observed that YHWH stands at the centre of attention in Exod. xvii 14-16. This is evident, first of all, from the fact that while the divine name YHWH did not occur at all in Exod. xvii 8-13, in Exod. xvii 14-16 it is employed repeatedly (YHWH tris, xvii 14, 15, 16; YH, xvii 16a; Moses and Amalek are mentioned twice each). Moreover, in Exod. xvii 14 YHWH takes the initiative and vv. 15-16 constitute Moses' response. In the light of these two distinctive differences between Exodus xvii 8-13 and xvii 14-16, it is obvious that xvii 14-16 occupies a particular, climactic position in the narrative as a whole.

5.2. In this special position *Exod. xvii 14-16 functions as the interpretation and actualisation of the incident narrated in Exod. xvii 8-13.*

The mighty hero Moses (cf. Exod. xvii 8-12) intones a lofty Te Deum, in which he emphatically declares that YHWH is his personal source of orientation and acknowledges the victory of Amalek to be the work of YHWH in the name which he assigns to the altar (Exod. xvii 15b). Through this name the (apparently) magical action of Exod. xvii 10-12 becomes a divinely directed event. This is underscored in the explanation of the name which Moses gives in Exod. xvii 16a. In this explanation Moses typifies the altar as a memorial (*yād*) "on the throne of YH", whereby he confesses that YHWH was present with him when he intervened as a "magician" in the battle against Amalek.

In my opinion, the verses 14 and 16b stand out in the concluding interpretative unit Exod. xvii 14-16. They serve to elevate the occurrence reported in Exod. xvii 8-13 above its historical time and location, as well as above its compositional place within the thematic frame of the Hexateuch: the fulfilment

---

[33] Cf. G.W. Coats, "Moses versus Amalek", *VT.S* 28 (1975), pp. 29-41 (37); Valentin, *op. cit.*, p. 171.

[34] Cf., e.g., A. Rofé, "Classes in the Prophetical Stories: Didactic Legenda and Parable", *VT.S* 26 (1974), pp. 143-164, and see Exod. xv 25; xvii 5f.

of the promises to the patriarchs. As a result, the pericope under consideration acquires eschatological overtones[35]. Indeed, through Exod. xvii 14, 16b the incident of Exod. xvii 8-13 becomes a paradigm of the manner in which YHWH combats and shall always combat the enemy, wherever that may be. In other words, the narrative about the victorious battle against Amalek, a story about a dire distress and its "magical" outcome, are pressed into the service of a theme of enduring significance, namely: YHWH is waging a permanent battle against Amalek, the cipher of the enemy from the beginning[36].

Finally, analysis shows that Exod. xvii 14-16 is constructed of elements from various literary sources: xvii 14, 16b and xvii 15, 16a (which are intimately connected with xvii 8-13). *While Exod. xvii 15, 16a contain the interpretation of Exod. xvii 8-13, xvii 14, 16b represent its actualisation*. Yet both strands are intrinsically intertwined. As a result of this interlacement, the altar of Exod. xvii 15 acquires a more comprehensive function. It not only retains the memory of the past (YHWH's assistance in the victorious battle against Amalek) but it also directs the reader's attention to the present and future, to YHWH's continuous conflict with "Amalek" (Exod. xvii 14, 16b). As an additional result, Moses' confession also acquires lasting significance. It becomes an exhortation to later generations to choose YHWH as their point of orientation when "Amalek" threatens, as did Moses.

---

[35] These overtones were detected, for example, by TPsJ on xvii 16, in which YHWH's extermination of Amalek is related to the generation of this world, to the generation of the Messiah and to the generation of the world to come; cf. Rashi on vs. 16 and Nachmanides on vs. 9. In patristic literature Amalek is the symbol of Satan and evil powers which are conquered by Jesus (the Greek translation of the name Joshua) and must be resisted by Christians; see, e.g., Origen, *Homiliae in Exodum* XI; Gregory of Nyssa, *Vita Mosis* II, 147ff.; cf. J. DANIÉLOU, *Sacramentum futuri*, Paris 1950, pp. 203ff.

[36] Cf. the qualification of Haman as an Agagite (Esther iii 1; cf. Num. xxiv 7; I Sam. xv 8 etc.). Exod. xvii 8-16 is read at the feast of Purim (*M Meg.* III 6). Moreover, like his patriarchal ancestor Esau (Gen. xxxvi 12), Amalek is also identified in Rabbinic literature with idolatry and its adherents, with everyone and everything that is inimical to YHWH, with Rome, etc.; see, e.g., *Mech.* II, 159; *Zohar Exodus* 65b, 66a, 67a; cf. the similar use of "Babel"; see S. UHLIG, "Die typologische Bedeutung des Begriffs Babylon", *AUSS* 12 (1974), pp. 112-125.

# THE LIFE SPANS OF THE PATRIARCHS

BY

C.J. LABUSCHAGNE

*Groningen*

The exceptionally high life spans allotted to the ante- and post-diluvian patriarchs (Gen. v and xi), have always been a baffling problem. No less problematic, however, is the length of life attributed to the three Israelite patriarchs, Abraham (175 years – Gen. xxv 7), Isaac (180 years – Gen. xxxv 28) and Jacob (147 years – Gen. xlvii 28). Everybody realises that such longevity is unnatural and improbable and that the amazing numbers, varying from 365 to 969 for the ante-diluvian and from 148 to 438 for the post-diluvian fathers, do not denote real life spans, but should be explained otherwise. There is general agreement among scholars that these numbers somehow functioned in a chronological system[1], of which there were at least three: that of the Masoretic tradition, the Samaritan Pentateuch and the Septuagint.

U. CASSUTO has shown that the life spans of the ante- and post-diluvian and of the Israelite patriarchs are either exact multiples of 5, or else multiples of 5 with the addition of 7. He maintains that the chronology of Genesis depends on the Sumerian and Babylonian Kings List and is founded on the dual principle of the sexagesimal system and the addition of 7[2]. C. WESTERMANN, on the other hand, believes that the number system in Gen. v and xi does not depend upon the Sumerian or the Babylonian Kings List, but was developed independently[3]. However, he seems to be unable to explain the numbers as such.

---

[1] See e.g. the article, "The Chronology of the O.T.", by S.J. DE VRIES in *IDB* 1, pp. 580-599, especially pp. 581f., who cites some literature. See also the literature cited in C. WESTERMANN, *Genesis 1-11* (BK I, 1), pp. 468 and 741 and further K. STENRING, *The Enclosed Garden*, Stockholm 1966; G. LARSSON, *The Secret System*, Leiden 1973; R.R. WILSON, *Genealogy and History in the Biblical World* (Yale Near Eastern Researches 7), New Haven 1977; G.F. HASEL, "The Genealogies of Gen. 5 and 11 and their Alleged Babylonian Background", *Andrews University Seminary Studies* 16 (1978), pp. 361-374; M.L. *Rosenzweig*, "Life History Data in the Bible, from Abraham to Joshua", *Judaism* 29/115 (1980), pp. 353-359, and cf. L. KÖHLER, *Der hebräische Mensch*, Darmstadt 1980, pp. 4, 28f. and see the commentaries on Genesis; the contribution by L. Löw, "Die Lebensalter in den jüdischen Literatur", *Beiträge zur jüdischen Altertumskunde* 2 (1875), cited by H.W. WOLFF, *Anthropologie des Alten Testaments*, München 1973, p. 338, was not available to me. WOLFF, by the way, does not discuss the extraordinary life spans.

[2] U. CASSUTO, *A Commentary on the Book of Genesis* I, Jerusalem 1961 (reprinted 1972), pp. 252ff., especially pp. 259f.; and II, Jerusalem 1964, pp. 250ff.

[3] C. WESTERMANN, *op. cit.*, pp. 473-480; 743f.

A major step forward towards their explanation is an important study by M. Barnouin[4], who brought Babylonian astronomy into the discussion. He studied the life spans of the ante-diluvian patriarchs in the light of astronomical mathematical calculations of the synodic periods of the planets. His work was carried further by C. Schedl, who points out that the knowledge of the "conjunction" of two planets ("serving" together) is attested in the Jewish tradition and must have been known to the writer of Genesis, because the life spans of three patriarchs in Gen. v correspond to the synodic periods of five planets (to the nearest decimal)[5]:

Jupiter + Saturn = 399 + 378 = 777 (Lamech)
Venus + Saturn = 584 + 378 = 962 (Jared)
Mercury + Mars = 116 + 780 = 896(5) (Mahalalel)[6]

The number of years attributed to Enoch, 365, corresponds to the days of a solar year. That accounts for the life spans of four ante-diluvian fathers. The highest life span, that of Methuselah, 969, is explained by Schedl as the sum of the periods of all the planets (10 years and 9 months = 129 months) added to seven times 120 (120 years is the maximum span of human life – cf. Gen. vi 3):

$129 + 840\ (7 \times 120) = 969.$

But there are still five ante-diluvian patriarchs' life spans to be accounted for, that of Adam (930), Seth (912), Enosh (905), Kenan (910) and Noah (950). Schedl's explanation of these numbers is ingenious, but not convincing, because it is too complicated. He adds up different numbers of days of the solar year (365 days, or 350 days of the cyclic solar year, or 312 working days) + different month-years (317 "light" month-years, or 350) + three types of "Schalttage" (235, 243 and 248) with the following result:

| | |
|---|---|
| Adam: | 365 + 317 + 248 = 930 |
| Seth: | 360 + 317 + 235 = 912 |
| Enosh: | 312 + 350 + 243 = 905 |
| Kenan: | 312 + 350 + 248 = 910. |

I would suggest that we apply Schedl's idea of the super maximum life span of $7 \times 120 = 840$ years to these numbers, as in the case of Methuselah, and

[4] M. Barnouin, "Recherches numériques sur la généalogie de Gen. V", *RB* 77 (1970), pp. 347-365.

[5] C. Schedl, "Der brennende Dornbusch: der Kosmos als Erscheinungsbild Gottes", in A. Resch (ed.), *Kosmopathie* (Imago Mundi VIII), Innsbruck 1981, pp. 677-711, especially pp. 697ff.

[6] For the astronomical data cf. Barnouin, *op. cit.*, p. 357, where further literature on the cuneiform material is mentioned.

subtract 840 years from these life spans. This results in the following normal lengths of life:

930 – 840 = 90 years for Adam
912 – 840 = 72 years for Seth
905 – 840 = 65 years for Enosh
910 – 840 = 70 years for Kenan
950 – 840 = 110 years for Noah

The origin of these normal life spans is unknown, but they seem to have been the starting-point of the chronological system. To these normal life spans were added the super maximum of 840 years in order to bridge the gap between Creation and the Flood.

What strikes us here is Noah's normal life span of 110 years, because it corresponds exactly to the length of life attributed to Joseph (Gen. l 22, 26). The "saviour" of mankind and the "saviour" of the tribes of Israel in Egypt had the same length of life. This may be no more than coincidence. Joshua, the hero of the conquest, also lived 110 years (Josh. xxiv 29). We will return to this life span further below.

For the significantly lower life spans of the post-diluvian Semite patriarchs, Shem (600), Arpachshad (438), Shelah (433), Eber (464), Peleg (239), Reu (239), Serug (230), Nahor (148) and Terah (205), there is still no satisfactory explanation. CASSUTO's principle of the sexagesimal system, augmented by the addition of seven or multiples of seven, which he applied to the ante-diluvian life spans, does not function here. It seems to me, for the time being, that there is no principle governing these numbers, except a chronological one: to fill the gap between the prehistoric ante-diluvian patriarchs and the "historic" figure of Abraham. It is significant that the Samaritan text and the Septuagint, though they differ from the Masoretic text with regard to the age at the successor's birth, are in agreement with *MT* with regard to the total life spans, except for Terah's age, 205 years, where the Samaritan text has 145 years[7].

Turning now to the life spans of the Israelite patriarchs, we see that the lengths of life attributed to Abraham, Isaac and Jacob are well below that of the majority of the post-diluvian fathers (Peleg with his relatively low life span of 148 years is an exception). However, their "ages", 175, 180 and 147, still exceed the maximum span of normal human life as ordained by God before the flood (Gen. vi 3): 120 years, an age specifically attributed to Moses (Deut. xxxiv 7). The age of Joseph, 110 years, can be regarded as normal, since it lies within what was considered to be a normal human life span. According to Egyptian standards an age of 110 years was the ideal human life

[7] See CASSUTO, *op. cit.*, pp. 258f.

span[8]. This may have been the reason for allotting to Joseph this life span. In Old Testament times the ideal age seems to have been 100 years (Is. lxv 20). The average length of life, according to the psalmist, is 70, or 80 years at most (Ps. xc 10).

How do we explain the improbable life spans of the three Israelite patriarchs? Commentators either ignore the difficulty and write about these ages as if they were normal, or they recognise the problem, but refrain from trying to solve it. CASSUTO is an exception. He explains the life spans as being in accordance with one of the principles in the early chronology: the use of multiples of 5, or multiples of 5 with the addition of 7. This is certainly true with regard to the four patriarchs and even in the case of Ishmael (137 years – Gen. xxv 17) and of Sarah (127 years – Gen. xxiii 1). However, in my opinion, this principle does not explain the life spans satisfactorily, neither does M.L. ROSENZWEIG's suggestion that a year is here really 6 months[9]. We must look for another explanation. It is important to note that for chronological purposes the life spans as such have no function. The different *stages* of their lives, however, serve this purpose: to calculate the years from Abraham's birth (through his entry into Canaan and Jacob's descent into Egypt) to the Exodus[10]. Nevertheless, the life spans must have some meaning, symbolical or other.

The principle of the absolute maximum human life span of 120 years, which SCHEDL applied to explain the life span of Methuselah, and which I used above to explain the "ages" of the ante-diluvian fathers Adam, Seth, Enosh, Kenan and Noah, can be applied to Abraham, Isaac and Jacob, but not to Joseph. Subtracting the maximum life span of 120 years from the "ages" of the three patriarchs, we get the following picture:

| | | |
|---|---|---|
| Abraham | $175 - 120 = 55$ | years |
| Isaac | $180 - 120 = 60$ | years |
| Jacob | $147 - 120 = 27$ | years |

These numbers can of course be regarded as real life spans, but they do not seem to explain anything and must be discarded. They do not appear to have any symbolic meaning either. This may be the case with regard to Sarah's life span: $127 = 120 + 7$, the maximum life span increased by 7, the number of fullness[11]. Ishmael's life span can be explained in the same way: $137 = 120 + 17$ – for the symbolic meaning of 17 see below.

---

[8] See J. VERGOTE, *Joseph en Égypte*, Louvain 1959, pp. 200f. and Th.N. GASTER, *Myth, Legend and Custom in the Old Testament*, New York 1969, pp. 222 and 380, note 1.

[9] M.L. ROSENZWEIG, *op. cit.* (see note 1).

[10] See table 2 in *IDB* 1, p. 582.

[11] CASSUTO, *op. cit.* I, p. 59, explains 127 as a round number (120) + an even greater number (7) and points out that the number of provinces in the Persian empire is given as 120 in the book of Daniel (vi 2), but increased by 7 ($120 + 7 = 127$) in the book of Esther (i 1; viii 9; ix 30).

New light has been shed on the riddle of the life spans of Abraham, Isaac and Jacob by J. MEYSING[12], who refers to a certain SCHILDENBERGER for his observation that the numbers 175, 180 and 147 appear to have been fashioned in accordance with a distinct pattern. This discovery was brought to the notice of the scholarly world by S. GEVIRTZ[13]. The pattern is the succession of multiples of the squares of the numbers 5, 6 and 7. These numbers, in an *ascending* sequence, are multiplied by the *descending* sequence of the uneven numbers 7, 5 and 3, which results in the following arrangement of the numbers, constituting a distinct pattern:

| | |
|---|---|
| Abraham | $175 = 7 \times 5 \times 5$ |
| Isaac | $180 = 5 \times 6 \times 6$ |
| Jacob | $147 = 3 \times 7 \times 7$ |

The range of the uneven, multiplying numbers *starts* with 7, while the range of the squared numbers *ends* with 7. This particular arrangement of the factors of the three life spans cannot be mere coincidence. It must be a matter of deliberate calculation. Until now the origin of this pattern has not yet been discovered. Since I am convinced that there is more to it than simply a play of wits, I offer the following explanation. Assuming that the numbers 175, 180 and 147 are not the *starting point* of the graded arrangement of the factors, but their *result*, we have to answer the question as to the origin of these factors. The answer to our question occurred to me, when I realised that the sum of all three sets of factors always amounts to the same number, *17*:

| | |
|---|---|
| Abraham | $175 = 7 \times 5 \times 5$: $7 + 5 + 5 = 17$ |
| Isaac | $180 = 5 \times 6 \times 6$: $5 + 6 + 6 = 17$ |
| Jacob | $147 = 3 \times 7 \times 7$: $3 + 7 + 7 = 17$ |

It is quite evident that the starting-point of the arrangement is the number *17*. The most obvious arithmetic analysis of *17* is $7 + 10$. The most logical division of 10 is $5 + 5$. In order to compute the symbolic age of Abraham the author used the most logical and obvious division of *17* $(7 + 5 + 5)$ as factors: $7 \times 5 \times 5 = 175$. Following this pattern, and in order to bring about a hierar-

[12] J. MEYSING, "The Biblical Chronologies of the Patriarchs", *Christian News from Israel* 14 (1963), p. 26.

[13] Stanley GEVIRTZ, "The Life Spans of Joseph and Enoch and the Parallelism *šib'ātayim – šib'īm – w$^e$šib'āh*", *JBL* 96 (1977), pp. 570-571. I do not agree with his suggestion that Enoch's life span should be analysed as $365 = 10^2 + 11^2 + 12^2$, neither do I accept his analysis of Adam's years as $930 = 30^2 + 30$, since both numbers can be explained in another, more plausible way. I also think GEVIRTZ is wrong when he states that "numbers may have been made to serve as the groundwork, on occasion, for nothing more meaningful than a play of wits ... rather than signifying anything more profound or mysterious". It might be observed that C. WESTERMANN does refer to GEVIRTZ's article in the bibliography (BK I, 3, p. 182) but refrains from discussing its contents.

chy, *17* is divided into $5+6+6$ (the *lower* number, 5, signifies the hierarchy) for the life span of Isaac: $5\times6\times6=180$. Following the same procedure, the factors for the computation of the age of Jacob are $3+7+7$, resulting in $3\times7\times7=147$.

With regard to the life span of 110 years attributed to Joseph, GEVIRTZ has remarked that 110 is the sum of this particular sequence of consecutive square numbers: $5^2+6^2+7^2=25+36+49=110$. He wrote that this "may be no more than coincidence"[14]. However, J.G. WILLIAMS, reacting to GEVIRTZ's remarks, argues convincingly that there is more to this than mere coincidence[15]. Adducing ample evidence to show that Joseph symbolically brings the patriarchal narratives of Genesis to completion and "combines and embodies many of the features of the portrayals of the preceding patriarchs and matriarchs", he gives Joseph, with his life span of 110 years, his rightful place in the hierarchical sequence and arranges the pattern of the consecutive square numbers as follows:

| | |
|---|---|
| Abraham | $175=7\times5^2$ |
| Isaac | $180=5\times6^2$ |
| Jacob | $147=3\times7^2$ |
| Joseph | $110=1\times5^2+6^2+7^2$ |

Joseph is "the *successor* in the pattern (7 – 5 – 3 – 1) and the *sum* of his predecessors ($5^2+6^2+7^2$)". This seems to me the correct explanation of the life span of Joseph. That a life span of 110 is also the ideal length of life according to Egyptian standards may be nothing more than a happy coincidence[16]. It

[14] S. GEVIRTZ, *op. cit.*, p. 571.

[15] James G. WILLIAMS, "Number Symbolism and Joseph as Symbol of Completion", *JBL* 98 (1979), pp. 86f. I might remark in passing that C. WESTERMANN also refers to this article without discussing the contents (see BK I, 3, p. 234).

[16] The same goes for the fact that $1+17+17+17=52=2\times26$ – see my contribution "The Literary and Theological Function of Divine Speech in the Pentateuch", *Congress Volume: Salamanca 1983* (SVT 36), Leiden 1985, pp. 154-173, cf. p. 171. However, this does not detract anything from my further observation that the numerical values of the extraordinary names Isaac, Jacob and Joseph are multiples of the symbolically very important number *26*! – see my article, pp. 171f. This aspect is a subject for further study in which the results of the work of O. GOLDBERG, *Die fünf Bücher Mosis, ein Zahlengebäude*, Berlin 1908, should be taken into serious consideration. Is it mere coincidence that the sum of the numerical values of the names of the ten patriarchs before Abraham, i.e. from Noah to Terah, is a multiple of *17* ($58+340+605+338+272+113+276+509+264+608=3383=199\times17$)? This was brought to my notice by Mr. E.J.C. Tigchelaar, my former assistant. Is it nothing more than coincidence that the numerical value of the name *Sarai* (the only matriarch of which the life span is mentioned) is a multiple of *17* ($510=30\times17$)? Is it mere coincidence that the sum of the life spans of Abraham and Sarah, Isaac and Jacob is a multiple of *17* ($175+127+180+147=629=37\times17$)? That the sum of the life spans of the four patriarchs (612) is a multiple of *17* ($36\times17$), however, appears to be a coincidence, since there is another principle operating here, as we have seen. Is it mere coincidence that Joseph was *17* years old when his story begins (Gen. xxxvii 2) and that *17* words are used to tell us (Gen. xlvii 28) that Jacob stayed in Egypt *17* years and is it coincidence that 68 ($4\times17$) words occur in the section about Abraham's death (Gen. xxv 7-11)?

is impossible to say whether Noah's "normal" life span of 110 years and Joshua's 110 years (see above) have been fashioned on the basis of Joseph's age.

If my explanation, that these four life spans all derive from the number *17*, is correct, there still remains the question as to the reason why this particular number was chosen as the starting-point for the computation of the life spans of the Israelite patriarchs. The best supposition, in my opinion, seems to be that it was selected because of its symbolic meaning. As I have explained elsewhere[17], the number 17 represents the numerical value of the name YHWH and at the same time that of *kābōd*, "glory". The symbolic meaning of 17 is most probably that it signifies YHWH's presence. If so, then the intention of the author of Genesis in choosing this number could have been to express YHWH's presence in the lives of the four Israelite patriarchs.

---

[17] See my article referred to in note 16, pp. 157f. and cf. also C.J. LABUSCHAGNE, *Deuteronomium* IA (POT), Nijkerk 1987, pp. 39f.

# THE ARK NARRATIVE RECONSIDERED[1]

BY

K.A.D. SMELIK

*Utrecht*

Research on the Ark Narrative (hereafter: AN)[2] in the book of Samuel was until recently dominated by the ideas of ROST as found in his study from 1926: *Die Überlieferung von der Thronnachfolge Davids*[3]. According to ROST, the editor of the book of Samuel inserted a narrative from the tenth century B.C.E. ROST called this account "die Ladeerzählung". It was written by a priest for the benefit of visitors to the Ark Sanctuary in Jerusalem who wanted to know how the Ark had arrived in this spot[4].

ROST's thesis was accepted by many scholars[5] – though with modifications. I do not intend to give a comprehensive survey of scholarly opinion on AN, but will mention some recent studies. In 1971, FOHRER published an ar-

---

[1] This article is a re-worked and updated version of a lecture which I held at the 1985 International Meeting of the Society of Biblical Literature at Amsterdam. I am grateful to Wendie Shaffer for editing the English.

[2] A survey of the different opinions from B. STADE until G. FOHRER is given by F. SCHICKLBERGER, *Die Ladeerzählungen des ersten Samuel-Buches*, Würzburg 1973, pp. 17-25. Cf. also H.J. STOEBE, *Das erste Buch Samuels* (KAT), Gütersloh 1973, pp. 127f.

[3] Reprinted in L. ROST, *Das kleine Credo und andere Studien zum Alten Testament*, Heidelberg 1965, pp. 119-253. AN is discussed on pp. 122-159. Cf. also SCHICKLBERGER, *op. cit.*, p. 25: "Die größte Wirkung auf die vergangenen Jahrzehnte hat zweifelsohne die Arbeit von L. Rost ausgeübt".

[4] Cf. ROST, *op. cit.*, p. 151: "Die Erzählung diente dem Zweck, den Besuchern des Heiligtums, besonders wohl den Festpilgern, die Bedeutung der Lade darzulegen, was am besten geschehen konnte durch die Erzählung ihrer wunderbaren Schicksale. [...] Vielleicht war auch das seltsame Kästchen mit den fünf goldenen Mäusen noch vorhanden in der Schatzkamer des Heiligtums, die wohl gegen einen entsprechenden Obolos besichtigt werden konnte".

[5] Cf. P.K. MCCARTER, Jr., *1 Samuel: A New Translation with Introduction, Notes & Commentary* (The Anchor Bible), Garden City 1980, p. 23: "This hypothesis has been among the most durable of modern scholarship", and H. TIMM, "Die Ladeerzählung (1 Sam. 4-6; 2 Sam. 6) und das Kerygma des deuteronomistischen Geschichtswerk", *EvTh* 26 (1966), pp. 509-526, p. 517, n. 17: "Der Nachweis dafür [for an independent AN; KS] hat Leonhard Rost erbracht". It is remarkable that TIMM, who elaborates upon the theological interpretation of AN in the Exilic period, does not show any doubt regarding the validity of ROST's thesis. More doubt is noticeable in STOEBE, *op. cit.*, p. 87, R.A. CARLSON, *David the Chosen King: A Traditio-Historical Approach to the Second Book of Samuel*, Uppsala 1964, p. 61, especially n. 5 ("ROST's hypothesis is completely anachronistic"), and R.P. GORDON, *1 & 2 Samuel: A Commentary*, Exeter 1986, pp. 24-26 and more strongly p. 92.

ticle[6] in which he confined the oldest version of AN to a few verses in I Samuel iv, v and II Samuel vi[7]. He distinguishes five earlier stages in the development of the story before the present text. His main argument for this literary surgery lies in the variety of terms by which the Ark is designated in these chapters of Samuel[8].

A detailed analysis of I Samuel iv-vi was published by SCHICKLBERGER in 1973[9]. According to him, an eleventh-century B.C.E. narrative (which he called the "Katastrophenerzählung") was expanded to a "Ladeerzählung", but only after the fall of Samaria in 722 B.C.E. This version was later inserted, with some modifications, into the Deuteronomistic History.

Although SCHICKLBERGER argues that ROST's thesis "ist nicht mehr aufrecht zu halten"[10], CAMPBELL nevertheless basically follows ROST's analysis in his 1975 dissertation[11]. He offers, however, a different explanation for the purpose of the story. It is not a *hieros logos* destined for curious pilgrims, rather it marks the end of the pre-Davidic epoch in Israel's history as YHWH's doing and it indicates that YHWH looks favourably upon the new political situation, to wit the Davidic dynasty in Jerusalem[12].

In agreement with SMEND's thesis concerning a triple Deuteronomistic redaction, VEIJOLA[13] ascribes the insertion of AN into the Deuteronomistic History to DtrG. DtrG added (according to VEIJOLA) in I Samuel iv all passages relating to Eli's sons, to wit the verses 4b, 11b, 17bα, 19aγ, 21b-22a and in II Samuel vi verse 21aβ. He was also responsible for the combination of I Samuel i-iii with iv-vi and the passages in ch. ii which connect this narrative with AN[14].

---

[6] G. FOHRER, "Die alttestamentliche Ladeerzählung", *JNWSL* 1 (1971), pp. 23-31.

[7] These are: I Sam. iv 1b-4a, 10-11a; v 1-2, 10* and II Sam. vi 1-2, 12.

[8] "Am ehesten wird den verschiedenen Bezeichnungen die Annahme gerecht, daß in der Ladeerzählung mehrere Erzählungsschichten vorliegen, die verschiedene Bezeichnungen verwendet haben und verschiedenen geschichtlichen Situationen entstammen" (FOHRER, *op. cit.*, p. 25). According to FOHRER, his approach is above all supported by the fact that the Ark is renamed in II Sam. vi 2. Actually, it is not, at least in the Masoretic text: FOHRER's interpretation is based on an emendation of the first *šem* ("name") in *šām* ("there"). It is interesting to note that FOHRER's pupil J. MAIER, *Das altisraelitische Ladeheiligtum* (BZAW 93), Berlin 1965, pp. 45-50 had already proposed in 1965 that the oldest version of AN could be recognised by the designation "the Ark of God", while "the Ark of YHWH" would be characteristic of the later "Lade-Erzähler".

[9] See note 2. A detailed criticism of SCHICKLBERGER's view is given by P.D. MILLER, Jr. and J.J.M. ROBERTS, *The Hand of the Lord: A Reassessment of the "Ark Narrative" of 1 Samuel*, Baltimore – London 1977, pp. 2-6.

[10] SCHICKLBERGER, *op. cit.*, p. 235.

[11] A. CAMPBELL, *The Ark Narrative (1 Sam 4-6; 2 Sam 6): A Form-Critical and Traditio-Historical Study*, Missoula 1975. A detailed criticism of CAMPBELL's view is given by MILLER and ROBERTS, *op. cit.*, pp. 7-9.

[12] Cf. CAMPBELL, *op. cit.*, p. 202.

[13] T. VEIJOLA, *Die ewige Dynastie: David und die Entstehung seiner Dynastie nach der deuteronomistischen Darstellung*, Helsinki 1975.

[14] Cf. *ibid.*, pp. 101f.

All these scholars agree on one point: the extant text of Samuel is the work of an editor who used older sources or traditions. They believe it is possible to reconstruct these sources and traditions by removing parts of the extant text. It is remarkable, however, that their literary-critical analyses produce dissimilar results. This raises the question as to whether it is useful to apply such an approach.

A different approach is found in the 1977 publication by MILLER and ROBERTS[15]. They do not try to divide the extant text into various literary strata and moreover show a keen eye for the structure and theological message of the narrative as a whole. They do not agree with ROST and others that the beginning of AN is to be found in I Samuel iv 1. They assume that some verses of I Samuel ii were also part of the narrative which they date as eleventh-century B.C.E.[16]. They also propose another correction to ROST's thesis: in their view AN ends with I Samuel vii 1.

In 1980, I published an article in Dutch called "De Ark in het Filistijnse land" (The Ark in the Land of the Philistines) and in 1983 another called "De intocht van de Ark in Jeruzalem" (The Entry of the Ark into Jerusalem)[17]. In these publications I investigated the historicity of I Samuel iv-vi[18] and II Samuel vi and their literary function in the context of the entire book of Samuel. I dated the narratives in the exilic period and suggested that the author[19] had a theological interest more than a historical.

Similar conclusions can be found in VAN SETERS' book *In Search of History* (1983)[20]. He argues that I Samuel i-vii "is the work of Dtr combining two themes, the story of Samuel and the Ark Narrative. They were never independent documents, and it is scarcely possible [...] to recover earlier stages in the tradition of these themes, if they ever existed"[21].

In the present article seven arguments are given in order to show that it is highly improbable that a separate self-contained AN dating from an early period in Israelite history ever existed. Subsequently, the literary purpose of the stories about the Ark in I Samuel iv-vi and II Samuel vi will be clarified in the context of the book of Samuel.

---

[15] See above note 9. Their study has been severely criticised by J.T. WILLIS in his article "Samuel Versus Eli: 1 Sam. 1-7", *ThZ* 35 (1979), pp. 201-212.

[16] Also P.R. DAVIES, "The History of the Ark in the Books of Samuel", *JNWSL* 5 (1977), pp. 9-18, especially p. 11, opposes the view that ch. 4 is the beginning of AN.

[17] Published in *Amsterdamse cahiers voor exegese en Bijbelse theologie* (= *ACEBT*) 1 (1980), pp. 42-50 and 4 (1983), pp. 26-36.

[18] When in this article the designation "I Samuel iv-vi" is used, I Samuel vii 1 and 2 are included (unless otherwise stated).

[19] In this article the singular "author" is used for convenience sake. In my opinion, the Book of Samuel was written by a group of authors.

[20] J. VAN SETERS, *In Search of History: Historiography in the Ancient World and the Origins of Biblical History*, New Haven – London 1983.

[21] *Ibid.*, p. 353.

## The (non-)existence of a separate ark narrative

I propose seven arguments to account for why a separate self-contained AN never existed:

1. AN contains many historical improbabilities as was noted by Kosters in 1893[22]. This precludes the possibility that the author of AN was a contemporary who wanted to record events of which he was an eye-witness.

2. AN is "a thorough-going theological narrative"[23]. Only by cutting out a considerable part of the story can we reconstruct an account which is no more than the record of an unfortunate incident in Israel's early history. The reconstruction of AN by Fohrer is a clear example of this approach which is based on circular reasoning: passages which reflect a theological interest are removed from the extant text: the truncated text is then presented as a very early narrative in which the original author – unlike the editor – was clearly not interested in theological problems[24].

3. The *Sitz im Leben* of a separate AN is rather unclear. If it is a document originating from the Ark Sanctuary in Jerusalem, important parts of the account are missing. It is not explained in the text when the Ark was built, when the battle at Aphek was fought, nor what happened to the Ark in the period between its arrival in Kirjath-jearim and its departure from Baalath-judah during the reign of David. The beginning of the account is missing and the main characters of the narrative are not introduced to the reader. We may try to solve this problem by removing all passages featuring Eli, his sons[25] or Michal[26]. This seems rather arbitrary. However, if there were no separate AN and these chapters from the beginning formed an integral part of a comprehensive story about Eli, Samuel, Saul and David, then there would be no missing passages. Nor would there be any need for the biblical authors to introduce Eli, his sons, David or Michal in these chapters, since they had already been introduced into the narrative.

4. It is significant that there is no agreement among biblical scholars about the beginning and end of AN. According to Rost, it begins with I Samuel iv

---

[22] W.H. Kosters, "De verhalen over de ark in Samuel", *ThT* 1893, pp. 361-378. See also Davies, *op. cit.*, p. 9: "highly improbable in certain aspects" (cf. *ibid.*, p. 16).

[23] See Miller and Roberts, *op. cit.*, p. 69.

[24] Thus I Sam. vi 5-9 is considered to be an insertion by Dtr because these verses clarify the theological message of the story; cf. Timm, *op. cit.*, p. 524, especially n. 33.

[25] See, e.g., H.W. Hertzberg, *Die Samuelbücher übersetzt und erklärt* (ATD), Göttingen 1968, p. 34; Fohrer, *op. cit.*, p. 26 and Veijola, *op. cit.*, pp. 101f. Davies (*op. cit.*, pp. 11-14), however, gives an elaborate argumentation as to why the centre of interest in the original version of ch. iv (at least in his reconstruction) lies with Eli and his family. All references to the loss of the Ark are in his view editorial expansion.

[26] This suggestion made by Rost, *op. cit.*, pp. 150, 212-215, was accepted by many scholars; see the survey by D.M. Gunn, *King David: Genre and Interpretation*, Sheffield 1982², p. 73. Gunn himself considers II Sam. vi to be a combination of AN and a separate Michal-story.

1 and it ends with II Samuel vi 19. Some scholars[27], however, disagree with Rost by excluding II Samuel vi completely from AN, whereas Miller and Roberts have argued (as noted before) that certain verses from 1 Samuel ii were also part of AN[28]. If we assumed there was never an independent AN, this problem would also be solved. The same applies to the complicated question of the boundary between AN and the so-called *Succession Narrative*[29].

5. There is no reason why we should assume that I Samuel iv-vi and II Samuel vi were based on earlier sources or traditions. They do not contain any specific, historical information which a later author could not have found in a chronicle relating to the early history of Israel or which could not have been gathered or invented by himself. The practice of carrying off images of gods as spoils of war[30] which is an important motive in AN, is not confined to the eleventh century B.C.E.; it is attested as early as the Old Babylonian period, and it continued into the Persian period. The most important example of this mentioned in the Hebrew Bible is the looting of the Jerusalem Temple in the sixth century B.C.E.[31].

Moreover, there are no conspicuous shifts, gaps or illogical contradictions in the story. The variety of names designating the Ark could be the result of the author's literary technique[32] rather than a combination of earlier material, especially as Fohrer is unable to offer a clear-cut division of the text into various sources, each one using a different name for the Ark[33]. In the third place, when we do not remove such important characters as Eli and his sons in I

[27] Cf., e.g., Schicklberger, *op. cit.*, pp. 129-149 and Miller and Roberts, *op. cit.*, pp. 22-26. See also McCarter, *op. cit.*, pp. 24f.

[28] Cf. also McCarter, *op. cit.*, pp. 24f. Van Seters, *op. cit.*, pp. 348f., gives, however, an argument as to why the suggestion of Miller and Roberts does not entirely solve this problem. Willis, *op. cit.*, shows that one cannot separate passages concerning Eli and his sons from those concerning Samuel: "the lives of Eli and Samuel are inseparably intertwined" (*ibid.*, p. 204).

[29] See the critical remarks by Van Seters, *op. cit.*, p. 280.

[30] Comparative materials are assembled by Miller and Roberts, *op. cit.*, pp. 9-17.

[31] For this reason I cannot accept the argument by Miller and Roberts, *op. cit.*, pp. 73-75 (accepted by McCarter, *op. cit.*, p. 25) that AN must have been written before David's defeat of the Philistines reported in II Sam. v 17-25, because the theological problem about the Philistine victory described in the narrative was only a burning issue in that period. If AN is a retrojection of sixth-century issues into the eleventh (as I hope to prove at the end of this article), this argument is no longer compelling.

[32] Cf. the treatment of these chapters in L.M. Eslinger, *Kingship of God in Crisis*, Decatur 1985, pp. 161-227.

[33] He speaks about "ein verhältnismässig klares Bild" (*op. cit.*, p. 26), but he has to emendate "the Ark of the Covenant of YHWH" and "the Ark of the Covenant of YHWH of Hosts which dwells between the cherubims" into "the Ark of [our] God" in I Sam. iv 3 and 4 (vs. 5 is secondary in his opinion) and to divide original from secondary designations of the Ark as "the Ark of God". "The Ark of God" is original in I Sam. iv 3 (emendation), 4a (emendation), 11a, v 1, 10; II Sam. vi 2, 12, but secondary in I Sam. iv 4b ("The Ark of the Covenant of God"), 11, 13, 17, 19, 21, 22; II Sam. vi 4, 6, 7 and vii 2. The secondary occurrences of "the Ark of God" outnumber the original in such a way that the designation "verhältnismässig klar" appears to be rather optimistic.

Samuel iv or Saul's daughter Michal in II Samuel vi, there is no dissonance between these chapters and the rest of the book: the same characters are involved and, as we shall see, there is also a thematic connection between AN and the book of Samuel as a whole, that is, the rejection of the house of Eli and that of Saul, and the election of the Davidic dynasty.

6. It is extremely difficult to understand how AN was saved from oblivion, if it were really composed in the eleventh or tenth century B.C.E. SCHICKLBERGER would like us to believe that the "Katastrophen-erzählung" was handed down in Israel for over two hundred years before it arrived in Jerusalem. But why should Israelites preserve an account of the vicissitudes of the Ark in the eleventh century, if this had no theological message and the Ark had become part of the Judaean and not the Israelite cult? Moreover, epigraphical finds in Israel dating from before the eighth century B.C.E. are extremely rare. Can we nevertheless assume that literacy was general in pre-monarchical Israel? This is highly improbable[34]. It is a further argument against the view that AN was written by a contemporary. Israelites did not write at that time.

7. This leaves the possibility that AN was transmitted orally, an assumption, however, that is also improbable. The extraordinary expectations some biblical scholars had of the memory of the ancient Israelites were scarcely based on sound evidence. If we consider the way historical information has been transmitted in rabbinic literature (which had an initial oral phrase), we have no reason to be very optimistic about the mnemonics of their Israelite ancestors[35]. The present text, moreover, does not show any trace of an initial oral phase.

We conclude that there are no compelling reasons to assume the pre-existence of an AN before the composition of the book of Samuel. We shall therefore investigate I Samuel iv-vi and II Samuel vi as an integral part of the book of Samuel.

## A SURVEY OF I SAMUEL IV-VI

I Samuel iv-vi seems to interrupt the story of Samuel's life which began in I Samuel i and which is continued in I Samuel vii 3 onwards. Moreover, Samuel is nowhere mentioned in these three chapters. Surely this indicates that I Samuel iv-vi was originally an independent literary unit?

However, perhaps this would be jumping to a conclusion. I Samuel iv-vi cannot be omitted from the book of Samuel. Even before Samuel, Eli is intro-

---

[34] Cf. K.A.D. SMELIK, *Historische Dokumente aus dem alten Israel*, Göttingen 1987, pp. 9, 22-24.

[35] Cf. also A. LODS, "Le rôle de la tradition orale dans la formation des récits de l'Ancien Testament", *RHR* 88 (1923/4), pp. 51-64, especially pp. 51f.

duced in I Samuel i, first as father of Hophni and Phinehas (vs. 3) and subsequently as priest (vs. 9). The mention of Hophni and Phinehas in I Samuel i 3 may appear superfluous, but it is not: it prepares the reader for the second half of ch. ii, where their wicked behaviour is rebuked and their doom announced. The contrast between Eli's heirs and the future prophet Samuel[36] is emphasised by introducing them actually during the story of Samuel's birth. The words of the unnamed prophet in I Samuel ii 27-36 also have a clear literary function: they give a clue as to how the story will continue. Hophni and Phinehas will both die on the same day and another priestly family will be elected instead of Eli's house.

So it is necessary that the sequel to I Samuel i-iii should contain an account of the fall of Eli's dynasty. And as this doom is connected with the capture of the Ark, another story had to be inserted concerning the vicissitudes of the Ark in Philistine hands. As soon as the Ark has returned to Israel, the story of Samuel's life is continued. Samuel effects the conversion of the people, after which the Philistines are no longer victorious; they are defeated and cease to encroach on the territory of Israel (I Sam. vii 13). In this way, ch. vii is a counterpart of ch. iv[37]. It is not by carrying the Ark into the battlefield but by confessing its sins, that Israel is saved from its enemies.

But why no mention of Samuel in ch. iv-vi? Why in fact should he be mentioned[38]? In what precedes, he is excluded from the judgement on Eli's house; his power as a prophet increases steadily as the death of Eli and his sons approaches. At the final moment it seemed better, therefore, to place Samuel on the sidelines and to concentrate on the downfall of the Elides. It is interesting in this respect that in ch. iv the author pays far more attention to the misfortunes of Eli and his family (vv. 11b-22) than to the capture of the Ark (vs. 11a). He concentrates once more on the Ark only after the Elides have met their doom. In the same way, he focuses on Samuel only when the adventures of the Ark are completed. In other words: it is possible to see the absence of Samuel in I Samuel iv-vi as a literary decision of the author rather than propose that the text should be divided into different strands.

The beginning of ch. iv of the Masoretic text, however, raises some questions. We can translate the beginning of vs. 1 as follows:

> And the word of Samuel came to all Israel
> and Israel went out towards the Philistines to battle.

Does the author want to suggest that because of Samuel's word Israel went to

---

[36] The contrast is indicated three times by the author in juxtaposing a verse concerning Samuel with one concerning Hophni and Phinehas in I Sam. ii 11/12, 17/18, 25/26.

[37] See also P.D. Miscall, *1 Samuel: A Literary Reading*, Bloomington 1986, p. 36, and McCarter, *op. cit.*, p. 149.

[38] Cf. also Van Seters, *op. cit.*, p. 349 and Willis, *op. cit.*, p. 212.

battle? This would fit in ch. vii, but not here. It seems better, therefore, to separate the first line from the second and to read it as conclusion of ch. iii and as a reference to ch. vii[39].

The second question is then: why did the Israelites begin fighting the Philistines? This is exceptional in biblical narrative. It is usually the Philistines who are the aggressors[40], while the Israelites merely defend themselves. For this reason, many scholars[41] want to emend the Hebrew text by following the Septuagint and read (as the New English Bible): "And the time came when the Philistines mustered for battle against Israel, and the Israelites went out to meet them ...". But, when we retain the Masoretic version as *lectio difficilior*[42], it becomes possible to answer the question of the elders in vs. 3: "Why has the LORD smitten us today before the Philistines?" The answer would be: He did so because the Israelites took the initiative in attacking the Philistines without waiting for a divine command. In the author's ideology this is not the right way for Israel to wage war against enemies: one has to wait for YHWH's initiative and approval. This is made clear in various passages in the Hebrew Bible[43]; I Samuel vii is particularly clarifying, and is, as mentioned above, a counterpart to ch. iv. In this narrative Israel first returns to YHWH and banishes all idols; then Samuel prays aloud that YHWH will save Israel. In response, YHWH throws the Philistines – who had begun hostilities by marching against the Israelites – into confusion. The Israelites have only to pursue the fleeing enemy and to slaughter them – the Philistines are unable to defend themselves after YHWH's intervention. This is how the Israelites should behave when threatened by the enemy – at least in the ideology of the biblical authors.

But in ch. iv the Israelites do not behave in this way. Even after their initial defeat, they do not turn to YHWH, although they know that He is responsible for the Philistine victory[44]. Instead, they fetch the Ark in the hope that this cult-object[45] will deliver them from the power of their enemies. We might see this as an act of piety, but I do not think that was the author's intention. The elders (unlike Samuel in vii 3) do not admonish the people to placate the anger

---

[39] Cf. P.R. Ackroyd, *The First Book of Samuel* (Cambridge Bible Commentary), Cambridge 1971, p. 45.

[40] Cf. I Sam. vii 7; xiii 5; xvii 1; xviii 30; xxiii 1, 27; xxviii 1, 4; xxix 1, 11; xxxi 1; II Sam. v 17, 22.

[41] Cf., e.g., H.P. Smith, *A Critical and Exegetical Commentary on the Books of Samuel* (ICC), Edinburgh (1899) 1969, p. 31.

[42] The version in the Septuagint is clearly a harmonisation of the original version to the common theme of the Philistines as attackers.

[43] Cf., e.g., I Sam. xiii 8-14.

[44] Cf. Eslinger, *op. cit.*, p. 165, but I do not agree with this author's conclusions in this respect.

[45] The subject of "and he will deliver us from the hand of our enemies" in iv 3 is the Ark and not YHWH (*contra* Stoebe, *op. cit.*, p. 130, 3c and Eslinger, *op. cit.*, p. 167).

of YHWH; instead they expect the Ark (and not YHWH Himself)[46] to bring certain victory. For them, salvation depends on the presence of a cult-object, not YHWH. It is therefore obvious that the Israelites will be defeated for a second time as indeed happens in vs. 10. All the more obvious because in their panic when they discover that the Ark has been brought into the camp of the Israelites, the Philistines admit their fear of the god(s) of Israel:

> Woe to us!
> Who will deliver us out of the hand of these mighty gods?!
> These are the very gods that plagued Egypt
> with all the plagues in the wilderness! (iv 8)

The Philistines, while showing themselves typical pagans by referring to the Ark as the Israelite gods (plural) and by confusing the plagues in Egypt before the Exodus with the sojourn of Israel in the wilderness, do at least acknowledge YHWH's power. The reference to the plagues in Egypt connects this verse with Exodus xv 14 ("the inhabitants of Philistia"), with the words of Rahab in Joshua ii 9-11 and the words of the Gibeonites in Joshua ix 9f. In contrast to the Israelites who are inclined to forget YHWH and to put their trust in others, the Philistines remember how terribly YHWH can smite His enemies; nevertheless, they take courage and without turning to their own gods for support[47] they join battle and are victorious.

The Israelite defeat does not surprise the reader, and for a third reason[48]. In vs. 4 it has already been stated that Eli's two sons accompany the Ark when it is brought to the Israelite camp. Since we know that they will shortly perish because of their sinful behaviour, we can expect (having read vs. 4) that the author will use the presence of the Ark during the battle at Eben-ezer/Aphek as an opportunity for having them both killed there, as indeed happens: "The Ark of God was taken and the two sons of Eli, Hophni and Phinehas, were slain" (iv 11).

In the sequal Eli's death is also recounted in a very skilfully arranged scene. His daughter-in-law perishes too, but before her death she is able to call her son Ichabod, "No-glory-left"[49]. This name is indeed a fitting summary of

---

[46] See the preceding note.

[47] Cf. STOEBE, *op. cit.*, p. 132: "Das ist deswegen nötig, weil sonst die Gefahr bestanden hätte, daß einer den Verlust der Lade als Unterliegen Jahwes vor den Göttern der Philister verstand".

[48] This is the only reason given by McCARTER, *op. cit.*, p. 109, as he supposes that "In the ideology of Israelite warfare the presence of the ark in battle was tantamount to the participation of the deity on Israel's behalf" (*ibid.*, p. 105). Maybe this holds for the common Israelite ideology, but it is not the ideology of the biblical writers. Cf., however, *ibid.*, p. 126, where McCARTER qualifies his view and states that YHWH also wanted "to demonstrate his power in the land of his enemies".

[49] This is a rather typical scene; cf. Ph. DE ROBERT, "Le gloire en exil: Réflexions sur I Samuel 4, 19-22", *RHPR* 59 (1979), pp. 351-356, especially pp. 351f., who draws attention to Gen. xxxv

this part of the story. YHWH's rejection of the Elide dynasty leads to its tragic end just as the coming rejection of Saul will lead to the downfall of his house[50].

In this respect it is interesting to note that the messenger who ran from the battlefield and reached Shiloh with the bad news, is called a Benjaminite. His name is not given, but in ancient Jewish exegesis he is identified with Saul[51]. This identification is not without reason. As McCarter remarked: "it is uncharacteristic of biblical narrative to provide such details gratuitously"[52]. I think that the unexpected introduction of a Benjaminite at this point in the story alludes to the election of another Benjaminite in ch. ix. That is also the reason why this scene in iv 16-17 has a quite striking parallel in II Samuel i 3-4, as indicated by McCarter[53]. In the latter passage an Amalekite brings the bad tidings of Saul's death to David. It is another invitation to the reader to compare the story of the house of Eli with that of Saul and his descendants.

Having dealt with the house of Eli, the author turns in v 1 to the Ark which was taken by the Philistines. The Ark is now given a new and appropriate designation, to wit, "the Ark of the God of Israel"[54]; possibly we should translate the Hebrew by "the Ark of the gods of Israel" in order to emphasise more strongly the Philistine setting of the story. Although the enemy carries off the Ark as booty[55] to the temple of Dagon at Ashdod, they do not have much reason to rejoice in their victory, nor in the capture of the Ark, as appears in the sequel to the narrative. Early the next day the priests discover the idol of Dagon fallen face downwards before the Ark: in a position of adoration[56]. They replace their idol, but the next day it has again fallen face downwards before the Ark, this time with its head and both hands broken off. As "hand" symbolises "power"[57], the meaning of this incident is clear: the pagan god is rendered powerless before YHWH. The seemingly victorious god loses head and hands and has to prostrate himself before his real master, the God of Israel. Furthermore, the Philistines themselves will soon realise that they have only defeated Israel, and not its God.

The occurrence of plagues in I Samuel v 6-12 is a variation on the plagues in

---

16-20 and to II Sam. iv 4. With reference to the possible translations of the name Ichabod cf. McCarter, *op. cit.*, pp. 115f.

[50] Cf. also Van Seters, *op. cit.*, p. 351.

[51] Cf. Pseudo Philo, *Liber antiquitatum biblicarum* LIV, 4; Midrash Shemuel 11:1.

[52] Cf. McCarter, *op. cit.*, pp. 113f. He adds, however: "but in this case the point escapes us".

[53] Cf. *ibid.*, p. 113.

[54] Cf. Van Seters, *op. cit.*, p. 350.

[55] Cf., however, M. Delcor, "Jahweh et Dagon ou le Jahwisme face à la religion des Philistins, d'après 1 Sam. v", *VT* 14 (1964), pp. 136-154, especially p. 143.

[56] Cf. McCarter, *op. cit.*, p. 124.

[57] Cf. *ThWAT* III, col. 421-455, especially col. 446.

the book of Exodus[58], but of a more comical nature, if we accept the interpretation of the inflicted illness being haemorrhoids, as the Masoretes have obviously done[59]. This ironic tendency is also apparent in the preceding scene when the idol of Dagon prostrates itself before the Ark[60].

From Ashdod the Ark is transported to Gath and from there to Ekron: "in reality a terrible triumphal procession for the Ark and so for God"[61]. In utter distress the Philistines ask their priests and soothsayers how to get rid of the Ark, this time designated as "the Ark of YHWH" (vi 2) – the Philistine knowledge of biblical theology is improving[62]. This also appears in the elaborate answer of the priests and soothsayers[63]. They recall the Exodus story (cf. iv 8), especially Pharaoh's stubborness, and they give instructions about the best way of sending the Ark back to Israel. They propose an ordeal[64] in order to know who was responsible for the plagues. The Exodus-theme[65] is also present in the detail that gold offerings are to accompany the Ark on its way back home; it reminds the reader of the booty the Hebrews took with them when leaving Egypt[66].

The cows in front of the wagon carrying the Ark know what is expected of them – they go straight in the direction of the Philistine-Israelite border, as the priests and soothsayers had predicted. The Philistine princes who follow this small-scale Exodus, witness the rejoicings of the Israelites when they see that the Ark has returned to their land. The Philistines know now that it is YHWH who has done them this great injury[67].

The return of the Ark to the land of Israel is, however, not without danger as appears from the fate of the seventy[68] inhabitants of Beth-shemesh who are struck down by YHWH. Finally, the Israelites realise that the Ark is not a weapon to be used at pleasure: YHWH is not the servant of His people. On

---

[58] Also the expression in v 12: "and the cry of the city went up to heaven" seems to be an adapted version of Ex. ii 23; cf. S.R. Driver, *Notes on the Hebrew Text and the Topography of the Books of Samuel*, Oxford 1966 (reprint of the second edition), p. 53.

[59] Cf. Smith, *op. cit.*, pp. 40f. (he does not, however, follow the Masoretic interpretation and like many others thinks that a bubonic plague is meant).

[60] Cf. also Stoebe, *op. cit.*, p. 143; Hertzberg, *op. cit.*, pp. 39f.; and Ackroyd, *op. cit.*, pp. 47, 54 and 56.

[61] Ackroyd, *op. cit.*, p. 56.

[62] Cf. also Miscall, p. 32.

[63] Such details are, of course, unmistakable clues proving the fictional nature of the presupposed AN.

[64] The milch-cows are separated from their young. "This will make it clear that only a divine power could drive the wagon away from Philistia towards the city of Beth-shemesh" (Ackroyd, *op. cit.*, p. 59).

[65] Cf. also Stoebe, *op. cit.*, pp. 143 and 150.

[66] Cf. Ex. xi 2; xii 35f.

[67] Cf. the prediction of the soothsayers in vi 9.

[68] I Sam. vi 19 (MT) has two different numbers of casualties: seventy and fifty thousand men; seventy seems to fit better. Cf., however, Miscall, *op. cit.*, p. 34.

the contrary, no one is safe when confronted with the symbol of this mighty God as will appear also from the story in II Samuel vi[69]. In this way, the elders' false estimation of the situation in I Samuel iv 3 is finally corrected.

The reader has a considerable wait before he or she again hears about the vicissitudes of the Ark. In this phase of the story it is not transported any further than Kiriath-jearim on the road to Jerusalem – the final goal of the journey – which it reaches only in II Samuel vi.

## The three themes of II Samuel vi

It is very important when interpreting II Samuel vi to take the wider context into account. In the preceding chapter v, David is anointed king over Israel, he captures Jerusalem and builds a palace there, sons and daughters are born to him in this city and he twice defeats the Philistines. In ch. vii David wants to build a temple for YHWH; this privilege is not granted to him, but the prophet Nathan gives him the promise of an eternal dynasty. In viii 1 we are told that David defeats the Philistines for a third time. So we find three major themes present in this section: "palace/temple", "dynasty" and "war against the Philistines". These themes are also to be found in ch. vi, though, as we shall see, in a different order.

In the first verse of ch. vi it is suggested that another battle against the Philistines is to be fought: "And David again gathered together every young man in Israel, thirty thousand". But contrary to the reader's expectation, David does not intend to wage war but to fetch the Ark from Baalath-judah in order to bring it to Jerusalem. The Ark – left there[70] in I Samuel vii 1 – can now continue its journey to the city which YHWH has elected to be the dwelling-place for His Name and which David captured in the preceding chapter. It had not been previously possible because Saul, placed by the author in the role of failing king, was unfit for the task of conquering this city: it had to be done by David[71]. And even David was not entitled to build the Temple, as appears in ch. vii; this will be done by Solomon[72]. Nevertheless, the warlike opening verse of ch. vi is not out of place. When David and his men fetch the Ark,

---

[69] See the death of Uzzah in II Sam. vi 6-8.

[70] Baalath-judah is another name for Kiriath-jearim; for the corruption of this name in MT see Driver, *op. cit.*, pp. 265f. and Gordon, *op. cit.*, p. 231.

[71] The mention of the Ark in I Sam. xiv 18 presents a problem in this respect. A possible solution in my article in *ACEBT* 1 (1980), p. 50, n. 4. Stoebe's question (*op. cit.*, p. 166): "Wie konnte das Interesse an der Lade so gering sein, daß sie in der Zeit Sauls völlig in Vergessenheit geriet?" is impossible to answer as long as we accept the historicity of the accounts concerning the Ark in the Book of Samuel. But if we regard them as literary works of art, the answer becomes simple enough: the biblical authors had to place the Ark on the sidelines as long as Saul, and not David, was king.

[72] Cf. II Sam. vii 13; I Kings v 5; viii 19.

they bring to an end one of the results of the Philistine victory at Eben-ezer/ Aphek. So the theme of "war against the Philistines" is already present in the first verse of the chapter.

The second theme found in ch. vi is the building of a sanctuary for YHWH. David's men put the Ark "in its place inside the tent that David had pitched for it, and David offered whole-offerings and shared offerings before YHWH" (vi 17). A tent is not, however, a suitable permanent accommodation for such an important cult-object; clearly, more fitting housing is required and indeed, eventually, the Ark will be placed in Solomon's temple (II Kings viii 6). For this reason, it is illogical to regard II Samuel vi as the concluding part of an AN (as suggested by Rost): the conclusion of the Ark-story is in II Kings viii 6-11.

A striking feature of II Samuel vi are the many allusions to a fertility rite [73]. It is suggested to the reader that at the end of the chapter David's wife Michal will give birth to a son who will be a fitting heir to the Israelite throne since he will be David's son and Saul's grandson. Because of this expectation the centre of the narrative is not the entry of the Ark in Jerusalem, but the meeting between David and Michal to which vs. 16 is a preparation. However, after Michal has shown herself a second Saul through her words to David (vs. 20) and thus unfit for the role of Queen Mother, she remains childless to her dying day. Whether this was the effect of barrenness imposed on her by YHWH or of continence on David's part, is a matter of dispute in biblical scholarship [74]. The author leaves the question open; possibly he wanted to suggest that it was the wish of both YHWH and David. The reader's expectation that a son of Michal and David would become the new king of Israel and unite the two royal lines, is thus thwarted. The rejection of Saul as king applies also to his descendants. Thus, the future of David's dynasty (the third theme) remains unsettled. The reader has to wait until the first two chapters of the book of Kings.

## The purpose of the stories about the Ark in Samuel

As the author was not primarily interested in recording historical events, why did he insert these stories about the Ark into the book? I believe he wished to convey a theological message.

---

[73] These are: David wearing a linen ephod and dancing without restraint (vs. 14); Michal looking down through a window (vs. 16); David blessing the people (vs. 18) and returning to bless his household (vs. 20) and David giving food to every man *and woman* (vs. 19; note the cake of raisins, a fertility symbol in Hos. iii 1 and Songs of Songs ii 5). Cf. also Carlson, *op. cit.*, pp. 87-96, N. Poulssen, "De Mikalscène; 2 Sam. 6, 16. 20-23", *Bijdragen* 39 (1978), pp. 32-58, and my article in *ACEBT* 4 (1983), pp. 26-36.

[74] For a survey of different opinions see my article in *ACEBT* 4 (1983), p. 36, n. 42.

In connection with the story about the Ark in Philistine hands, he probably wanted to teach the reader that YHWH will deliver Israel only in His own good time. The Israelites should not trust in the Ark if it were a charmed weapon. The symbol of God's presence among His people is not a guarantee against defeat. YHWH is prepared to have Israel defeated and His Holy Ark captured by the uncircumcised if Israel is following its own path[75].

On the other hand, the reader should not conclude from this defeat that YHWH is weaker than the gods of the enemy. Thus the idol of Dagon has to prostrate itself before the symbol of the God of Israel, when the Ark is brought to Dagon's temple. By His own hand YHWH saves the Ark from the Philistines and effects its return to Israel. Even then a horrifying accident has to occur before the Israelites realise how terrifying God's power is.

This being the message of I Samuel iv 1-11, v and vi, the following question arises: to what particular events is the author reacting? Not, as has already been said, to an Israelite defeat in the eleventh century, but what then? In this respect it is important to note that Eli's daughter-in-law exclaims: "The Glory has gone into exile from Israel!" What exactly does this mean?

The expression also occurs in Hosea x, a prophecy announcing the fall of Israel in 722/0 B.C.E. We find in vs. 5: "... its glory, because it is carried into exile from there". In this context "its glory" designates "the calves of Beth-aven [= Bethel]". The next verse (vs. 6) explains that the images are carried to Assyria as tribute to the Great King. The possibility that I Samuel iv 21-22 refers to Hosea x cannot be altogether excluded but is not very probable. The "calves of Beth-aven" are described in a most uncomplimentary manner, both in Hosea and in Kings, while for the biblical narrators the Ark represented an acceptable cult. It is hard to imagine that the Ark and Jeroboam's calves would be placed in the same category.

But if we turn to Ezekiel viii-xi, we find a more convincing answer to our question about the "glory" that was led into exile[76]. These chapters describe how the Glory of the God of Israel (or YHWH)[77] first leaves the Temple and afterwards Jerusalem on the eve of Jerusalem's capture by the Babylonians in 586 B.C.E.[78]. The capture of the Ark by the Philistines is actually an allu-

[75] Cf. also the summary of our story given in the – according to the dating by H.J. Kraus, *Psalmen I* (BKAT), Neukirchen/Vluyn 1966, pp. 540f. – post-exilic Ps. lxxviii 56-66.

[76] Cf. Ackroyd, *op. cit.*, p. 52.

[77] When we keep in mind the abovementioned theory of Fohrer concerning different literary strata in AN, it is interesting to note that in Ezekiel the designation "the Glory of the God of Israel" (Ez. viii 4; ix 3; x 19; xi 22 and xliii 2) also alternates with "the Glory of YHWH" (Ez. i 28; iii 12, 23; x 4 [2×], 18; xi 23; xliii 4, 5 and xliv 4). Cf., however, W. Zimmerli, *Ezechiel I* (BKAT), Neukirchen/Vluyn 1969, p. 204.

[78] Cf. also De Robert, *op. cit.*; he is, however, not of the opinion that I Samuel iv was inspired by Ezekiel (as I suggest), but just the other way round: Ezekiel viii-xi is an echo of I Samuel iv 19-22.

sion to the pillage and destruction of the Temple of Jerusalem, the Ark being comparable with the holy vessels and the Philistines with the Babylonians[79].

As a sixth-century context is most suitable for the story about the Ark in Philistine hands[80], so we also get a clue as to where the author found his inspiration. In Jeremiah vii (cf. xxvi) the inhabitants of Jerusalem are warned not to trust in the doctrine of the inviolability of the Temple, which was propagated by the Jerusalem priesthood. YHWH is prepared to have His sanctuary destroyed by Israel's enemies if the people do not mend their ways. In order to prove this the reader is reminded of the fate of YHWH's sanctuary at Shiloh. It is not stated in the text in which period the destruction of this sanctuary occurred; according to archaeological evidence it was probably the Assyrian period[81]. Our author suggests, however, by giving Eli his domicile at Shiloh that Jeremiah vii 12 refers to a much earlier period in Israel's history. I suggest that he wrote I Samuel iv-vi as a counterpart to the text in Jeremiah[82]: the theological message of Jeremiah's prophecy is developed into a story about the capture of the Ark in a much earlier period[83].

If we understand the biblical narrator rightly, he wants to suggest that Israel must put its faith solely in YHWH and not in the doctrine that Jerusalem and the Temple will never be captured by an enemy. Moreover, he explains that the defeats of 597 and 586 were not the result of a supposed inability on YHWH's side to save His people, but of His wrath. The reader may be sure that when YHWH reconciles Himself with His people, He will defeat the

---

[79] We see in I Sam. iv-vi the same ambivalent attitude towards the Philistines as in the book of Jeremiah towards the Babylonians: they are both playing their role in God's scheme and they both are nevertheless humiliated and thus punished for their arrogance.

[80] It is interesting to compare our conclusion with ACKROYD's remark on I Sam. iv 21 (*op. cit.*, p. 52): "To later readers the parallel with the situation in the time of the Babylonian exile would be evident" (cf. *ibid.*, p. 63). This does not seem to be a coincidence; the "later readers" being the first readers of the text, the reference to the events of 586 B.C.E. was intended by the authors from the start. As regards the date of I Sam. iv it is also interesting to note that in two passages in the book of Jeremiah the exile of a divinity is mentioned, to wit, that of Kemosh (Jer. xlviii 7) and Milcom (Jer. xlix 3).

[81] For this reason the exile of Ephraim is mentioned in Jer. vii 15 as elucidation of the reference to the destruction of the Shiloh sanctuary in vs. 12. *Contra* J. DAY, "The Destruction of the Shiloh Sanctuary and Jeremiah vii 12, 14", *SVT* 30 (1979), pp. 87-94. Cf. also R.A. PEARCE, "Shiloh and Jer. vii 12, 14 & 15", *VT* 23 (1973), pp. 105-108. I do not agree with him that the text in Jeremiah refers both "to the events c. 1050 B.C. and to those of 732-722 B.C.". Clearly, only one event is alluded to.

[82] Another interesting text in Jeremiah in this respect is iii 16: After the exile when Israel will receive from God shepherds after His own heart, the people "shall say no more: The Ark of the Covenant of YHWH; neither shall it come to mind; neither shall they remember it; neither shall they resort to it; neither shall it be made anymore". This text belongs to a later stage in the composition of the book of Jeremiah; is it an allusion to I Sam. iv 3 or was it another source of inspiration to the author of I Samuel iv?

[83] Retrojection of contemporary issues into the past is a fairly common procedure in biblical narrative; see K.A.D. SMELIK, "De Hebreeuwse Bijbel als historische bron", *ACEBT* 8 (1987), pp. 9-22, especially p. 18.

Babylonians and bring back the Temple vessels, as promised in Jeremiah xxvii-xxix. The Glory of the God of Israel (or YHWH) will return to the Temple (Ez. xliii 1-5).

It is even possible that the initiative of the Israelites in beginning the war against the Philistines in I Samuel iv is a reflection of the Judaean rising against Babylon which led to the destruction of the Temple and the carrying away of its vessels in 597 and 586. If this is the case, we compare I Samuel iv with Ezekiel xvii, where the prophet rebukes the Judaean king Zekediah for this rebellion. These allusions must have been rather obvious to the first readers of I Samuel iv-vi.

There is, however, a second theme in I Samuel iv: the fall of the Elide dynasty. This theme is also present in the preceding chapters, there in continual contrast with the theme of Samuel's election to be YHWH's prophet. We are told that Eli's sons commit several sins against YHWH[84] and that Eli was not able to restrain them[85]. From ii 29 it even appears that Eli participated in the double-dealing of his sons, but the text is not very clear[86]. Because Eli failed to keep his sons under control, he too is condemned. In the words of the man of God who visited Eli in ch. ii: notwithstanding the fact that he was elected to be YHWH's priest, Eli honoured his sons above YHWH and thus forfeited God's eternal blessing (ii 28ff.).

This part of the story has been explained as an allusion to the replacement of the Elides by another priestly family[87]. In the context of the book of Samuel the prophecy in ii 35 is, however, in the first place an allusion to the rejection of Saul and the election of David, the "faithful priest" standing for the faithful king[88]. Thus the passages about the fall of the house of Eli prepare the reader for the predominant theme in the book of Samuel: the replacement of one king by another.

This theme is also found in the conclusion of II Samuel vi. We have already seen that when we interpret II Samuel vi not as the concluding part of a separate AN, but as a component of the book of Samuel as a whole, the story focuses not only on the arrival of the Ark in Jerusalem as a preparation for building the Temple but also on the quarrel between David and Michal which leads to the repudiation of Saul's daughter. In this conflict, Michal represents her deceased father and is thus designated "the daughter of Saul" in vv. 16,

---

[84] Cf. I Sam. ii 12-17, 22, 29 and iii 13.

[85] Cf. I Sam. ii 25, 29 and iii 13.

[86] Cf., e.g., Stoebe, *op. cit.*, pp. 116f.

[87] Cf., e.g., J. Dus, "Die Erzählung über den Verlust der Lade 1 Sam. IV", *VT* 13 (1963), pp. 333-337 (Zadokites).

[88] In the context of the Deuteronomistic History, the fall of the house of Eli is paradigmatic of the destruction of the Judaean kingdom; in both cases the failure of Israel's leaders brought about the suffering of the people and the exile of the most sacred cult-objects.

20 and 23, instead of "the wife of David"[89]. In this way the central theme of the second part of I Samuel, to wit, the contrast between Saul and David, is resumed – Michal taking over the role of Saul.

Finally the conflict between the two spouses results in a complete rupture between David and Michal. She will not become the mother of David's heir: another heir is needed. In this way the rejection of Saul and his house, announced in I Samuel xiii and xv is completed, and the subsequent theme, that of David's succession, is introduced.

The literary style of the author when he intertwines three different themes (the Ark/Temple theme, the replacement theme and the succession theme) into one narrative, is eminently skilful. The earlier story featuring the Ark is also excellently written. In particular, the contrast between the despondency of ch. iv and the comedy of ch. v achieves a fine effect. The author succeeds in presenting a profound theological message through a compelling story that combines dramatic scenes with comic relief.

---

[89] See I Sam. xix 11 where the latter designation does occur in a context where Michal opposes her father in favour of her husband.

# PSALM LXXX: FORM OF EXPRESSION AND FORM OF CONTENTS

BY

N.J. TROMP

*Utrecht*

## TEXT

2 Give ear, O Shepherd of Israel,
thou who leadest Joseph like a flock!
Thou who art enthroned upon the cherubim, shine forth
3 before Ephraim and Benjamin and Menasseh!
Stir up thy might
and come to save us!
4 Restore us, O God;
let thy face shine and we shall be saved!

5 O LORD God of hosts,
how long wilt thou be angry
with thy people's prayer?
6 Thou hast fed them with the bread of tears,
and given them tears to drink in full measure.
7 Thou dost make us the scorn of our neighbours;
and our enemies laugh among themselves.
8 Restore us, O God of hosts;
let thy face shine and we shall be saved!

9 Thou didst bring a vine out of Egypt:
thou didst drive out the nations and plant it.
10 Thou didst clear the ground for it;
and thou didst cause it to take deep root and to fill the land.
11 The mountains were covered with its shade;
the mighty ceders with its branches;
12 it sent out its branches to the sea,
and its shoots to the River.
13 Why then hast thou broken down its walls,
so that all who pass along the way pluck its fruit?
14 The boar from the forest ravages it,
and all that move in the field feed on it.

15 Turn again, O God of hosts!
Look down from heaven, and see;
have regard for this vine,
16 this stock which thy right hand has planted,
and the son that thou madest strong for thyself.
17 They have burnt it with fire, they have cut it down;
may they perish at the rebuke of thy countenance!
19 Then we will never turn back from thee;
give us life, and we will call on thy name!
20 Restore us, O LORD God of hosts!
Let thy face shine and we will be saved!
(RSV and KJ)

"Semioticians stick to their guns; but that is a poor strategy for attracting people", a colleague confided to me. That is: time and again semioticians start enunciating their theory and its terminology, as if their readers are stubborn ignoramusses. And in reproducing their analyses they hold on to their models and jargon, suggesting that a new and intricate presentation of seasoned and straightforward ideas is the secret of their trade. My colleague's advice meant: write the results of your analyses down in a way others can understand.That will enable them to compare the output of the semiotic approach to the one of current methods.

I will put that advice into practice here, be it with some hesitation. For firstly a well-known impasse looms ahead. If we offer a new interpretation, we will be confronted with the reproach of pretending to be superior to our predecessors; as if a similar reproach was not addressed to established methods when they emerged. If we present current views in a new terminology, we may be upbraided of making simple truths complicated. As if from a scholarly point of view it is not only the results that count, but at least also the systematic and verifiable way to reach them. Which implies indeed that elements of a semiotic approach have been cultivated *avant la lettre*.

Because of standing by the theories of A.J. GREIMAS, the main stream of the Paris school did not develop adequate models for analysing literary texts by allowing for the vital link between the form of the expression and the form of the content. The expression was hardly studied systematically in view of its relations with deeper levels of texts with their syntactical and semantic components. J. GENINASCA has taken this task in hand, with remarkable results. I will make use of this approach here in a somewhat haphazard way[1].

[1] According to S. LEVIN (*Linguistic Structures in Poetry*, The Hague 1973[4]) coupling, which is a model of the special unity of structure as to content and expression in poetry, is present when

## II. The form of the expression

The application of Geninasca's model to biblical poetry entails some problems. First of all it starts from a poetic tradition in which prosodic laws are well established. And knowledge of them enables the analyst to determine positional equivalences which put us on the track of semantic equivalences. As to the phonological aspect one is familiar with certain rules pertaining to assonance in the broad sense of the word. In this way we can discover differences which are semantically suggestive and stimulate further research in that direction. It need not be argued here that in the biblical field research is still in its infancy, although pioneer studies were published in the last few years. As to my knowledge no analysis focusing on the connection between the form of the expression and of the content in Old Testament poetry is extant, we must be content to scout the field and ask some relevant questions here.

### *1. Strophic structure and vs. 15*

What role is played by vs. 15 in Psalm lxxx? It is congenial to the refrain because of the double divine name (as in vs. 8), of the use of the root *šûb* in the imperative and of a parallel imperative which is semantically related to the one appearing in the refrain ("look down and see"; "let your face shine upon us"). As the psalm does not strike up with it, the burden does not mark the beginning of the strophes, but their conclusion. If we take vs. 15 as a variation on the refrain, the architecture of Ps. lxxx looks this way:

str. 1: vv. 2-4; str. 2: vv. 5-8; str. 3: vv. 9-15; str. 4: vv. 16-20.

---

two elements in a text converge: as to the content, when in two instances equivalence of its substance (semantics) goes together with equivalence of its form (comparable syntagmatic position); as to the expression, when twice equivalence of its substance (phonology) is combined with equivalence of its form (position on the metrical axis, i.e. metrical position). Geninasca (1971) enlarges this principle in maintaining that a similar convergence possesses heuristic value as soon as we are dealing with equivalences both as to the form of the expression and of the contents, in other words, when an equivalent metrical position goes together with an equivalent syntagmatical one. Then the regularity of the expression's form arouses expectations which the enuntiator may effectively disturb by deviating from the set pattern, in that way putting the reader on the track of semantical transformations. Each relation of content and expression may result in a homology, i.e. "a rigorous formulation of reasoning based by analogy"; the homology manifests the isomorphism of the relations existing between two places on both levels (see A.J. Greimas and J. Courtés, *Semiotics and Language, An Analytical Dictionary*, Bloomington 1982, pp. 144f.).

Selected bibliography: J. Geninasca, *Analyse structurale des Chimères de Nerval*, Neuchâtel 1971, Introduction; *idem*, "Découpage conventionnel et signification", in A.J. Greimas, *Essais de sémiotique poétique*, Paris 1972, pp. 45-61; *idem*, "Pour une sémiotique littéraire", in: *Actes sémiotiques, Documents* (Paris), IX, 83, 1987, pp. 7-24.

The results of exegetical research will not be mentioned here completely; see H.J. Kraus, *Psalmen 60-150* (BK XV/2), Neukirchen 1978[5], pp. 717-725; G. Ravasi, *Il libro dei Salmi* II, Bologna 1983, pp. 671-689; on Ps. 80, see N.J. Tromp, "La métaphore engloutie. Le langage métaphorique du Psaume 80", *Sémiotique et Bible* 47 (sept. 1987), pp. 30-41.

The quantitative relaions between the strophes merit further consideration: we expect to find some regularity in them, based on the laws of Hebrew poetry. In establishing the exact structure of the lines, however, we are facing uncertainties.

In vv. 2-3 MT reads two tricola, followed by a bicolon in vs. 4; in view of its length, vs. 5 also must be taken as a tricolon, although MT does not do so. In vv. 15-16 the situation is unclear: if we maintain vs. 16.2, the verses count 5 cola, i.e. two bicola followed by a monocolon, or a bicolon with a tricolon. The result is as follows:

str. 1: 2 tricola, 1 bicolon (BHK: 4 bicola);
str. 2: 1 tricolon, 3 bicola;
str. 3: 7 bicola;
str. 4: 1 tricolon, 4 bicola.

This looks rather chaotic: there is an apparent lack of regularity. We find no basic structure which may be deviated from in a significant way. An alternative solution consists in considering vs. 15 not to be a varied refrain. Merely counting the cola on the basis of a regular 3 + 3 meter, and making no decision as to the division in lines, we find this structure:

str. 1 (A1): vv. 2-4 (8 cola); str. 2 (A2): vv. 5-8 (9 cola);
str. 3 (B1): vv. 9-14 (12 cola); str. 4 (B2): vv. 15-20 (13 cola)[2].

## 2. *The relations between the strophes*

Accepting the Masoretic division in vv. 5 and 15, and elsewhere following BHS, we obtain two groups of strophes, A and B, on the basis of the number of cola. Both comprise two strophes, the second of which is marked by the first line being a tricolon, suggesting the boundary between the two strophes of the same group. The coherence of A1-A2 and of B1-B2 is reinforced by these groups of strophes, rather than the individual ones, being concluded by the refrain.

Starting from this structure we can characterise its components syntactically in this way:

A1 is a supplication (a direct manipulation);
A2 is a reproach about the present situation (dysphoric sanction);
B1 is a description of the past, debouching into a reproach about the present;
B2 is a supplication (a direct and indirect manipulation).

---

[2] As to the strophic division authors do disagree. The proposed structure resembles the one presented by A. ROEFER, "The End of Psalm 80", *Tarbiz* 29 (1959), pp. 113-124.

So we find a syntactical conformity, i.e. an equivalence as to the form of the content, which runs parallel with a positional equivalence of limit and non-limit strophes:

A1:A2 = B2:B1 = manipulation:sanction.

This discourse as a totality is bordered by the element which is essential in the enuntiators' narrative programme. They realise a performance which consists in enunciating a discourse that intends to act upon God. The performance they induce God to carry out is manifested in the refrain as making his face shine, an effect of which will be the transformation of the enuntiators: "and we will be saved".

It might be straining the evidence to maintain that, because vs. 15 is not the conclusion of B1 but the beginning of B2, the reader must feel deprived of the expected refrain after B1, the absence of which would underline that the situation is judged beyond hope, beyond supplication. What we may say, however, is this. As far as being a refrain, vs. 15 drastically changed, it turns up late (after 12 cola only, not after 8 or 9, as before), and is not a monolithic utterance as in vv. 4 and 8, but is intertwined with the fabric of B2. I will return to this point.

This infraction of an established pattern constitutes a deviation in the form of the expression which arouses the expectation that something similar will be true for the form of the content also.

The relation between A2 and B1 appears to be climactic: in A2 the lament is predominating, but it results in an entreaty (vs. 8), while in B1 the lament carries more weight because of the internal contrast between past (blessing: 9-12) and present (curse: 13f.), and by the absence of the refrain, which is expected after a strophe of this size, and whose wording is familiar by now.

This is not the only difference between A2 and B1, making the repetition of the dysphoric sanction significant. One notices that in A2 the damaging actions are reproduced in the form of rather neutral observations, whereas they are introduced by the interrogative "wherefore?" in B1, a question as to God's motive for action. This question which seems to prevail upon God to react, suggests there is not any answer to it; and in fact no answer is forthcoming, as it is not manifested in the text. Moreover, there is a diversity between A2 and B1 as to the acting subject. In A2 (6-7) God himself is the acting subject in three sentences: he realises personally a dysphoric programme or he enables the adversary to do so; in vs. 7.2 only the enemy himself is directly active. In B1 (13f.) this proportion is reversed: one action is ascribed to God, three actions are put down to human agents directly. Which is a serious condition: after all God is the shepherd and the "planter" of his people: he can be appealed to. From human adversaries no compassion can be expected.

Given a free hand they will finish off their victim (17.1). It seems in fact that they are allowed to give rein to their fury, because God turns away from his people. This may explain why this strophe is not concluded by the familiar refrain and more specifically, why its supplication, when alluded to, has "turn back" instead of "restore us", the heart of the matter being God's aversion from his people.

God's performance is represented as a process in so far as A2 manifests an inchoative aspect of his activity (wrath) and his performance is expressed in durative verbal forms (6f). In B1, too, there is an inchoative aspect (the breaching of the walls), while the others' activities are manifested as iterative by the verbal forms (*yiqtol*). Moreover, there is an element of repetition in the three syntagmata consisting in three lexemes each: pass-by/road/plucks; boar/wood/ravages; wild beast/field/devours. The terminative aspect, the complete destruction, must be near; it is suggested by 17.1 (burnt) and 19.2 (give us life). The supplication for a saving intervention, however, shows this suggestion to be a rhetorical overstatement.

As to the relation between A1 and B2, they are similar as they are marked by the manipulation. A1 is the opening part of the discourse, as nothing precedes it. B2 not only concludes the psalm, it also constitutes a reprisal of A1 and a sequel to A2 and B1. In order to be significative, the repetition of A1 in B2 must be different from A1 itself. The example of the refrain indeed shows how subtle the difference may be: in this case there is only a slight change as to the form of the expression. The main difference must derive from its position related to the section it concludes and to the development of the manipulative process.

Sections A1 and B2 contain four imperatives each:

A1: give ear; shine forth; stir up; come;
B2: turn; look down; see; visit.

The implied position of the addressee is different in the two cases:

A1: God is invisible (non-paraître + être);
B2: God is totally absent (non-paraître + non-être);
A1: God is actively, although dysphorically, committed;
B2: He is willingly neutral, letting matters take their course;
A1: God is related to his people;
B2: God has broken relations with his people.

The sanction of God's programme is more bitter in A2 than in B1. This explains why the manipulation is more intensive in B2 than in A1; in A1 we find four imperatives, in B2 also four, which are reinforced this time by the addition of three, more indirect manipulations: "may they perish", "let thy hand be", "give us life" (Hebrew: *yiqtol*). Moreover, B2 is concluded by the two imperatives of the refrain (20), which constitutes an inclusion of a kind with vs. 15 (*'lhym ṣb'wt, šûb*). There is a hidden manipulation in vs. 17.2, which means: "make your face menacing so that they perish", a direct contrast with "make your face shine, so that we will be saved". The verb *pqd*, "to make an active appearance", is specified towards the adversary and towards the enuntiators. The latter express the wish that God's hand may protectively rest upon their representative, in order that he may live; the former may participate in the menacing face of God in order that they may perish. Up till now God's obfuscated face is the cause of Israel's plight.

In A1 the manipulation rather intends the transformation of God: he is to listen, to appear, to come into action; in B2 the transformation in the humans is predominating (17-19). Both rationally and emotionally this is explained by the contribution of A2 and B1. There is some reason, consequently, to maintain that the relation between A1 and B2 is a climactic one, as is true for A2 and B1, *ergo* for A and B. This is affirmed by the refrain, which finds its strongest form in vs. 20 (three divine titles)[3]. For the first time the tetragrammaton appears in the refrain here; interpreted as "the one who is actively present", it is semantically related to the verb *pqd*. It may very well have an optative meaning in this case[4], in other words: the Lord is called upon to verify his name YHWH and to show his presence by his saving intervention. In this sense vs. 20 constitutes an inclusion with vs. 15 and the culminating final chord of the psalm. The supplication proceeds from "return" to "make us return" (15.20): a climax which summarises the object of the supplication. And unexpectedly the latter entreaty obtains a double charge. Verse 19 namely runs: "We will not turn back from you", a promise which may be understood as an implicit confession of guilt. Therefore "make us return" will also have a moral meaning. For that reason God's wrath is not as unaccountable as vs. 13 suggests, and not as indefinitely lasting as vs. 15 seems to imply. In order to reinforce the supplication the present plight is presented more dramatically than conditions justify. The luminous face is a token of grace and forgiveness, while the obfuscated face expresses a just wrath and punishment.

Further we notice a change of metaphors. The vine is skilfully converted into a "sprout", which not only individualises the vine, but also tends towards a lexicalised metaphor (such as *nēṣer*) for a human being. Thus the appearance of the "son" is prepared[5].

Everything goes to show that the manipulation of B2 is a radical transformation of the one in A1, a fact which is brought about by the intervention

---

[3] Compare F. Delitzsch, *Die Psalmen*, Leipzig 1894$^5$, p. 535 and Kraus, *op. cit.*, pp. 718f.

[4] See P. Joüon, *Grammaire de l'hébreu biblique*, Rome 1947$^2$, par. 79e4.

[5] It is unlikely that Hebrew *bēn* means "twig" here, as proposed by D. Hill, "Son of Man in Ps. 80 v. 17", *NT* 15 (1973), pp. 261-269: p. 263, n. 2. For vv. 15 and 17, see also B. McNeil, *NTS* 26 (1979-80), pp. 419-421.

of the preceding sections A2 and B1. In this way B2 is the climax of the discourse.

Consequently there is a relation of homology between limit and non-limit strophes, A1 and B2 being in a limit position in the poem, and A2 and B1 in a non-limit position. An observation on the meter may consolidate this hypothesis: it is remarkable that A2 and B2 each count one more colon than A1 and B1, a fact which marks the limits between the quantitatively equal groups of strophes (A and B). The impression that A1 and B2 belong more together than A1 and B2 finds a counterpoise in the datum that the first lines of A2 and B2 seem to be tricola. (In vs. 5 it is semantically evident that the sentence constitutes one line; in vs. 15 I follow MT in placing the four imperatives within one line.) In this way the distance between A1 and A2, between B1 and B2 is enlarged, and the one between A2 and B2 diminished.

## II. The form of the content

### *Israel, Joseph, Ephraim, Benjamin and Menasseh*

As L. Jacquet notes, only northern tribes are mentioned here: there is no talk of Judah, Jerusalem or Temple[6].

The LXX title *hypèr toû 'Assurìou* suggests that these translators connected the psalm with some Assyrian invasion of the Northern Kingdom. Of course the descriptions of the current plight (6f., 13f. and 17) and the entreaties (4.8 etc.) play a role in this. Jacquet lists at least eight proposals as to the date of the text's origin, ranging from Achab's time to the Maccabean period. As to the place of origin (Shilo or Jerusalem) the discussion centres around the title *YHWH ṣb'wt*[7].

This debate is characteristic for the historico-critical method, its procedure, its interests and its claims. Some critical remarks must be made here, however. On the one hand every standpoint as to date and place of origin remains uncertain in this case. On the other the psalm is no more nor less than a particular and subjective way of digesting objective circumstances. That is why even an intimate knowledge of the latter does not constitute the decisive key towards its meaning and sense. Moreover, although his perspective remains an historical one, Jacquet is right in stating: "Reste que, dans la suite, les Juifs durent réutiliser le Psaume, quitte à l'adapter lors des désastres qui survinrent . . ."[8]. The essential question pertains to the meaning of the text rather than to its application (reference).

Starting from the personal names Israel, Joseph, Ephraim, Benjamin and

---

[6] L. Jacquet, *Les Psaumes et le coeur de l'homme* II, Gembloux 1977, p. 566.
[7] *Ibid.*, pp. 566f.; O. Eissfeldt, "Psalm 80", in *KS* III, Tübingen 1966, pp. 221-232.
[8] *Ibid.*, p. 567.

and Menasseh, we ask what they contribute to the meaning of the text.

The genealogical relation between them is the following: Israel represents the first generation, Joseph and Benjamin the second, Ephraim and Menasseh the third. In this view the position of Benjamin is curious: this member of the second generation is put on one level with representatives of the third and is enclosed by them. This creates a distance between the two couples of brothers, between Joseph and Benjamin, between Ephraim and Menasseh. Which is the thematic importance of this literary fact? Are we dealing with individuals or with tribes, co-existing entities or with successive generations? We can ascertain that in biblical narratives the persons mentioned have or are brothers, and that in each case the relation between them is upset. Israel obtains the rights of the first-born from Esau; to his father Benjamin replaces the lost Joseph (Gen. xlii 38); Menasseh is subordinated to Ephraim (Gen. xlviii 22). The strange trio Ephraim – Benjamin – Menasseh might show that genealogical priority, based on birth, is of no consequence here. Two generations are called in one breath, as if they were contemporaries, and the youngest is put in the first place, to be followed by the junior of two brothers, who again obtained priority. First a certain simultaneity is suggested as to Israel and Joseph, this because of their parallel position, then Ephraim, Benjamin and Menasseh are put on line with each other. In fact some simultaneity between all of them is presented as self-evident: because God is the shepherd of the first, he is to take care of the last. In other words: the genealogical dissimultaneity is undone. We will see that this motif is coupled with another inversion, through which an individual represents a collectivity. We wonder whether a similar phenomenon returns somewhere in the psalm. It would seem that we come across an analogous situation in the allegory of the vine. We are reminded of the vicissitudes of Israel *cum suis*: the vine is a simple plant among the peoples in Egypt; by the grace of YHWH it grows in a way to surpass peoples and countries. But at present it is reduced to near-nothingness (13f.; 17.1). The solitary plant became a forest ("vom Weinstock zum Weinberg", KRAUS writes), just as the patriarchs of vv. 2f. became tribes/collectivities; but now the history of grace has turned into an history of rejection: the vineyard has been reduced to a plant, a mere sprout (*kannâ*), a lonely son. This poor remnant of a mighty people remains the man of God's right hand, the son of man, once made strong by God (cf. 9-12). But this very state of inferiority is a reason for God's intervention, which favours the downtrodden above those that burn them, the younger above the older. YHWH puts down the mighty, he exalts the lowly. The solitary representative of the people is the object of God's grace, he is the king sitting at God's right hand, "is per quem dextera tua nos salvare volet"[9].

[9] F. ZORELL, *Lexicon Hebraicum*, Rome 1964, p. 314B.

The king is as much an individual as the patriarchs of vv. 2f. are individuals. He is the incarnation of the people, and in him past history, exemplified by the patriarchs, should repeat itself. The exceptional stylistic position of Benjamin in vs. 3 is revealed to be a privileged position by the allusions to it in vv. 16.2 and 18.1. Apparently the praying people wants to identify itself particularly with Benjamin.

Whatever this particular interpretation is worth, it shows the approach of semiotics. The problem of the proper names is not broached as an isolated detail, to be unriddled as such from without, but as part of the discourse. To be sure, we start from an hypothesis, taken from other discourses, but it is only accepted as valid when its tenability is tested on the basis of the concrete text as a whole. Knowledge of the cultural universe of the psalm is therefore presupposed, but it is not automatically applied to the object under discussion, but tested on it. Which is done by checking whether the themes of the inversion of genealogical priority in favour of the younger and of the conversion of the individual into a collectivity recur in the text. Besides, the remarkable literary position of Benjamin in vs. 3 points to vv. 15f., where the infraction of the regular form of the expression marks a decisive transformation in the relation between the enuntiator and God, namely the identification with Benjamin, the one who is entitled to God's saving intervention, because he has got into low water. In this way the "text-immanent" approach of semiotics may be understood and put in perspective[10].

## III. Conclusion

We now return to the conclusion arrived at in part I, and examine closely its relation to the findings of part II. The analysis of part I showed that there is a homological relation of this kind: A1:A2 = B2:B1 = limit:non-limit = manipulation:sanction = reinstatement:demolition = life:death.

This looks rather like an abstract wording of the figurative isotopy than of the thematic one. In other words, it resumes the general situation the psalm refers to, which is the condition of misfortune and the people's reaction to it. Against this background the thematic isotopy is projected, i.e. the transformation of a people that considered itself superior to others because of being a mighty power, into a people that acknowledges its inferiority and entrusts itself to the grace of God. The figurative isotopy can be found in kindred

[10] The semiotic approach analyses its object in its final shape and aims at discovering and verifying its significance from the structure of its content; literary criticism rather intends to explain the present state of the text by tracing the history of its growth into its final shape. An eloquent example of the latter is the study by W. Beyerlin, "Schichten im 80. Psalm" in H. Balz and S. Shulz (eds.), *Das Wort und die Wörter* (Festschrift G. Friedrich), Stuttgart 1973, pp. 9-24.

Psalms, those of public lament and entreaty. It is the result of a generic approach to these texts, which is characteristic for form-criticism. The thematic isotopy, the specific angle under which it is illuminated, is proper to the individual psalm, the one under discussion. The latter was arrived at in part II. History is illustrated in our Psalm as a series of precedents creating an obligation as to the present plight. Through the course of history YHWH has established a pattern of behaviour: he created a tradition of intervening out of mere grace in favour of the inferior and the powerless. The very distressing conditions of God's powerless people are the trump played by the enuntiators; now they can effectively appeal to the precedents of history. In this way a disadvantage is turned into an advantage; weakness has become strength (II Cor. xii 9).

We can conclude by specifying the homology: A1:A2 = B2:B1 = limit:non-limit = future:present = manipulation:sanction = restoration:demolition = action out of grace:action out of wrath = preference for the inferior:slight of the superior. In this reasoning, guilt does not fit; that is why it is acknowledged indirectly and as an afterthought: "We will never turn back from you!"[11].

---

[11] The author wants to acknowledge the stimulating criticisms made by his fellow-members of SEMANET, Dr. G. Lukken, Drs. J. Maas and Drs. P. de Maat.

# PSALM XXIII

*Some regulative linguistic evidence*

BY

N.A. VAN UCHELEN

*Amsterdam*

Through the ages and every day anew Psalm xxiii pre-eminently has afforded consolation and support to the believer. The words and imagery of this short and rich text will certainly accompany the faithful reader "all the days of (his) life". To this psalm particularly applies, what in general has been stated: "(...) compositions like the psalms have been contextualized in many situations from the time they were first composed (...) right down to modern times"[1].

But the very same short and rich text obviously does not guarantee a clear and unambiguous interpretation. On the contrary, no psalm apparently has given rise to so many divergent opinions and interpretations as the psalm of the good shepherd.

In a well-documented article Ch. O'CONNOR once again gives a survey of early and more recent considerations as to the structure of Psalm xxiii[2]. Though the survey is not exhaustive, the writer nevertheless reviews some ten studies by giving "a bird's-eye view of the various proposals concerning the fine and/or gross structure of Psalm 23"[3]. However, none of the proposals as to the so-called fine structure or gross structure happens to be the same.

---

[1] See John F.A. SAWYER, *Semantics of Biblical Research* (Studies in Biblical Theology, Second Series 24), London 1972, p. 7; the writer points out the "avoidance of particularity" in the language of the Psalms (p. 15) which allows a "wide applicability of biblical tradition" (p. 16), with the result that the religious text can be "contextualized in an infinite number of situations in the synagogue and the church, and in the private experience of individual members of these and other religious communities" (p. 15). See also M.S. SMITH, "Setting and Rhetoric in Psalm 23", *Journal for the Study of the Old Testament* 41 (1988), pp. 61-66, esp. 64: "It is this lack of explicit referentiality that has helped to inspire so many to apply this psalm to their own life journey".

[2] In 1983 he already defended as a doctoral thesis in Louvain *Psalm 23: A Closer Look. A Text-Critical, Form Critical, Word and Surface-Structure Study, Including a Consideration of its Data and a Commentary*; the more recent study is: "The Structure of Psalm 23", *Louvain Studies* 10, 3 (1984), pp. 206-230. For a more complete bibliographical survey see also M.S. SMITH, *op. cit.*, pp. 64, 65.

[3] The fine structure regards the marking off of colons, whilst the gross structure reflects strophic demarcations.

Every scholar appears to have his own reasons for his own division of the psalm, be it in colons, in strophes or in both. For the sake of completeness O'CONNOR adds his own "diagram of the overall structure of the psalm" (p. 230) to the review of previous studies. His diagram, it has to be remarked, also demonstrates a different division, in that it does not correspond with any of the foregoing proposals.

This evident lack of agreement does not only concern the structure; scholarly studies also show many points of difference as to the imagery of the psalm. To be precise, there is not so much question as to the imagery, the metaphorical language as such, but the difference of opinion concerns the number of separate images which are to be found in the psalm. Does the psalm contain three images, namely of the herd, the traveller and the guest (VAN DER PLOEG; also, but differently: BRIGGS and WEISER), two images, namely of the shepherd and the host (B.W. ANDERSON, CALES, KRAUS, MITTMANN, RIDDERBOS) or only one image, namely of the shepherd (VAN UCHELEN; also, but differently: MORGENSTERN and KÖHLER)[4]?

Does the psalm in its shortness and richness speak to the scholars in diverse manners or do the scholars speak of the shortness and richness of the psalm in diverse manners?

Of course it is not easy to decide to what extent the differences in interpretation are to be seen as the results of the particular properties of the text or how far they are the outcome of distinctive cultural and academic approaches[5]. However, it would be too easy to suggest that the great variety in opinions and interpretations supports those ideas in modern literary criticism which hold that "each reading suppresses and highlights certain features of the text according to the interpretive assumptions of the community in question. According to such views, there is no such thing as a literal interpretation of a text. What seems literal is merely a reading that is persuasive from within certain accepted cultural assumptions"[6].

The richness of a number of divergent opinions as to the structure of the psalm may be tempting; to this reader, however, it seems to be necessary to return once again to the text of the psalm. Before accepting that one reading

---

[4] For more possibilities or varieties, see M.S. SMITH, *op. cit.*, p. 61; SMITH seems to have overlooked the studies of O'CONNOR.

[5] For the possible causes which lead to differences in interpretation of literary texts see Jan VAN LUXEMBURG, Mieke BAL, Willem WESTSTEIJN, *Over literatuur*, Muiderberg 1987, ch. 2, pp. 33-56. As O'CONNOR in his survey deals with a rather long period of investigation, from KISSANE (1953) to MITTMANN (1980), a certain amount of differences in the interpretation of Psalm 23 can be expected. But a lack of even the slightest sign of consensus of opinion calls for further investigation.

[6] See H. EILBERG-SCHWARZ, "When the Reader is in the Write", *Prooftexts* 7, 2 (1987), pp. 194-205 (book review of Jose FAUR, *Golden Doves With Silver Dots* (Semiotics and Textuality in Rabbinic Tradition), p. 197.

is no more true to the text than the other, we have to venture a new return to the properties of the text of the psalm. The basis for such a return is textual empiricism[7]. The guiding principle of a critical return to the text will be the question what is the inherent property of the text of Psalm xxiii or which language-elements are inevitably proper to the text of this psalm? That is to say, which elements from the point of view of the text of the psalm are hard-core items in comparison with sequences of colons or patterns of strophes?

One such inalienable feature of the text is the presence of two nominal phrases[8], which both form important links in dominant places in the text, namely in vs. 1b (*yhwh r'y* and in vs. 4c (*ky 'th 'mdy*).

Their nominal character gives to the verses an affirmative and assertive tenor; they function as statements which up to now have not come up for discussion. Their emphatic dominance is greatly enlarged by the fact that both nominal phrases are directly combined with verbal phrases in the negative, namely vs. 1c (*l' 'ḥsr*) and vs. 4b (*l' 'yr' r'*).

From a syntactic point of view the combination of the phrases in vs. 1 and 4 results in sentences which have a parallel construction: two nominal phrases in the positive coupled with two verbal phrases in the negative. Semantically, in both sentences the linking has the very same consequential effect: in vs. 1 the statement *yhwh r'y* has as a consequence *l' 'ḥsr* and in vs. 4 the *l' 'yr' r'* is the result of the statement *ky 'th 'mdy*.

From a rhetorical point of view both sentences show a chiastic correspondence in that in vs. 1 the sequence is a nominal phrase followed by a verbal phrase, whilst in vs. 4 the verbal phrase precedes the nominal phrase. In their close syntactic and semantic relation the sentences nevertheless maintain their own character: formally by the difference between the colon-pattern (2+2) in vs. 1 and the colon-pattern (3+3) in vs. 4 and substantially by the different subjects of the nominal phrases, namely in vs. 1b the third person singular and in vs. 4c the second person singular.

The correspondence of linguistic and rhetorical features gives to the sentences their respective dominant places and expresses their own function of couplings in the text of the psalm[9]. The micro-structure, so to speak, of the two sentences interacts with the macro-structure of the text:

---

[7] See Geoffrey THURLEY, *Counter-Modernism in Current Critical Theory*, London 1983, ch. 8, esp. p. 122: "Fundamentally, an empiricist criticism insists that the role of the critic is to show the text for what it is".

[8] Admittedly, a third nominal phrase occurs (vs. 5: *kwsy rwyh*) but on the basis of its syntactic construction and its rhetorical context this phrase does not seem to have a dominant place in the structure of the text comparable to the other two (vs. 1 and 4).

[9] Within the framework of a logotechnical analysis C. LABUSCHAGNE has hinted at the so-called "balansmodel" of Ps. xxiii: the phrase *ky 'th 'mdy* (vs. 4c) is the numerical middle and the thematic kernel of the psalm, being preceded by and followed by 26 words: *Deuteronomium* Ia (De prediking van het Oude Testament), Nijkerk 1987, p. 33; in his brief excursion he refers

Vv. 2-4a continue and elaborate on their own diction vs. 1 by constantly keeping up the characters of vs. 1: the third person singular of 1b and the first person singular of 1c. This elaboration is most expressively to be found in the sequences: "*He* makes *me* to lie down" (2a), "*He* leadeth *me*" (2b) and "*He* leadeth (!) *me*" (3b).

Vv. 4d-6 in the same way and in their own diction form a continuation and elaboration of vs. 4b, c by consistently relating to each other in the following verses the characters of the dominating sentence of 4b, c, namely the second person singular to the first person singular: *Thy* rod and *thy* staff they comfort *me* (4d); *Thou* preparest a table for *me* (5a); *Thou* anointest *my* head (5b)[10].

The description of the linguistic and rhetorical state of affairs up till now on the one hand has shown a significant coupling of sentences and on the other hand an interacting convergency with subsequent sentences of the text. In a continuing analysis and a closer attention to the language dimension of the text[11] the distinctiveness of this coupling of sentences as well as its close relation to the subsequent sentences can be stressed.

The nominal phrases (1b and 4c) function as the topic of the text: they are postulated as the *modus ponens* for they put in front what is known to addresser and addressee. Their common knowledge, presupposed by the topic[12], is the starting point of the further textual communication. What the psalm is about is determined in advance: it is the name of God and the effectiveness of the name of God.

In their grammatical-syntactic arrangement the so-called nominal phrases

---

to R. Oost (cf. note 16); see also J. Smit Sibinga, "Gedicht en getal. Over de compositie van Psalm 6", *Nederlands Theologisch Tijdschrift* 42, 3 (1988), pp. 185-207, esp. 206; also J. Bazak, "Numerical Devices in Biblical Poetry", *VT* 38, 3 (1988), pp. 333-337, esp. 334-335 regarding Ps. xxiii 4 ("numerical devices in order to emphasize central sentences").The analysis of mathematical aspects of a text surely has its merits; however, if they are not combined with a linguistic and rhetorical analysis, mathematical kernels will be disconnected from their actual surrounding context. The close correspondence of vs. 4 with vs. 1 and their integral interaction with the text as a whole cannot be ignored, not even in a numerological framework.

[10] The regular interchange of this pattern (second person and first person) is broken off in 6c (first person and third person); however, from another angle, the mentioning of the name *yhwh* causes 6c to return to 1b; this device of *inclusio* stresses in its own way the main motif of the psalm: the (effectiveness of the) Name of God.

[11] For an analysis fo the literary devices of the text, see, besides the studies and commentaries referred to in O'Connor and Smith (note 2), also my: *Psalmen* I (De prediking van het Oude Testament), Nijkerk 1986$^3$, pp. 158-162 and "Psalm 23, Een lied van vertrouwen", *Toonsoorten van de Schrift*, Hilversum 1983, pp. 33-36.

[12] Cf. J. Culler, "Presupposition and Intertextuality", in: *The Pursuit of the Signs. Semiotics, Literature, Deconstruction*, London 1983$^2$, pp. 100-118; the nominal phrases 1b and 4c function as "logical presuppositions" with implicit reference to other, prior texts; "We may or may not find in earlier poems sentences similar to those presupposed; that is in no way crucial. They function as already read; they present themselves as already read by virtue of the simple fact that they are presupposed" (p. 114).

are closely related to each other. From a semantic point of view they additionally form a tight interrelation in that the same meaning of the same Name is involved. Without violating the meaning and the tenor of the text apparently we could easily interchange vs. 1b and 4c: *(ky) 'th 'mdy / l' 'ḥsr* to be followed by *yhwh r'y / l' 'yr' r'*[13].

The verbal phrases of the psalm (namely 1c and 4b; especially 2-4a and 4d-6) form the comment or the focus of the text[14]. They follow as the *modus exponens* and have to be considered as an elaboration on the nominal phrases. In continuation of what is stated beforehand as common knowledge they later on give in their own diction further particulars.

Continuing and elaborating in their own way on the nominal phrases, the verbal phrases of the psalm underline their importance and dominance. As topics the nominal phrases appear to function as dominant links, which contain regulative evidence as to the reading of the further particulars of the text.

Reading these further particulars, namely the elaborations in 2-4a and 4d-6, from the point of view of topic and comment, we inevitably once again come upon the metaphorical language and the possible number of separate images of the psalm.

The topic as the *modes ponens* has an indicative mood and does not contain any metaphorical language[15]. The comment as the *modus exponens*, to be found in the above-mentioned elaborations, shows a rich imagery and contains nothing but metaphorical language. This statement has been contradicted by several scholars, who hold that contrary to the first (2-4a) the second elaboration (4d-6) is not metaphorical but literal. Thus MITTMANN argues in favour of a "Doppelläufigkeit von Bild- und Sachrede"[16], for it is his convic-

[13] Cf. T.A. VAN DIJK, *Macrostructures. An Interdisciplinary Study of Global Structures in Discourse, Interaction and Cognition*, Hillsdale, New Jersey 1980, p. 4: "The notion of topic for a passage of a text seems to involve a kind of semantic invariance". However, from a textual point of view, namely the text of the psalm as a whole, the interchangeability does not make any sense: each nominal phrase has its own continuation and elaboration. For textual topic-functions, see also VAN DIJK, *Taal en Handelen. Een interdisciplinaire inleiding in de pragmatiek*, Muiderberg 1978, pp. 89-91. As to the character and role of vs. 1b see also S. MITTMANN, "Aufbau und Einheit des Danklieds Psalm 23", *Zeitschrift für Theologie und Kirche* 77, 1 (1980), pp. 1-23, esp. 20: "Die exponierte Stellung verleiht ihm (sc. der Zweier "Jahwe ist mein Hirt") den Charakter eines Mottos, eines übergreifenden Leitsatzes, der sich nicht nur in der ersten Strophe, sondern den ganzen Psalm hindurch entfaltet". MITTMANN apparently did not observe the linguistic and rhetorical correspondence with vs. 4 and therefore overlooked the structural dominance of these verses for the text of the psalm as a whole.

[14] Admittedly, the comment as further enquiry already starts in the verbal phrases 1c and 4b; in this function they give initial particulars, respectively elaborated in 2, 3, 4a and 4c, 5, 6.

[15] This statement, of course, can be contradicted in as far as 1b is conceived of as an image.

[16] See MITTMANN, *op. cit.*, esp. p. 2. Of the same opinion is R. OOST in his "De structuur van Psalm 23", *Amsterdamse Cahiers* 7 (1986), pp. 96-100; he divides the psalm into a poetical-metaphorical (1b – 3 + 4) and a liturgical-situational (5 + 6) strophe. See also M.S. SMITH, *op. cit.*, who by recapitulating through structure, movement and imagery deals with "the issue of the poem's unity on the levels of both historical background and rhetoric", namely vv. 5-6 and vv.

tion "daß dieses Lied in seiner zweiten Hälfte nicht im Bilde spricht, sondern ungeachtet (*sic!* v.U.) der metaphorisch gesteigerten Diktion eine Realität beschreibt". The psalm has to be conceived of as "ein Danklied, dessen Anspiegelungen auf Mahl und Tempel (vs. 5-6) den institutionellen Raum und Rahmen dieser Gattung, die Dankfeier mit dem Opfermahl im Gotteshause, vergegenwärtigen" (p. 2).

Sticking, however, to the topic as apparently being "das Bekannte" and the comment consequently being "das Neue"[17] we must repeat the question: what images does the text employ and what do they stand for?

In the first half of the psalm we find as topic: there is no want, for God is the shepherd through the fields (1b, c); this reassurance of not being in want is elaborated on by means of metaphors in the comment (2-4a): green pastures, still waters, paths of righteousness and renewal of life are enumerated[18].

In the second half of the psalm we find as topic: there is no fear of evil, *r'*, for God is in close attendance within the fold (4b, c); this lack of fear is amplified by favourable expressions in the comment (4d, 5, 6): comfort by rod and staff, preparation of a table, anointing with oil, overflowing of the cup, in short: the presence of goodness, *ṭv*.

The metaphorical force of the comment in the first half of the text does not deal with pastures, waters, paths and the soul but with the effectiveness of God as a shepherd: there is no want. The metaphorical force of the comment in the second half is that the text does not deal with rod, staff, table, oil and cup, but by these expressive terms portrays the effectiveness of God who is nearby: there is no fear of evil, only the presence of goodness.

The imagery of the psalm appears to be unambiguous: the image of God as the shepherd through the fields goes hand in hand with the image of God, who is nearby within the fold. The predominant idea expressed by the figurative language is the effectiveness of the Name: *yhwh* as the one *'mdy*.

Close attention to the language-dimension of the poetic text[19] of Psalm 23 has resulted in a configuration of linguistic and rhetorical elements which have a dominant place and prominent function in the psalm because of their

---

1-4. His recapitulation, however, seems to be founded on intertextual concepts rather than on textual analysis.

[17] Cf. W. SCHNEIDER, *Grammatik des biblischen Hebräisch*, München 1976², p. 163, where he also uses the terms "Thema" and "Rhema".

[18] Though they belong to "the level of imagery" (p. 62). SMITH, *op. cit.*, curiously enough remarks: "All these physically experienced phenomena", evidently forming part of "the external physical journey" (p. 64).

[19] For a language-oriented literary criticsm (p. 6) as a cyclic motion of literary and linguistic observations (p. 7) being the interdisciplinary study of language as used in literary texts (p. 18), cf. P. VERDONK, *How Can We Know the Dancer From the Dance? Some Literary Stylistic Studies of English Poetry* (Doctoral thesis at the University of Amsterdam, 1988).

correspondence and convergency. Though some elements are given more prominence than others all are related to each other and give the text its own organisation. This organisation is realised on several levels[20], which are complementary in as far as they shape the intentionality of the psalm. The description of this textual organisation intends to familiarise the reader with "the poem's intentionality, its built-in, self-declaring interpretation"[21].

"Fine structures" as an outcome of the marking off of colons and "gross structures" as a result of the patterning of strophes (see note 3) are secondary, so to say external structures, if structures at all when emerging from theoretical extra-textual schemes. As primary structure has to be considered the internal organisation of sounds, words, phrases and sentences, which in their coherence and cohesion form the text. In describing this text we have come upon the configuration of linguistic and rhetorical elements which form its inalienable and inherent property. The textual organisation of these properties has "heuristic-interpretative value"[22] in as far as it guides the reader in his endeavour to find out what the words on the page are about.

---

[20] As basic levels are operative phonology: patterns of phonemes which have rhyme-force, e.g. in the verbal forms of 2a, b and 3b; lexis: sequences of lexical items which have foregrounding force, e.g. the nominal forms in 2a, b and 3b; grammar: syntactic constructions which have semantic force, as e.g. described with regard to the topical part of the psalm, vv. 1b, c and 4b, c. Cf. R. FOWLER, *The Languages of Literature. Some Linguistic Contributions to Criticism*, London 1971, ch. 14: Linguistics and the analysis of literature, pp. 219-237, esp. 223, 224, and also 234: "'The poem itself' as a formal unit is a composite in which the relationship between its components are more vital than the distinctions, and a composite which is greater than the sum of its parts"; "The primary structure, pattern, unity, of poems is produced by the establishment of *significant* relationships (...)".

[21] Cf. G. THURLEY, *op. cit.*, p. 104; also p. 23: "The fallacy is to regard form and content as differentiable entities ('two types of property within the text', p. 25) causally related within the text, rather than as simply different ways of talking about the same thing ..."; p. 27: "Now this view, strictly speaking, commits us to the concomitant view that the role of the critic is not interpretation, but description: what the critic should do is not interpret the work, but to familiarise the reader with its language".

[22] Cf. I.J.F. DE JONG, *Narrators and Focalizers. The Presentation of the Story in the Iliad.* Amsterdam 1987, p. 34.

# INDEX OF BIBLICAL REFERENCES